IMPERIAL JAPAN

1926–1938

by

A. MORGAN YOUNG

1938
WILLIAM MORROW & COMPANY
NEW YORK

IMPERIAL JAPAN
COPYRIGHT — 1938

By A. MORGAN YOUNG

PRINTED IN THE UNITED STATES
BY THE POLYGRAPHIC COMPANY OF AMERICA, N. Y.

PREFACE

MANY are the books on Japan: they mostly follow a prescription, reviewing different aspects of a country which is strangely unlike the lands of Christendom, though it has entered into economic competition with them. I have here tried to present something rather different. Encouraged by the fact that *Japan in Recent Times, 1912-1926,* has been found useful by other makers of books as well as by readers who sought to increase their knowledge, I have attempted here to present a sequel—though it is only part of the same story in the sense that it continues the record. A reign that seemed likely to be quiet and humdrum has proved so full of happenings that it has been difficult, even at slightly greater length, to record these eleven years as adequately as the previous sixteen. But for readers who would like the facts rather than my gloss upon them, here is a book full of them. During ten of the eleven years I was seldom absent from the editorial desk of the *Japan Chronicle,* so there was little about current events that did not come my way, and I have tried to select from the mass the most significant and most closely related. Sometimes so many things were happening at once that it has been impossible to observe a strict chronology and the subject rather than the date has had to be considered.

As in my previous book I have adhered to the Japanese custom of putting the surname first and the personal name after; also, where titles are concerned, I have used the highest attained instead of explaining that the Mr. of one day was the Baron of the next.

CONTENTS

CHAPTER I

A NEW ERA

FOLLOWING a Chinese custom, Japan begins a new era with each reign. When the Taisho era ended on Christmas Day, 1926, "Taisho" was made the posthumous name of the deceased Emperor, and the new era was named Showa. Taisho meant Great Righteousness, and the reign of sixteen years had been distinguished by the number of scandals and the greatness of the corruption in its history. Showa might be translated "Peace made Manifest," and was to be marked by a constant prating about Japan's sacred mission of keeping the peace of the Far East, and by a progressive breaking of that peace and a cynical disregard of truth and justice.

Yet the reign began with a sense of disillusionment and almost of exhaustion. The damage caused by the great earthquake of September 1923 was only partly repaired, and Mr. Inoue Jonnosuke, who had been Governor of the Bank of Japan and was to be Finance Minister, declared early in 1927 that the £400,000,000 profit which Japan had made out of the Great War, had been frittered away and not left a trace. There was so much hardship and it was so hard to get money that this may have seemed to be the case, but actually the war profits had transformed the economics of the country, and had changed it as completely as it was changed by the revolution of 1868.

Apart from economic effects, Japan's prestige in the world was enhanced; she took part in the councils of Europe to a degree never formerly imagined, and the Washington Conference in 1922 had given her the hegemony of Northeastern Asia. For the first time there was a government which might be called democratic. Its leading spirit had been Mr. Hamaguchi, an honest and courageous Finance

Minister, with Gladstonian conceptions of economy. He had already suffered in health through his fight for sound finance, and on the death of his Chief, Count Kato, had taken the Home portfolio. But this change did not end the struggle against the army's demands for more and more money, for the experiences of the Great War had led to new and more expensive ways of fighting, and Japan had found herself behind the times.

Another very notable character in the Kato Cabinet was Baron Shidehara, the Minister for Foreign Affairs. It is not too much to say of Baron Shidehara that he is the only modern statesman in Japan whose will and conscience bade him deal fairly by China and whom opportunity and courage enabled to do so. It was no easy task that he set himself, for, as the Chinese learnt the difficult business of becoming nationalistic, by which alone they could preserve the integrity of their State, they became increasingly "difficult" to deal with, for there were many points of friction, and they became less amenable. A desultory war between North and South was going on. So far there had been continuity of government at Peking, and though the Kuomintang, with its headquarters still in Canton, had a better claim to represent the people than had the Government in Peking, it would have been against Baron Shidehara's principles of non-interference to accord it the recognition that it sought before it had really vindicated its claims.

The young Emperor of Japan came to the Throne in the closing days of 1926. The new year began portentously for China, though just what was portended nobody knew. The Kuomintang had fought its way northwards to Hankow, and there, on January 5, 1927, a Chinese mob swept through the British Concession with a mighty uproar. The totally inadequate force of marines that had been landed from a British warship found itself worse than useless. It is possible that resolute gunnery would have dispersed the mob, but the officer in command saw that there was a directing power behind this seeming disorder, and refrained from action.

With heroic self-restraint the marines endured insult and assault. Mr. Eugene Chen, who was at that time the Foreign Minister in the Kuomintang Government, while disclaiming any incitement, undertook to call the mob off and protect the British residents so long as they made no attempt to protect themselves. There was nothing for it but to accept the offer, and the surrender of the concession logically followed, being effected by the Chen–O'Malley Agreement on February 19th.

That a history of the reign of a new Japanese Emperor should begin with an encounter in China between Chinese and British forces is not an irrelevant divagation. Mr. Engene Chen had a very strong bias against Britain, and succeeded, both in Canton and in Hankow, in alienating the sympathy of British officials from the Kuomintang. On the other hand, he had a confidence in Japan which could only have been justified had Baron Shidehara possessed a permanent tenure of the Foreign Office instead of a very precarious incumbency. His capture of the British Concession was a personal triumph, but it was not the way to achieve the succession of retrocessions which it was hoped would follow. He declared to one interviewer that had the British fired a shot, the whole community would have been exterminated, and to a representative of the Japanese news agency he said: "We assure you that you may dismiss all apprehensions that the Kuomintang Government is planning to do the same thing in the Japanese Concession that it did in the case of the British Concession in Hankow. Such a thing is not dreamed of by the Kuomintang." But Chen was backing the wrong horse.

There had been a serious quarrel between Canton and Hongkong, and the possibility of exploiting this was being discussed in Japan, along with the chances of the Kuomintang being reasonable on the subject of Japan's desires in Manchuria if Japan supported it in China, when Baron Shidehara's speech on foreign relations at the opening of the Diet on January 18, 1927, put the whole Chinese ques-

tion, for the moment, on a higher plane that it had hitherto
occupied. Japan was anxious, he said, to see the re-estab-
lishment of order and security in China. Friendship for
China dictated this wish, which was also necessary for the
commercial interest of Japan. But the end could be attained
only by Chinese initiative; compulsion from without could
only do harm. Japan could only lend her support to Chinese
endeavours and provide opportunity for their fulfilment.
With this object in view she had prohibited the supply of
arms and the advancement of loans that could be used for
the promotion of civil strife. These restrictions were a necessary part of any sincere non-intervention. China must devise
her own internal policy and appoint her own governors.
Success in these tasks would promote her prestige beyond
her own borders; but China had a historical background
of several thousand years; she had a national life peculiarly
her own; and no imposition upon that national life of
political or social institutions devised by foreign nations to
suit their own convenience could possibly succeed. Nor
could it be imagined that the Chinese would long acquiesce
in foreign intervention or submit to foreign dictation. In
any case, whatever institutions China might adopt for herself, Japan, with her own history and her own ideals, would
have the will and the capacity to uphold her own system
of government immutable for all ages.

The last phrase was an echo of the words of Ito's
Commentary on the Constitution regarding the Throne of
Japan, and the sentence referred to the possibility, which
then seemed to be imminent, of China adopting Communism
as the basis of her political system. Those who were customarily loudest in asserting the unique loyalty of Japan
were also first in professing a panic fear of the dangers
involved to Japan in China becoming Communistic, and
demanding that this be prevented.

Chinese "unification" was not yet complete. The victorious army, under General Chiang Kai-shek, proceeded
to Shanghai. The British authorities had surrendered the

Hankow Concession; but they had not surrendered their interests in Shanghai, and hurriedly sent a military force to defend them. Eugene Chen, disappointed at not being able to repeat his triumph, denounced this attempt "to subjugate the Southern army," but the Shanghai Defence Force subjugated nobody. No lives were lost through its presence, and the only collisions that the Southern army had were with a few of its own countrymen in the native city. The Northern troops who had been camped in the neighbourhood left for the North with as little equipment as possible. Baron Shidehara had let it be known that it was against his policy to send any Japanese reinforcements, and the Japanese naval men on the spot assisted in the easy task of persuading the Northerners to leave without fighting.

A Southern army which took possession of Nanking was not so well in hand as that which had hurried on to Shanghai, and Baron Shidehara's policy was put to a severer trial there. From Nanking, too, the Northerners decamped, and it was subsequently attempted to put all the blame for the disorders there on the departing troops; but the weight of evidence was against this explanation. Mob law prevailed for a time. Mr. Morioka, the Japanese Consul, who was sick, was dragged from his bed, and escaped with great difficulty, but saved the imperial portrait and the more important of the consular papers. In the general confusion a few British and Americans were killed, but no Japanese. That the casualties were so small was due principally to the British and American warships which hurried to the scene, and, at a critical moment, put a barrage of shells between the group of foreigners and the mob about to attack them.

Baron Shidehara still stayed his hand; the Nationalists had undertaken to be responsible for the safety of foreigners, and the Japanese Foreign Minister, aware that order could never be restored in China if there were constant foreign interference, decided that, for the sake of the larger issues, such risks must be run by foreigners as they would run in other countries during a time of civil commotion. The distressed foreigners were brought down to Shanghai, the Japanese very glad of their deliverance. Mr. Chen made much anti-British capital out of the incident, and for a time Japan was almost popular in China.[1]

Dissensions had by this time appeared in the Nationalist ranks. Dr. Sun Yat-sen had insisted upon permitting Communist co-operation, but the Communists, under the inspiration of Borodin, were now running the party instead of merely co-operating. Instead of going back to Hankow to settle with them, Generalissimo Chiang Kai-shek set up a Kuomintang Government at Nanking on April 18, 1927, and, realising that no Chinese Government run by Communists could hope for recognition by any country except Russia, decided to purge the party of Communism. Borodin and the other Russians went flying back to Moscow, and thither too went Mr. Eugene Chen. Nationalist historians in China deal rather scantily with the purge, but the Powers approved both of its severity and of its oblivion.

Japan showed no disposition to abandon her concession in Hankow or to subscribe to the principles of the Chen–O'Malley Agreement. Besides, her principal interest was in Manchuria, and the Kuomintang influence had only just reached the Yangtse. For their immediate problems the Japanese could still deal with the Northern Generals, who would usually listen to a financial argument.

At the end of 1926 Marshal Chang Tso-lin, Superintendent of the Three Eastern Provinces (Manchuria), yielded to a temptation that he had hitherto avoided, and took up his quarters in Peking as Generalissimo, and maker and unmaker of Presidents. It was a fatal move for him. Its cost alone compelled him to abandon the excellent currency policy that he had formerly maintained, and the Mukden

---

[1] In 1937, when Admiral Little protested against the jeopardising of European life and property in Shanghai by the landing of a Japanese army, Admiral Hasegawa replied, "It's no more than you did in 1927," which was apparently accepted as a sufficient answer.

notes became the most instead of the least depreciated in China. And because he could not keep his eye on Japanese doings in Manchuria so well as he had done in Mukden, he had to be stiffer in his diplomatic attitude, so that the Japanese did not reap the benefit from his absence for which they had hoped.

Thus at the outset of the new reign events in China became the dominant interest. Another indication of what was to come was a typical patriotic outburst. Japan is cursed more than any country with the type of patriot whose sole claim to distinction is the violent denunciation of better men than himself. It happened during the last long illness of the Emperor Taisho that the Marquis and Marchioness Tokugawa, than whom there were no finer types of natural and inherited nobility in Japan, gave a charity dance. After the Emperor died, the patriots stirred up such indignation that the Marquis and Marchioness were glad to retire to a distant rural estate till the trouble blew over. There was to be more of this sort of patriotism than ever before.

While the great majority find full occupation in the earning of a living and the care of a family, and eccentricities are the marks of a small minority, some of the Japanese eccentricities are so quaint as to merit notice. It was at the beginning of the new reign, for instance, that "doll diplomacy" began. Whether the idea first germinated in an American or a Japanese mind matters little. Japan had always been famous for dolls, and some very charming ones were made in America. It began with exchanges from the children of one country to the children of the other. In Japan the business was carried through with a solemnity that belongs to the youth of the world. The dolls were taken round the country and in their presence distinguished old gentlemen in frock coats lectured school children on the cultivation of international friendship, symbolised somehow by these small ambassadors of good will. Maintaining a diplomatic silence, the dolls were really quite useful in providing a topic for platitude, and enabling speakers to avoid such thorny questions as immigration and import tariffs.

It went on a long time and reached its climax in 1935, when Mayor La Guardia of New York sent two full-sized tailor's dummies as Mr. and Mrs. America on a visit. These arrived by the *Asama Maru* early in June, did the usual tour, and, dressed in Japanese costume, returned by the *Heian* on the 29th of the same month. The highest point of absurdity being reached, doll diplomacy then came to an end.

The great majority of people found times hard, but many still had money to spare and wasted it in various ways. The little blue parakeet called budgerigar had a great vogue and would sell for as much as a thousand yen (£100). Dogs of various sorts were fashionable, but the commercial element introduced by large brown pigeons and angora rabbits made these less popular. Dancing, however, became all the more popular by being commercialised, and dance halls were profitable. There was a great deal of controversy in official quarters regarding these new institutions, and they were strictly regulated, no "sitting out" being allowed, and the taxi-dancer taking a ticket for every dance from her partner. As a social phenomenon the dance hall was all to the good. The geisha, as a professional entertainer, had deteriorated, and was spoken of officially as though she belonged to the same class as the prostitute. The dance hall to a certain extent re-established the distinction between an entertainer and a prostitute, and provided many young men for the first time with that escape from both segregation and indulgence which is the most agreeable characteristic of Occidental society. Dancing, moreover, was a far cheaper form of entertainment than that provided by geisha, so the geisha were left more and more to the elderly and well-to-do, who in public assemblies would inveigh against the immoralities of the modern dance. A high police official in Osaka was particularly zealous in getting dance halls abolished throughout the prefecture. Having retired, he proceeded to open one himself, within easy reach of the city but just outside the prefectural boundary.

In this period, too, cafés sprang up by the thousand, generally tiny places with fanciful names and garish lights, which dispensed bad tea, weak beer, stale cakes, and gramophone noises. The police regarded them with suspicion, the waitresses often being unlicensed prostitutes who defrauded the Government of lawful revenue, and they tried to regulate the cafés out of existence; but demand continued to ensure supply, and the line of least resistance for the police was to squeeze rather than suppress.

Though at the outset of the Showa era the Cabinet was more democratic and its members more honest than had been the case hitherto, the constitutional position of the Diet had not improved, yet while its behaviour deteriorated its prestige increased. Though deprecated by political essayists as defeating its own aims, violence gets results. Turbulence was not an Opposition monopoly in the session of 1927. Members of the Government party thundered against Seiyukai corruption, and, without mincing their words, accused General Baron Tanaka, the president of that party, of embezzling several millions of the Secret Service money. Such accusations admitted of no answer, since it was impossible to render an account of costs of espionage, but Tanaka had been Minister for War during the Siberian intervention, when the General Staff had had its share in the unbridled corruption that accompanied that adventure. The Minseito Government, which had a genuine desire for economy, found it impossible to stem the tide of spending. Every department wanted larger allotments than ever, and, declaring that it was maintaining a rigid economy, the Government got another record budget passed, and, with the usual rush of bills passed without discussion on the last couple of days, brought the session to a normal end.

To close the session with a spate of undebated legislation was the usual practice, most of the debating days being spent in vain interpellations or prolonged discussions on unimportant matters. The momentous events in China received little attention, but much time was spent on discussion of the latest version of the Religions Bill. The rulers of Japan, like rulers everywhere, believe that religion is an excellent thing for the lower classes, and are anxious that it be of the right sort. In drafting a bill which required the tenets of each religion to be presented in writing for official approval, the Government was displaying no illiberality. The greatest zealots in the official hierarchy were quite indifferent as to any eccentricity of belief so long as it left loyalty unimpaired. It was becoming more and more compulsory for certain classes, particularly soldiers and school children, to visit Shinto shrines and make obeisances at the proper times while the priests recited their incantations; but this was officially declared to be not an act of worship but only a token of respect towards the Imperial House. It was already becoming dangerous to deny the Gods or the historicity of the early Emperors, and was to become much more dangerous during the next few years. There was a great desire to obtain foreign recognition of Japanese fables. After the Imperial Enthronement in 1928, an official of the Household expressed to the assembled journalists reporting the event the gratification which had been felt when it was observed that even the envoys of Roman Catholic countries had bowed to the Kashikodokoro (the Imperial Household Shrine, in which the spurious Mirror, Sword, and Jewel of the Sun Goddess are placed for adoration), as respectfully as the most loyal Shintoist of them all. Perhaps they said, like Naaman, "In this thing the Lord pardon thy servant."

But the discussion on the Religions Bill did not touch these high matters. A point in the Bill that attracted criticism was that the priest, minister, or other responsible person in every place must be of educational qualifications not lower than graduation from a middle school. Of the popular Neo-Shinto sects several, with a collective following running into millions, were founded by illiterate peasants; but curiously enough, no objection was raised on their account. It was rather advantageous than otherwise to put obstacles in the way of further creations of the sort. The point was raised that some officers of the Salvation Army might be disqualified—a body of whose work the Empress Dowager approved and to whose support she had contributed.

Like much other legislation and regulation, the Bill was intended to assist the police in keeping a finger on the pulse of every kind of activity; but nobody was very keen on it except a few bureaucrats, and it was dropped; nor did any better fortune await its revival in subsequent sessions.

CHAPTER II

THE FINANCIAL CRISIS OF 1927

THE legislators having earned their salaries and the Diet being formally closed, the Government was in hopes of having nine months peace in which to get on with its administrative duties; but hardly had the session ended when a storm broke of which reverberations were heard all over the world. The firm of Suzuki stopped payment. It was the "wonder firm" of the war, and had accumulated legends which lasted only a little longer than its money. American magazines often published articles on "The Richest Woman in Japan"—sometimes "in the world"—with photographs of Mrs. Suzuki, a staid and comfortable widow lady, who directed countless enterprises of unthinkable wealth. But they never mentioned Mr. Kaneko, though the Japanese papers often mentioned Kaneko and forgot Mrs. Suzuki. The late Suzuki had left his widow a miscellaneous business including a steelworks that was almost moribund. He also left her his banto, or office manager, a little man of modest demeanour who dressed badly and shaved seldom in wealth and poverty alike; but Kaneko had vast ideas, though whether he was a Napoleon or a George Ponderevo was never certain. Suzuki's increased enormously during the war, handling business of every kind, and secured a good deal of Government patronage. The older rival firms declared war, and stuck at nothing. They did not stick, for instance, at saying that the reason why the Bank of Formosa advanced unlimited credit to Suzuki's was the friendship between Mrs. Suzuki and Count Goto, who founded the bank. After the war there was an armaments race, and Suzuki's bought metals for the supply of the Government arsenals. The Washington Conference in 1922 called a halt to the armaments race, and the Government left Suzuki's holding the metals. Enemies thought that the time had come to strike and inspired articles in the Press declaring that the firm was about to crash. Then came the great earthquake of 1923: the Government gave orders to the Bank of Japan to advance money liberally; the Bank of Formosa unloaded on to the Bank of Japan the bills it held against Suzuki's, and everybody breathed more freely for a space. In March 1927 the Bank of Japan told the Bank of Formosa that it would not hold these Suzuki bills any longer, especially as they did not arise out of the earthquake at all. Kaneko appealed to Mr. Kataoka, the Minister of Finance, pointing out that it was at his predecessor's instance that his firm had incurred its liabilities. The Minister was obdurate and Kaneko retired defeated, not knowing that he had wrecked a Government.

The Bank of Japan would wait no longer for payment, and the Bank of Formosa had to approach Mr. Kataoka. It was a "semi-official" bank and he could not let it down. So the Government drafted an Urgent Imperial Ordinance advancing 200,000,000 yen to the bank. This had to be passed by the Privy Council before it could take effect. Count Ito Myoji, a member of the Council, an old male harridan with a great reputation as a patriot, who had enriched himself out of every war and hated so honest a Government as that now in difficulties, thundered against the Ordinance, and, on April 17, 1927, the Wakatsuki Ministry resigned.

Bankruptcies are rare in Japan. Advances at low interest are made, debts are paid off over a long period without interest, and the firm is either kept in being or amalgamated with some other concern. There is something to be said for the smooth method; but Kaneko's enemies were out for blood and so were the enemies of the Government. The firm of Suzuki simply disappeared, but the Government had to advance 500 million yen to tide over the crisis instead of the 200 millions that would have saved the situation had the patriotic Count Ito not intervened.

There came a sudden break in the continuity of policy. Not long before the events just recorded, Mr. Takahashi had resigned the presidency of the Seiyukai, to which, along with the Premiership, he had succeeded when Hara Takashi was murdered in 1921. General Baron Tanaka, who, during his career as Minister for War, had found the jobbery of the Seiyukai to his liking, became its new President. He toured the country with Takahashi, who introduced him to numerous big meetings. Here he played the bluff soldier, and, when Takahashi had made his oration, he would rise and say that his own sentiments had been admirably expressed. Though Tanaka was very wealthy—which was hardly creditable in a soldier—and had great influence, he had been openly derided for corruption in the Diet and was hardly the man to restore confidence in a financial crisis—which, perhaps, was the reason why he persuaded Takahashi to undertake the burden of the Finance Ministry. Dr. Suzuki, an adroit professional politician, became Home Minister, General Shirakawa Minister for War, and Mr. Ogawa Minister for Railways.

The formation of a new Government and the advance of 500 million yen to the Bank of Formosa did not allay the financial panic. Bank after bank closed its doors, and the Government declared a moratorium. One of the greatest industrial concerns in the country—the Kawasaki Dockyard —which did so much work on Government order that it was regarded as itself a Government concern, shut down for lack of working capital, for the Fifteenth Bank, which financed it, failed badly. In Osaka 237 factories stopped working. But the printing press saved the situation: while General Tanaka was forming his Government the Bank of Japan was printing notes, and on April 21st it was announced that the issue was 2,318,000,000 yen, an increase of 639,000,000 in a single day. None of the banks that did foreign exchange business were affected, so, except for a slight decline in the exchange rate, which rather helped exports for a while, the repercussions abroad were not remarkable.

The new Government called a special session of the Diet on May 3rd to pass its emergency measure for financial relief, and General Tanaka made a formal declaration of continuity of policy, which, as might have been expected, was merely a prelude to an undoing of the work of the previous Cabinet. He even used a phrase of Baron Shidehara's, that he was in favour of all the legitimate aspirations of China.

The immediate crisis being averted, Takahashi resigned the Finance portfolio; he was growing old and he did not like the company he was in. He was succeeded by Mr. Mitsuchi.

Baron Tanaka then proceeded to destroy continuity of policy. First he dismissed the prefectural governors appointed by the Minseito. There was no peculiar turpitude here, for both parties indulged freely in this vicious practice, pro-testing that they considered it very harmful, but that such dreadful men had been put in by the other party that purity in the general election could only be secured if the Governors were such men as the Ministry could regard as fair and unbiased. The Governors assembled in conference at the capital, and Dr. Suzuki, the new Home Minister, said little about political purity but much on the great virtues of ancestor-worship and the intention of the Government to reform the administration of shrines. This was less a revela-tion of Suzuki's personal piety than an indication that the obligations of patriotism were to be enforced more strictly than ever.

Though Suzuki was not a military man, this was ominous, for the army in Japan is the arbiter in patriotism. To be ready to die for the Emperor is the first requirement of patriotism, and the opportunity is provided from time to time by the army. The military machinations had begun even during Baron Shidehara's time. He succeeded in main-taining peace on the Yangtse, but he was unable to prevent a strengthening of the Japanese garrison in Tientsin and Peking in readiness for any opportunity for aggrandisement that might present itself when the victorious Kuomintang continued its march northward.

No sooner was Tanaka in power than he dispatched troops to Shantung to intercept the Kuomintang army. But the Kuomintang was too discreet to challenge the Japanese, and called off the campaign for the year. There being no excuse for their remaining, the Japanese expedition returned home in September, and it was loudly proclaimed by the army's journalistic supporters that by its very presence it had preserved peace. Japan's leading journalist and historian, Mr. Tokutomi, was, as usual, all in favour of strong measures, and exclaimed indignantly that the Chinese seemed to think that Manchuria and Mongolia belonged to them. This, indeed, was as far as the Japanese policy went at that time. They could do as they pleased without much opposition in Manchuria and Eastern Inner Mongolia, but the Southerners were difficult people to deal with and they did not want them in the North.

Shidehara's China policy had had its effect on public thought. Dr. Yoshino, a liberal professor with a large following, declared that the protection of foreign communities within her gates was China's own duty and that these communities could not expect to be unaffected by China's own troubles. Mr. Nakano Seijo, a member of the Diet, pointed out that Great Britain, who had sent a force to defend Shanghai, no longer monopolised unpopularity but that Japan had recaptured it; a Minseito meeting on July 15th denounced Baron Tanaka's expedition; and the Press in general demanded a withdrawal of the troops because they were not needed and their presence had provoked another boycott. Should civil war appear in Shantung, they said, it would be much cheaper and better to withdraw the couple of thousand Japanese residents for a time than to send a Japanese army to enforce peace. These things are worth recalling because, though it was never true that the military party had lost its power in Japan, there was in 1927 an amount of independent civilian thinking which five years later it did not seem possible that there ever could have been.

CHAPTER III

TANAKA AND JAPAN'S MANCHURIA POLICY

MANY attempts had been made to detach Manchuria from China, so as to make Japanese pretensions to control easier. So long as the Peking régime lasted, a policy combining bribery and encroachment was working well enough. It was impossible to come out into the open and offer the Kuomintang recognition as the price of Manchuria, though many secret proposals to this effect were made; but the Kuomintang did not trust the Japanese Government sufficiently to accept the offers made in its name. Besides, there was a conscientious objection, and caution prohibited an immoral contract which was almost sure to be but a prelude to a succession of others. Indications that the Kuomintang was gaining the mastery over the whole of China filled the military men with apprehensions, for a victorious Kuomintang would be sure to raise difficulties in Manchuria.

A number of conferences were held in the early part of the Tanaka régime, partly in order to test the sentiments of the more influential civilian elements, including, of course, the great commercial interests. The most important of these was the Far Eastern Conference, which met on June 1, 1927, when General Muto, Commander-in-Chief of the Kwantung Army, insisted that there must be a more thorough exploitation of Manchuria and Mongolia. The Conference practically decided the fate of Manchuria, so far as regards its definite detachment from China, though the exact method still depended on the possibilities of opposition from the Kuomintang, and such picturesque details as the restoration of a Manchu Empire were improvised later.

So far as the public was concerned, which is kept informed of the proceedings even of the Cabinet and the Privy Council by judicious "leakage," the Conference was preoccupied with the unwillingness of the Chinese in Manchuria to lease land to Japanese, which, according to the Treaty of 1915, they could do. When Mr. Yoshida, Consul-General in Mukden, returned to his post after the Conference, he gave something like an ultimatum to Marshal Chang Tso-lin that if leases could not be obtained, then ownership must be the alternative. It was not explained how this would overcome Chinese reluctance to surrender occupancy, but was clearly a threat that recalcitrancy would be punished. Mr. Yoshida also prohibited the construction of railways which the Japanese might consider would compete with the South Manchuria railway, but rather inconsistently insisted that the Kirin–Hoinyung line, which would give an outlet through the north of Korea, be completed immediately. To promote this line there had been a Japanese loan of a very irregular kind, which was said to have been used by the Marshal's military establishment.

No general communiqué was issued to the Press regarding the findings of the Conference, so there was no close agreement between the reports of the different newspapers. It would seem likely, however, that the document published later in China as the Tanaka Memorial, and purporting to have been presented to the Emperor on July 25, 1927, actually represents the findings of the Far Eastern Conference. The Conference was called for the purpose of discovering how far officialdom could be depended upon to back the Government in a "positive policy" in Manchuria. It was found that the liberalism practised by Baron Shidehara had not penetrated far below the surface or received wide support, and that an aggressive movement was sure of popular backing. The Press for a while continued to criticise militarism, but the military were well assured that, when the time came to strike, there was nothing to fear from Japanese liberalism. The Shantung flurry having passed, the Far Eastern Conference was regarded as the beginning of a very definite forward movement in North China. General Chiang Kai-shek had his hands full for some months in completing the purging of the Kuomintang of its Communist elements. Marshal Chang Tso-lin was left in charge in Peking. In his absence from Mukden Japanese intrigue did its best to create disorder there, and the legend to-day is that Manchuria was in a state, economic and social, bordering on chaos. But Mr. C. Walter Young, who speaks with unrivalled authority on Manchurian affairs, extolled the peace and order maintained in Manchuria by Chang Tso-lin and the good financial standing of his Government in an article in the *Chinese Economic Journal* for July 1927.

By way of a start in Manchuria, Mr. Yamamoto Jotaro, energetic and full of ideas, and popularly regarded as representing the Mitsui interests in the Seiyukai, was appointed President of the South Manchuria Railway. Mr. Matsuoka Yosuke, ready of speech and determined in manner, was his vice-president, and was destined to attract rather more international attention than his qualities warranted.

The forward movement in Manchuria was gaining strength. It was announced in the Press that Mr. Yoshizawa, the Japanese Minister in Peking, was to settle all outstanding questions with Marshal Chang Tso-lin on August 24th, reminding him that Japan had saved him once again, as in 1925, by throwing her troops across the path of his Chinese enemies, and that some acknowledgment of such favours was due. (In 1925 they strongly denied interference, though Chang Tso-lin thanked them for it.) A black list of anti-Japanese Koreans in Chientao was also compiled and handed to the Marshal as something that it was his duty to deal with. But this year also saw the beginning of a new technique for handling Koreans for imperialistic purposes which later played an important part in the destinies of Manchuria.

Suddenly the Press, which yesterday had been demanding the withdrawal of troops from Shantung, to-day was eagerly backing expansion in Manchuria, the *Kokumin* in particular demanding an effective right to lease land in the north as

well as in the south. Mr. Saito, a director of the South
Manchuria Railway, returning from a tour, described how
the Chinese, driven by poverty and misgovernment from
Shantung and Chihli, were pouring into the more extensive
regions of North Manchuria. Speaking in October 1927, he
put the number of permanent settlers in the north at not
less than 700,000 for that year, and went on to point out
the great commercial opportunities that this afforded to
Japan, who must no longer concentrate on South Manchuria
but embrace the far vaster areas of North Manchuria as well.
To carry manufactures to that region and to bring raw
materials thence, railways must be constructed, and, "in
short, everything possible must be done to bring Japan and
North and South Manchuria closer together."

Japan proceeded to bring them together by constructing
a railway to Tsitsihar, which competed with the Chinese
Eastern Railway far more than any of the Chinese lines
that Japan complained of competed with the South Manchuria Railway. What Japan really objected to was not
competing railways, but railways that she had not constructed herself. If Marshal Chang Tso-lin wanted a new
line, everything was easy so long as he asked the South
Manchuria Railway to construct it for him, for this meant
remunerative work, liberal interest, and Japanese co-
operation in management. But when he constructed railways himself, without Japanese aid or co-operation, this was
held against him as a hostile act. Regarding the new line to
Tsitsihar, Japan supported him in ignoring the Russian
protests.

The policy of Mr. Yamamoto Jotaro became so "positive"
that the Powers began to prick up their ears, wherefore
Mr. Yoshizawa told the Pressmen in Peking that "Japan
has no intention whatever of adopting any positive decisive
policy towards Manchuria, nor does she plan anything like
invasion"—and the news being circulated from Peking
perhaps had a more reassuring effect than if it had come
from Tokyo. In China itself the statement was less reassuring,

for it was clear that the Far Eastern Conference was beginning to bear fruit. Mr. Yoshida, Consul-General in Mukden,
whose functions were ambassadorial rather than consular,
informed Mr. Mo, the Civil Governor, that anti-Japanese
movements, such as the collection of duties under the new
Chinese tariff and the construction of lines competing with
the South Manchuria Railway, must cease forthwith. Mr.
Yoshizawa in Peking delivered similar mandates to Marshal
Chang Tso-lin. Both invoked the decisions of the Far
Eastern Conference as their authority, which caused Mr.
Hamaguchi to say hard things of this "monstrous con-
ference."

The Chinese were getting restive under Japanese hectoring,
and there was a great public demonstration in Mukden.
It was explained in Japan that all the trouble was due to
the Chinese foolishly mistaking the Far Eastern Conference
as something aggressive, just as they mistook Japan's claims
to a "special position" and had mistaken the intention of
the Twenty-one Demands. In spite of Mr. Yoshizawa's
disclaimers of aggressive intent, Mr. C. C. Wu, the Nanking
Foreign Minister, told him that his mandates to Chang
Tso-lin were worse than the Twenty-one Demands. On the
other hand, we find a popular daily in Tokyo expatiating
on the popularity of Japan among the Mongolian princes,
and expressing the opinion that it was time to drop Chang
Tso-lin instead of holding him up.

In the autumn of 1927 Mr. T. W. Lamont, of Messrs.
Morgan & Co., paid a visit to Japan. He had been before,
in 1920, when he concluded the arrangements for a consortium for the rehabilitation of China by loans. On that
occasion Mr. Lamont's statements and those of Japanese
financiers as to what had happened differed remarkably,
and where the truth lay was never disclosed because China
refused to have anything to do with the arrangement by
which she was to find salvation at 9 per cent. Again in
1927 there was the usual feasting, with sugary speeches
about how much America loved Japan, proofs thereof being

that she bought Japanese silk, and, after the earthquake, lent Japan money at a higher rate than she had paid for fifty years. Having expounded his gospel that there is no higher form of philanthropy than to lend money at interest, Mr. Lamont returned whence he came. It was published abroad that Morgan's were to lend the South Manchuria Railway forty million yen.

Of the propriety of this transaction there was considerable doubt. At the time of the 1920 consortium the Japanese had wanted Manchuria and Mongolia excluded from its scope, but Mr. Lamont insisted that they must be included as part of China. It was stated in the Press that there was a gentlemen's agreement that the consortium should not lend money for projects in these regions in which Japan was so much interested. But now Mr. Lamont was ready to lend money to the S.M.R.[1] for the development of Manchuria. Mr. Yamamoto Jotaro soon confirmed the fact of the contract, but put the amount at thirty million dollars, to be issued at 97 and to bear 6 per cent interest. There were not lacking newspapers on both sides of the Pacific to extol this new proof that the door was still open.

A tremendous storm followed. The loan was denounced from one end of China to the other. An endeavour was made in Japan to show that it was only students and self-seekers who were making the fuss and that the Chinese authorities from Chang Tso-lin downwards were anxious to give Japan everything she wanted. In view of the facts, this interpretation was difficult to sustain. Lieut.-General Honjo, Japanese military attaché at Peking and adviser to Chang Tso-lin, reported that the Marshal was quite abusive in his remarks on Japan's policy in China; General Yang Yu-ting, his Chief of Staff, told the Pressmen that the loan would have been welcome enough but for the fact that Japan was opposing the construction of lines of economic

[1] See C. Walter Young, *Japan's Special Position in Manchuria*, Johns Hopkins Press, pp. 267, 285, where it is pointed out that "positive" evidence of the gentlemen's agreement is lacking.

advantage to China and insisting on lines of strategic advantage to Japan, which drew indignant protests from Mr. Yoshizawa and lengthy explanations as to Japan's rights. Yang returned to the charge and said that China was capable of constructing her own lines and was, in fact, doing so.

For the time being China scored. The Chinese argument that the Morgan Loan would be a subsidy to Japanese imperialism, and that in any dispute the safety of American money would be the first care of the Department of State, could not be ignored. The Chinese Foreign Minister filed a formal protest at Washington on December 5th; Morgan & Co. made what excuses they could, and dropped the loan. Mr. Hamaguchi, with much reason, denounced Tanaka's military antics as having depreciated Japan's prestige in China, and the Tanaka policy was certainly proving expensive. There was a slowing down of enterprise in Manchuria and of the reconstruction of earthquake-stricken Tokyo, and there was talk of "decisive measures" for recovering the Nishihara loans from China.

The bitterest dispute was over the joining of the Chang-chun–Kirin line with the North Korean railways. £2,000,000 had been advanced in 1918 as a bribe to get this work done, and the Chinese, having allowed the South Manchuria Railway to extend the Kirin line as far as Tunhua, refused to go further, standing on the treaty right to construct such railways as they chose, with the restriction that if they needed money they should first apply to Japan for it. Meanwhile the Japanese worked from the Korean end, and on October 10, 1927, the bridge over the Tumen (the boundary river) was opened. The *Manchuria Daily News* (published in English by the South Manchuria Railway) expressed the hope on this occasion that China would get over her "strategic obsession" and complete the railway.

CHAPTER IV

THE PROLETARIAT VOTES

As the year 1927 drew to an end, rumours were plentiful that another expedition would be sent to Shantung, but for the time being domestic politics took the lead in public attention. The Minseito party had the biggest representation in the Diet but not an absolute majority; and as the Tanaka Government could not be sure of the support of the minor parties, it was pretty certain that it would resort to the expedient of dissolving the Diet. Party meetings were therefore held to discuss the general election in advance and to draft "no confidence" resolutions. The Diet met for business on January 21, 1928, after the long holiday that follows the opening at Christmas. An attempt was made to get the "no confidence" vote put at the head of the agenda but it was frustrated. The formal speeches were proceeded with, Baron Tanaka delivering two, one as Premier and one as Foreign Minister, and, as customary, he gravely asked the House for its support during the session. Mr. Mitsuchi, the Finance Minister, expounded the financial situation. All the time the Chief Secretary stood near by, "in a respectful attitude," holding a package in a large purple silk napkin. Everyone knew what it was, but until it was unfolded the House howled like Pandemonium. Then silence fell, and, standing in a religious hush, the House heard the reading of the Imperial Rescript ordering its dissolution.

Some significance attached to the general election which followed. It was the first time the manhood of the nation had had the privilege of voting, and it was hoped that the electorate would be too numerous to be cajoled or bribed. Dr. Suzuki, the Home Minister, exhorted the prefectural governors to see that the elections were conducted fairly, and was shocked when the Opposition declared that this was equivalent to telling them that they must see that the Government candidates were returned. The police similarly were instructed to prevent improprieties of speech and publication, and naturally found that such improprieties were committed only by the Opposition. Minseito meetings were broken up, Minseito pamphlets seized, and Minseito posters torn down. A handbill, "Vote for those who got you the vote," was suppressed as improper. Perhaps with more reason, a pamphlet professing to give details of General Tanaka's embezzlement of three million yen of secret service money was confiscated. The General, at a political meeting, urged the necessity of eradicating habits of frivolity and decadence. At a Minseito dinner in a big hotel there was a sudden uproar at the discovery that one of the waiters was a police detective. An explanation being demanded of the manager, he excused himself on the ground that the man was so often there to spy on foreign guests that he had ceased to notice him.

In spite of the strictness of party discipline and the excess of organisation, the election was poorly conducted. There were far too many candidates, and the forfeits of those who did not secure the minimum number of votes amounted to a large sum. In the end, in spite of an amount of violence and coercion for which even the Premier and Home Minister found themselves obliged to express regret, the Seiyukai had a majority of only one or two over the Minseito, and the question arose whether an immediate dissolution would not be advisable. Of eighty-eight Proletarian candidates only eight were elected, and of Mr. Muto Sanji's Business Party, the only party with a real programme, only four; and there was a sprinkling of independents, some ready to be bought, others inclined to follow Mr. Ozaki Yukio, the most distinguished parliamentarian of them all. Neither side cared to seek an alliance with the Proletarians, so the Government made terms with Ozaki and the Business Party, and trusted to good party discipline to get it through the special session. Other measures were taken which precluded any idea of trouble from the eight Proletarian members.

These measures consisted mainly of a persecution of anything even savouring of radicalism. This is a subject that must be considered apart from this narrative of the first manhood suffrage election. The immediate steps taken were to make secret arrests of over a thousand people suspected of "dangerous thought," to proscribe the Farmer-Labour Party, the Labour Union Council, and the Young Proletarians' League. Gangs of patriotic ruffians beat labour leaders, without the police interfering, and there was a general terrorism to counteract the manhood vote.

Of course, neither police nor bullies were always discreet in their manhandling. After the election three Minseito leaders waited on the Premier and complained that mob law had prevailed throughout the elections, that the police had muzzled the Press, sealed the mouths of speakers, and given outlaws a free hand. The Premier promised that it should not happen again. Next day, when Suzuki Bunji was addressing a very mild and centrist Social Democratic Party, newly formed, a mob of ruffians stormed the platform and attacked him, the police contenting themselves with calling on the meeting to disperse. At Wakayama, at the same time, some patriotic ruffians settled a political difference with swords, killing their enemy and seriously wounding several of his friends. Justice was never done in this case. The world has discovered since then that official promises of decent behaviour are readily made but indifferently kept.

Meanwhile developments were taking place in China. The Nanking army and its allies were on the warpath again, with the determination to capture Peking. As early as December the question of sending another expedition to Shantung to stop it was under discussion, but mobilisation orders were not issued till April 19, 1928. Some ambiguous diplomacy preceded this. Yin Yu-ching, an emissary from the Southern group, now purged of Communism, had been in Tokyo in March, and, it was said, had promised that Manchuria would be given self-government if Japan sent no expedition this year to interfere with the progress of the

Southern armies. This was rather like the long-desired declaration that Manchuria was not an integral part of China; but its complete detachment had now been decided on, and the proposal was disregarded. The Diet met for a short special session on April 23rd, and so swiftly did events move that a clash at Tsinan was announced to the House on May 4th. But this attracted less attention than it deserved. The legislators were excited over domestic politics rather than adventures in China. To make the microscopic majority effective, the Government whips had to enforce a very strict discipline. The Opposition were equally determined, and Mr. Terada Ichinose, a Minseito member, attended the House in bandages, after being severely beaten by hired bullies of the Seiyukai.

But the Opposition did nothing to hinder the political terrorisation of proletarian politicians. It was striving towards democracy, but not to that extent. It had accusations against itself to face. Members of the Minseito declared that the government of the country was (or should be) based on the Imperial Diet, or "centred" on it, as the word was more usually translated. "Blasphemy!" shouted their enemies—it centred on the Emperor. It deserves record, in view of later degeneration, that at this time there were some members of the Seiyukai who had the decency to declare that they were averse to dragging the Imperial name into the dirtier passages of party politics.

The nearest that the Diet got to a protest against the persecution of advanced political thought was to protest, with some bitterness, against the fact that the Government did not lay before it the plan to strengthen the Peace Preservation Law by prescribing the death penalty where, heretofore, ten years' imprisonment had been thought sufficient. The Government took no chances: it hated the expression of the mildest liberal opinions, so it got its way by means of an Imperial Ordinance. The raid on March 15th, when over 1,000 Communists were arrested, did duty as a "state of emergency," and along with the tightening of the law, the Goverment saw to it that every liberal professor was driven out of the universities. After all, the chief duty of the special session was to pass the budget, which it did,— a record budget, "balanced" at 1,774,000,000 yen, with the help of bond issues of 200,000,000 yen.

CHAPTER V

THE MURDER OF CHANG TSO-LIN

SHANTUNG was still a "Northern" province, and the Japanese expedition's nominal task was to protect the couple of thousand Japanese residents in Tsinan, in case the advancing Southern forces collided with the Northern troops there. Everybody took it for granted, however, that the real task of the expedition was to prevent the Kuomintang army from advancing further north, though there was some talk of leaving Chang Tso-lin to his fate. It was complained that since he had left Mukden for Peking the financial condition and the currency of Manchuria had deteriorated; still worse, that the Marshal grew less amenable to Japanese advice, constructed railways that he wanted and left unconstructed the lines that the Japanese wanted. That feelings were far from cordial and were, in fact, approaching a crisis was shown by the fact that, when the Marshal ordered some troops from Mukden to Peking, in view of the approach of the Kuomintang army, the Japanese withdrew rolling-stock to the South Manchuria line so that the Manchurian troops were immobilised.

Accounts of what happened in Tsinan never made a coherent whole. General Chiang Kai-shek entered the city on May 2nd, and everything was amicably discussed, even to the taking away of the Japanese barbed wire fences, so that they should not excite the ire of the Chinese troops. The next day, the Japanese declared, the Chinese started looting; they also confessed that they arrested Chinese street orators, lest they arouse the temper of the people. The retreating Northern troops were convenient objects of blame for disorder, as they had been at Nanking over a year before. However it began, there was fighting on the 3rd, the 6th, 7th, and 10th, the consequence of which was that a large part of the city was destroyed, some two thousand Chinese were killed, as well as twenty Japanese civilians and twenty-seven soldiers. Marshal Chang Tso-lin sent word, asking for a suspension of hostilities. The gigantic Chang Tsung-chang, Governor of Shantung, and nominally an ally of Chang Tso-lin, retreated rapidly for the purpose, he declared, of making a last stand at Tientsin. But nobody regarded Chang Tsung-chang seriously except the unfortunate people whom he oppressed.

The main body of the Southern forces, instead of retreating as they had done the previous year, walked round Tsinan and resumed their advance northwards by rail. The Japanese thereupon advised Marshal Chang Tso-lin to return to Mukden and leave the Southerners to take Peking. If he resisted, they pointed out, he would probably be beaten, and the Southerners would pursue his retreat into Manchuria, where the Japanese could not tolerate any strife. Whether the Marshal would have held his own had be been left to himself, nobody can tell. He had a very good chance of smashing the Christian General, Feng Yu-hsiang, before turning to deal with the South, and he held a strong position. But the Manchurian troops, though the best fed and most regularly paid in China, had more than once proved singularly disappointing in the field. Besides, the Japanese had already taken steps to prevent reinforcements arriving. He had to obey. At 1.15 a.m. on June 3, 1928, after a year and a half as Generalissimo in Peking, he left the capital in his special train for Mukden. Entering Mukden at 5.30 a.m. on June 4th, his carriage was accurately bombed, and he died of his injuries in a few hours. The Japanese War Office issued a statement about Chinese who were challenged by Japanese sentries near the spot, and were bayonetted on attempting to escape, bombs being found on the bodies. But these were obviously neither the men nor the bombs that killed the Marshal.

The death of Chang Tso-lin was a shock. For more than twenty years he had held his own in Manchuria, accused by some ardent nationalists of being the tool of Japan, but actually the chief obstacle to Japanese encroachment. His bandit adventures in his younger days were recalled by foreign journalists to give a romantic touch to their articles and by Japanese writers when they wished to discredit him. He lived rather like an Oriental despot, surrounded by armed guards and familiars and with a polygamous household in the background, but he knew his own domain thoroughly and its good government was his principal concern. His predecessor in office, Chao Erh-hsun, was one of the ablest of Chinese statesmen, and Chang had been his loyal lieutenant and devoted friend. On his resignation in 1913, Chang Tso-lin succeeded him. Panegyrists of Japanese penetration in Manchuria have often ascribed to the existence of the leased territory in the far South and the South Manchuria Railway extending to Changchun the fact that Manchuria was the most peaceful and progressive region in China. Those who have any knowledge of the effect of such political juxtapositions will not be led into any error by this fable. The presence of Japanese, always ready to interfere and to assert their rights, made the task of governing Manchuria far more difficult than it would otherwise have been; but the Marshal kept the peace, paid his way, and adroitly resisted encroachment. His old chief Chao Erh-hsun lived on in Peking till 1927, when Chang Tso-lin was Generalissmo, and, when he died, Chang, by his generous provision for the funeral and the security of the family, testified to the constancy of their friendship.

Chang Tso-lin had a great distrust of Russians. With some of his men he fought on the Japanese side in the Russo-Japanese war—as a freelance, or "bandit," of course. Probably as powerful a reason as any which weighed with the Japanese in their policy of not interfering too much with him was their absolute assurance that, whatever else he might do, he would not intrigue with Russia. He had definite views regarding the development of Manchuria, and pre-ferred his own opinion in the matter of laying new railways

to those of Japan, though he was ready to accept the aid
of the South Manchuria Railway, both engineering and
financial, in laying lines of which they both approved.
Where the Japanese would not agree, his own engineers and
capital sufficed.

With the frequent changes and increasing ineptitude in
Peking he gradually lost patience. In 1926 he declared his
independence of the Peking Government, a step the significance of which has been dishonestly exaggerated. It meant
that he would not suffer interference, not, as propagandists
for Japan pretended, that he was announcing the creation of
an independent State. He held office from Peking and it
was as a Chinese citizen that he took charge in the Capital.
Some agreements with foreign Governments he made direct,
but confirmation by Peking followed.

Who killed Chang Tso-lin? The question reverberated
round Japan for years after the tragedy. No Chinese ever
doubted that it was a piece of the Japanese army's work,
but there seemed to be no good reason for it at that particular
moment. However, it is always difficult for those unac-
customed to murder to follow the mental processes of those
who adopt it as a policy. The great fact remained that in
spite of General Tanaka's two expeditions, the Kuomintang
were now masters of China, and it now seemed logical to
recognise the Nanking Government—if it would abandon
Manchuria.

Japanese writers have often jeered at the "Chang Dynasty,"
but one of the first acts of the Nanking Government, now in
control all over China, was to appoint Chang Hsueh-liang,
"the Young Marshal," to his father's post. There was some
dubiety in Japan regarding the Young Marshal. General
Tanaka reported to the Cabinet on July 17th, that Chang
Hsueh-liang had acknowledged the authority of the Nanking
Government, and had undertaken to adhere to Dr. Sun
Yat-sen's Three Principles and to fly the Nationalist flag.
But, he said, the real master of Mukden was General Yang
Yu-ting, the Chief of Staff—and it was taken for granted

that Japan would be able to manage him. Tanaka assured the Cabinet that any rough-handling of Japanese interests by the Nanking Government would be carefully watched. The next day Nanking denounced the Sino-Japanese treaty of commerce. As the United States had already recognised China's tariff autonomy and had made a new treaty of commerce with Nanking, it was rather difficult to deal with this denunciation in the only diplomatic form that General Tanaka really understood.

Things like this, as well as the hatred the army felt towards the Kuomintang now that it seemed likely to unify China, made the prospect of recognising the Nanking Government very disagreeable unless very advantageous terms could be arranged. Nor was the prospect sweetened by the Shakai Minshuto (Social Democratic Party) passing a resolution denouncing the Government's China policy, and demanding recognition of the Nanking Government and encouragement of Sun Yat-sen's Three Principles.

The Young Marshal's acceptance of and adherence to the Nanking Government remained the chief stumbling-block. To hoist the flag and openly proclaim allegiance was galling after all that had been done to detach Manchuria from China. Consul-General Hayashi in Mukden gave the Young Marshal an "ultimatum" on the subject, but could get nothing better than a promise to wait for three months. Tanaka, who, like most of Japan's military men, was a great believer in the power of money, suggested that if the Marshal wanted money, the South Manchuria Railway would be glad to advance him some; and he sent Baron Hayashi Gonnosuke, a former Minister to China, to try and persuade the Marshal not to throw in his lot with Nanking, though the mission was camouflaged as an act of courtesy—attendance at the funeral of Chang Tso-lin. Baron Hayashi argued that there was nothing novel in the detachment of Manchuria and in Japan's assumption of something like a protectorate, since she wanted this in 1915, and only desisted owing to China's objections. The time had now come to make these desires effectual. On August 8th he spoke very plainly to Marshal Chang Hsueh-liang, but the Young Marshal, with equal plainness, told him that he was resolved to acknowledge the authority of Nanking.

Viscount Kaneko and Mr. Tsurumi were sent to America to preach the gospel of an independent Manchuria. The forward policy had been boosted in Japan to such effect that the Minseito was wavering in its support of Baron Shidehara, though it had a very lively apprehension of the fact that Tanaka's methods in China had induced a boycott that had already diminished trade by thirty-two million yen. Toyama Mitsuru's "China Ronin" were doing some independent diplomacy, cajoling and bullying, and their help was so embarrassing that Tanaka told the Young Marshal that Consul-General Hayashi and Baron Hayashi were the only accredited bargainers.

The victorious Nationalist Government made things more uncomfortable by asserting itself. It seized a Japanese propagandist paper published in Chinese in Peking; and it demanded the punishment of General Fukuda for his massacres of Chinese in Shantung. Mr. Yoshizawa, the Japanese Minister in Peking, being home on leave in October 1928, made earnest representations to General Tanaka on the need for reasonable and friendly policies in China, but he was persuaded to adopt an unreasonable one, Japan insisting on control of the Shantung Railway as the price of withdrawal, so that it was not till March 27, 1929, that withdrawal really began.

The transference of the capital to Nanking and the ancient Northern Capital being renamed Peiping (Northern Peace) rather diverted interest for a time, and the preparations for the Enthronement of the young Emperor of Japan in November 1928 completely monopolised attention. When that function was over, interest was sharply revived by the news that, on December 29th, Marshal Chang Hsueh-liang had accepted the post of High Commissioner for the Four North-eastern Provinces, had sworn fealty to the Nanking

Government, and had hoisted the Kuomintang flag. Chang Tso-hsiang was named Governor of Kirin, Wan Fu-lin of Heilungkiang, and Tang Yu-lin of Jehol. The inclusion of Jehol with Manchuria, involving the renaming of the Three Eastern Provinces under the new style of the Four North-eastern Provinces, was a matter of administrative convenience which Nanking afterwards had cause to regret. It was noted as rather ominous that in the new appointments there was no mention of General Yang Yu-ting, who had previously been mentioned as Governor of Fengtien (the Mukden province) and had been referred to by General Tanaka as the real ruler of Manchuria. It was known that he was still in office and was in charge of the Mukden arsenal.

He was soon heard of. On January 10, 1929, the Young Marshal invited General Yang Yu-ting and Chang Ying-huai, head of the Peking–Mukden Railway, to a mahjong party at his mansion in Mukden. As they entered the room prepared for them they were shot dead by the Marshal's guards. It was announced that they had been executed. The Young Marshal saw to their honourable burial, and gave a hundred thousand dollars to the family of Yang Yu-ting, who, one of his eulogists declared, had given proof of his unalterable probity by dying a poor man.

A high Japanese official informed the Press that by these executions Chang Hsueh-liang had avenged his father's death. The Chinese garrison headquarters at Peiping had a very different story. The Chinese story was that Yang Yu-ting had conspired with the Japanese for the proclamation of a Manchurian Republic, of which he was to be head, and which was to include Chihli as well as the Four North-eastern Provinces. This was indignantly denied in Japan, but was a much more likely story than that of the dutiful son avenging his father's death. Throughout China it was believed that the Young Marshal had struck a heavy blow at Japan's plans. He certainly triumphed for the time being, but the hoisting of the Kuomintang flag at Mukden, instead of putting an end to the long machinations to separate

Manchuria from Intramural China, only made the army the more resolute to find an opportunity and to strike decisively.

Many of the best minds in Japan were profoundly disturbed by the murder of Chang Tso-lin, and those who declared most emphatically that it was impossible that the Japanese army could have done such a thing, were only trying to exorcise their own doubts. There were constant demands for a clearing up of the mystery. A Sino-Japanese joint inquiry had presented its report in December 1928, but this has never been published. Baron Tanaka asked the Peers, almost as a personal favour, to refrain from discussing it, and he told the Diet that the inquiry was not yet concluded. He bluffed through the Diet session of 1929, but the agitation still continued. It was shown beyond all explanation to the contrary that the spot where the murder had taken place was in the midst of an area for the protection of which the Japanese Kwantung army was responsible, and "punishment" was talked of. General Muraoka, the Commandant, and Mr. Kinoshita, Governor of Kwantung, both resigned. The matter was so serious as to involve reports to the Throne, and on July 1, 1929, the Tanaka Government resigned, unable to face the responsibility of having caused anxiety to the Imperial mind. Chang Tso-lin dead had proved more powerful than Chang Tso-lin living.

Tanaka did not long survive his fall from Office. On Saturday, September 28th, there was a Seiyukai banquet at which he presided, as cheerful and robust as ever. On Sunday even his enemies were shocked at the circulation of an "extra" announcing his death. Clouds had been gathering so thickly about the Seiyukai that the rumour spread that he had committed suicide, and this was so widely believed that his friend General Ugaki, the Minister for War, considered it necessary to give out a formal denial. None who knew Tanaka would credit such a rumour. He was a giant in physique and was never dismayed or depressed. He had left the party at a late hour, after a very convivial evening, and drove to the house of a concubine, in whose company he died very shortly afterwards—a mishap such as has been known before to happen to amorous and elderly gentlemen full of wine.

As the convenor of the Far Eastern Conference he laid plans for the subjugation of China which in other hands than his own have caused purposeless suffering to many millions and have brought infinite discredit on Japan. In his own military ventures he was peculiarly unlucky. He was directly responsible for the grandiose intervention in Siberia which cost 700 million yen, caused much misery, and left a legacy of hatred. At the cost of 100 millions he demonstrated in 1928 that Japan could go into China, destroy an inland city, and get away again; and his machinations against the Kuomintang secured that party's domestic supremacy. His administration was an orgy of corruption. But he goes down to history as a practitioner of bold policies and an apostle of Japanese expansion.

CHAPTER VI

LIBERALISM'S LAST EFFORT

TANAKA's last Diet session, in 1929, had been distinguished by almost continual disorder. In the House of Representatives it was one long series of loud denunciations of everything done by a government which was both unpopular and corrupt. The House, it is true, was disorderly by habit, but, though the tradition was strong that it was patriotic to be a bad and predacious neighbour and glorious to have the army in the field, these considerations did nothing to mollify it; and the promises of conquest in the future did not bring oblivion to the ineptitudes of the present. The House of Peers was more orderly but even more hostile, and many of its members were neither disinclined nor afraid to say exactly what they thought of the military idea of politics. The time was to come when even the House of Peers would be intimidated, but for the present liberalism was still vocal.

When Tanaka's resignation was followed almost automatically by the coming into power once more of the Minseito, with its President, Mr. Hamaguchi, as Premier, there was a general feeling of relief. Some had got into the habit of echoing the criticism of Baron Shidehara's foreign policy as weak, but its sharpest critics could not fail to see that Tanaka had spent a great deal of money and only got hatred and the first really effective boycott in history as a result of his strong-arm methods, so Shidehara's resumption of the Foreign Office portfolio was generally approved.

A strange figure, incongruous to most of his colleagues, occupied the important post of Home Minister, and a few words regarding him are necessary, for his presence in the Cabinet was one of those revealing flashes which show from time to time the gulf that still remains between Old Japan and Modern Europe. Adachi Kenzo, from his youth up, had been one of the strutting patriots the endurance of whom is the price that Japan pays for her extravagant exaltation of loyalty. As a young man he was sent by his patron Sasa Tomufusa to his native city of Kumamoto to stir up feeling against Marquis Okuma, who, in the opinion of Sasa and his school, was too complaisant towards the Powers with whom he was engaged in the difficult task of drawing up new treaties. A political gangster, inspired by Adachi's eloquence, threw a bomb at Okuma, after which he disembowelled himself. Okuma lost a leg. A shrine was erected in the gangster's memory, but Adachi had not yet become a great hero. He went to Korea, and in Viscount Miura, the Japanese Minister, he found a patron after his own heart. Miura, annoyed with the Queen because she did not trust him, sent for Adachi, and explained his plan to him. Adachi, accordingly, went once more to Kumamoto, a city famous for its gangsters, of whom he collected twenty-four who were instructed to raid the royal palace in Seoul, the Japanese Legation Guard standing by to see that they were not interfered with. A dozen of the gang were given special instructions to seek out the Queen and kill her. They raced through the rooms and corridors, seizing the terrified palace ladies and beating them to make them show where the Queen was. When one of them found her she wrenched herself out of his grasp and ran shrieking down a corridor towards the King's apartment, with the murderers in pursuit. Some held the King, while others ran their swords through the Queen. Without waiting to see whether she was dead, they rolled her up in bedclothes, drenched them with kerosene, which they had provided for the purpose, piled on billets of wood, and set all on fire, feeding the flames liberally with more kerosene till everything was consumed.

Nobody was punished for this horrible crime, but Prince Ito expressed bitter regret that he had appointed such a man as Miura. But the legend grew that Miura was an empire-builder, and he remained to the end of his life a political oracle, enormously respected. Adachi remained in politics, with this murder as his sole capital, and attained Cabinet rank under Count Kato. Presumably Hamaguchi had to promote the patriot still further. He earned his promotion. He dismissed all doubtful prefectural governors and replaced them with his own party henchmen, so that at the next election the Minseito got a big majority, and Adachi was called "the king of elections." As Home Minister he exercised the censorship with a heavy hand and chastised political thinkers with scorpions. He was a blot on a Cabinet which otherwise had qualities that raised it above any previously known in Japan.

Other notable members of the Cabinet were Inoue Jonnosuke (who had deplored the evaporation of Japan's war wealth), who became Minister of Finance; General Ugaki, Minister for War, and Admiral Takarabe, Minister for the Navy. The Defence Ministers had held these posts under Kato and Wakatsuki, and were reasonable and statesmanlike men, which, perhaps, was the reason why Tanaka did not have them when he held office.

The Seiyukai having lost its president, it became a matter of importance who should fill that post. That at this moment the Minseito stood much higher in reputation was due to accident rather than to its superior principles. Everything in the parties depended upon leadership: the parties themselves stood for no political ideals, and between the rank and file of either there was little to choose. When Prince Saionji had been president of the Seiyukai, it was the most respectable party. Under Hara (murdered in 1921) it had greatly increased in wealth and influence but had deteriorated in morals. The Minseito, founded (as the Rikken Doshikai) by Prince Katsura, had a most unpromising beginning, for Katsura's reputation was bad, but under Count Kato and Mr. Hamaguchi it took on some of their high character, while the Seiyukai, under Tanaka, became a byword for corruption. In Hara's time Takahashi and Tokonami helped to maintain the reputation of the Seiyukai.

just as in Hamaguchi's day a leader like Adachi cast over the Minseito a baleful mediæval glamour.

Japan's greatest parliamentarian, Ozaki Yukio, had grown disgusted with a party system that stood for nothing but spoils, and ploughed his lonely furrow; his "twin god of the Constitution," Inukai, had almost come to the same condition, but kept a personal following as head of a political "club." Mr. Tokonami, who had been Hara's Home Minister, had broken from the Seiyukai and formed a new party, the Seiyuhonto. He was the most honest and highminded of bureaucratic statesmen, and very keen on the promotion of a reasonable patriotism. Honesty and lack of fanaticism were a hindrance to party leadership, and, getting nowhere with his party, Mr. Tokonami dissolved it and formed a "club" instead. But he was always trying to form working agreements and angling for Cabinet appointments for himself. The veteran Ozaki Yukio remarked on the contrast between Tokonami's high personal character and the petty opportunism of his political tactics, and his advice to Tokonami was very much like a paraphrase of, "Seek ye first the kingdom of God and his righteousness, and all these things shall be added unto you." Tokonami had come back to the Seiyukai at last, but he became neither president nor Premier; Inukai, who for years had led the Kokuminto, most of whose members, on its dissolution, joined the Minseito, at last discovered that his principles were in conformity with those of the Seiyukai, and, after Tanaka's death, was elected president.

Inukai resembled General Baron Tanaka in no degree whatever except in the possession of plenty of courage, and even this quality was of a different temper. Honest, though very ready to accept contributions to his political fund, he did not regard politics as a field for plunder as had all Tanaka's friends. Physically almost a dwarf, and frail, he was fourteen years older than his herculean predecessor but was still full of fight. Though sometimes chauvinistic in his speeches, he was no admirer of military men; he always advocated the holding of the defence portfolios by civilian statesmen, and his first speech after becoming president of the Seiyukai was a vigorous denunciation of militarism.

Had the parties been as devoted to political ideals as they were destitute of them, there would probably have been more regard for continuity of policy. But seeing that Tanaka had deliberately destroyed the constructive work of the Minseito, the Minseito in its turn could hardly be blamed for reverting to its former policies. Nor could retaliatory tactics be altogether avoided. Seiyukai party henchmen put in as prefectural governors had to give place to adherents of the Minseito, and the prancing proconsul Yamamoto Jotaro, who had been made president of the South Manchuria Railway Company with a view to imperial expansion, was replaced by the railway expert and economist Dr. Sengoku, so that development might be orderly and finance should be sound. The Seiyukai traditionally followed a "positive" policy, which Tanaka had found agreeable as it meant a free spending of money. As soon as the Minseito returned to power, Hamaguchi began campaigning for economy, and almost immediately announced a reduction of the budget by eighty million yen.

When liberalism and the growth of democracy in Japan are under discussion, it would be easy for a critic to deny that either had obtained any foothold. Freedom of thought and of speech were always confined within very narrow grooves, and manhood suffrage made a very small contribution towards social emancipation. The liberalism of Hamaguchi was mainly centred on a Gladstonian economy combined with a rigid system of Protection; that of Baron Shidehara on good neighbourliness and a respect for other countries' rights, especially those of China. The two statesmen, backed by their colleagues, strove also for the effective authority of the Diet, and for control by the civil power.

The fate of rights and liberties to which their limited liberalism seemed to be indifferent may be surveyed elsewhere. Here, in the description of the effort to establish liberalism in the Japanese polity, it is better to keep to phases in which success, however transient, was achieved. For the world at large the London Naval Treaty of 1930 is little but the last feeble effort of the movement for naval disarmament. In Japan its importance rather lies in its being the last success scored in the effort to achieve civil control. The treaty maintained and even extended the ratio system, against which Japanese naval enthusiasts continually tried to stir up national feeling. At Washington in 1921, there was a certain glow at Japan being the only Power to parley in the gate with Britain and America. But as nationalism became a more morbid growth, the idea of inferiority to any other country became irksome. The strategic arguments against the ratio not being very impressive, it came down at last to a question of national dignity: it was intolerable for Japan to acknowledge inferiority.

The Government and even some of the naval officers were more reasonable, however; Admiral Takarabe, Minister for the Navy, the chief naval delegate, and Baron Wakatsuki, a former Premier, the civil head of the delegation, certainly gave no promise of being unreasonable when they got to London. General interest in Japan was only spasmodic, but there was something like a revolt in the navy. So far as outsiders could see, discipline was better and intrigue less prevalent in the navy than in the army, but there was something of the same tendency for the General Staff to regard itself as the Service, and to look on the Minister as a sort of liaison officer, whose chief duty was to make the Diet understand that it had to pass the estimates. Incidentally, the London Conference was the occasion of the first public broadcast from London to Japan, Baron Wakatsuki making a short report on progress; but it was when the newly elected Diet met on April 23rd, the day after the new Naval Treaty was signed in London, that the nation became aware of the sharp disagreements in high places on the subject. In accordance with custom, the Foreign Minister, Baron Shidehara, reviewed foreign affairs at the first meeting. He admitted that naval experts were not satisfied with the new treaty, but said that the Government had, nevertheless, after careful consideration of all the relevant facts, decided to participate in this international agreement.

This he amplified two days later, and the Minseito acclaimed the treaty as a great achievement, but the trouble was only beginning. Mr Inukai, President of the Seiyukai, asked indignantly how the Government could ignore the opinion of the Chief of the Naval General Staff that the Treaty left Japan insufficiently protected. It was freely declared that Admiral Kato, the Chief of Staff, was only awaiting the return of Admiral Takarabe before handing in his resignation as a mark of his disapproval. Those who regarded the Services as sacrosanct were very restive over the fact that the Premier had taken over the naval portfolio in the Minister's absence, and it was also remarked that General Ugaki was persistently absent from the Diet, so that the opinion of the War Office could not be elicited. Actually the Minister for War was seriously ill. There were lively rumours as to the trouble there would be when the Privy Council got to work. Some of the members hated the Minseito, and hated Baron Wakatsuki especially, whose Government they had helped to pull down in 1927.

The Press exploited the affair, less from convictions about naval defence than to promote sales. A lieutenant-commander happening to commit suicide just then, his rash act received fame as being due almost certainly to patriotic chagrin. Admiral Takarabe landed at Shimonoseki on his return, on May 18th, when a young man stepped forward and handed him a packet wrapped in a silk napkin. It was found to contain a dagger—a polite hint that he should commit suicide. More serious was a plot for direct action against the Admiral in Tokyo, nipped in the bud by eighteen precautionary arrests. Other arrests included a gang of bravoes who attempted to force their way into the house of the aged Admiral Togo to discuss naval defence with him.

Admiral Okada, a former Minister for the Navy, loyally

tried to bring Admiral Kato to a more reasonable frame of mind, visiting him again and again, and asking him, if he could not be reconciled to the idea of the treaty, at least to conform to the decent traditions of the service and resign quietly. Takarabe, for his part, refused to speak at all. Baron Wakatsuki, he said, was chief delegate, and he must await his return. Kato, however, could not contain himself so long. On June 11th he availed himself of his right of audience, reported his opinions to the Throne, and resigned. On the 17th Wakatsuki arrived, and was greeted by enormous crowds, who gave him an enthusiastic reception, showing that the naval propaganda had not yet made a great impression. Continued ill-health forced General Ugaki into resignation about the same time. He was succeeded in the War Ministry by General Minami, Commander-in-Chief in Korea. General Minami was all for vigorous action on the continent, and he led Japan into an adventure which may yet prove to be her ruin.

The Navy General Staff was a good deal in sympathy with its Chief, and took steps to rob the Government of its victory. It presented a supplementary estimate for a hundred million yen to make good the deficiencies in naval defence created by the London treaty! It is easy to prescribe a limit to tonnage but that does not necessarily limit spending. An air programme of two hundred millions to make good the naval deficiencies was also presented. The Government, in despair, jettisoned its promised reduction in taxation. The army was not behindhand. It demanded more and more money for mechanisation.

The war against civil control had begun in earnest, though not yet in the open. The War Council held repeated meetings, at which discussion was long and acrimonious, though it was said that Admiral Kato, who had flung in the apple of discord, remained silent. Admiral Togo was credited with an adverse opinion, and even Takarabe, it was said, had been badgered into a confession that he would have preferred an unlimited navy.

The constitutional position of the Privy Council was always a little uncertain. It was always claiming rights of veto, but as this function was purely obstructive, Governments of all complexions were inclined to ignore it whenever possible. It had raged more than once against General Baron Tanaka, who imperturbably apologised, like a Titan asking the pardon of pigmies, but did not reopen any question for the Council to discuss. When the War Council completed its report, accepting the Treaty, the Premier presented it only to the Throne. The Privy Council's president, Baron Kuratomi, demanded the report. The Premier flatly refused. A special committee of the Privy Council was appointed under the chairmanship of Count Ito Myoji, who was bitter almost to the point of insanity against the Minseito, to examine the treaty. It would be wearisome to recall the interminable discussions and passionate outbursts at the committee meetings. The Council commanded neither the respect of the ruling class nor the confidence of the people, and this was largely due to the man who insisted on saving the country by rejecting the treaty—Count Ito Myoji. A busy, talkative, self-important man, of humble origin, he had attracted the attention of his great namesake, Prince Ito, who took him into employment under his patronage. He seemed destined for a brilliant career when he became chief secretary to the Cabinet in 1892, at the age of thirty-five, and in that capacity he made himself feared and hated by his intrigues and his arrogance, while he gratified his vanity by making politicians dance attendance on him for everything they required. In 1895 he was sent to Chefoo to exchange the ratifications of the Treaty of Shimonoseki, after the Sino-Japanese War, and there he behaved more like a bully than a diplomatist. The Chinese asked for delay and he angrily told them that he would order the recommencement of hostilities if they did not finish the business at once. It is unlikely that Li Hung-chang believed that Ito had any such powers as this, but, after consulting with some foreign diplomats, he acceded, and Ito went back as proud as a turkeycock, receiving a barony for his achievement. But the display of arrogance was rather empty, for the European Powers advised Japan not to annex the Liaotung Peninsula, which had been the chief prize of the war. While Ito was storming, Li Hung-chang got assurances from the Ministers of the Dreibund that they would not permit Japan to wriggle out of the abandonment of Liaotung.

In the third Ito Ministry, Ito Myoji became Minister for Agriculture and Commerce, but held office only a few months. And now he showed that he had not even the Japanese virtue of loyalty to his chief and patron. Loyalty to the Emperor is a transcendental quality; loyalty to one's chief is the theme of popular romances and the peculiar virtue in which the Japanese believe that they excel.However, modern political intrigue forgot the obligations of feudal fealty, and Ito Myoji led his followers into the opposite camp; he was rewarded by Prince Yamagata, who had persuaded him to take this step, with a seat in the Privy Council, then a powerful body, closely related to the Genro, and apparently its destined successor; but, after the leading spirits among the Genro, Princes Ito and Yamagata, died, the Privy Council became a rather petulant assembly of superannuated bureaucrats.

If Ito Myoji thought his Councillorship would lead to greater distinction, he was mistaken. True, he became Viscount in 1907, and Count in 1922. It was remarked that each war brought him a degree of nobility and an accession of wealth, but his acquirements of wealth were even more mysterious than his elevations in rank.

He loudly declared his patriotism on all occasions, and proved it by the usual method of decrying that of others. As he waxed in age he increased in venom, becoming like a termagant whose tantrums, amusing at a distance, are embarrassing at close quarters. In 1927 his diatribes contributed greatly to the fall of the Wakatsuki Ministry; in 1928 he embarrassed the Tanaka Ministry by his intemperate denunciations of the Kellogg Pact; now in 1930 he showed himself a very miracle of irascibility in his attacks on the London Naval Treaty. Death at last quieted him in February 1934. Such was the character of one of Japan's more eminent modern patriots.

In the end, Mr. Hamaguchi spoke to the Privy Council briefly but firmly, and told them that the sooner they made up their minds to perform their duty of recommending ratification the better. On September 27th the Council did so, the Premier presented the treaty to the Throne on October 1st, and the ratification was immediately forwarded to London. Takarabe resigned the naval portfolio, but the rumour that this was the price of the Privy Council's consent was discounted by the fact that Admiral Abo, another member of the delegation who had recommended adoption of the treaty, succeeded him.

The Navy had to be placated with a big replenishment programme. Less than a month later, at a banquet held at the close of the annual naval manœuvres, Rear-Admiral Momotake made a speech denouncing the London treaty and the intellectuals who approved of it. This extraordinary outburst was received with cheers by the naval officers and with visible embarrassment by Ministers and other civilians present.

Opponents of the treaty persisted in their propaganda until "national self-respect" was found to demand the abolition of any acceptance of inferiority. Other countries suffered in a similar way. The group of moderate and far-seeing statesmen with international minds, who directed Minseito policy, found their difficulties increase as the tide of nationalist sentiment mounted, most of their followers being gradually lifted off their feet. Allowing for differences of time, place, and circumstance, one might detect a similar change in England in the same period.

It needed great resolution on the part of the Premier and his colleagues to pursue their policies in the face of all that opposed them. The Services, with all their great prestige, were against them; economy for the time being increased the hardships it was designed to cure; and honest finance had such effects that it was hard to believe it the best policy. Nor were the troubles all domestic. Immediately after the Hamaguchi Ministry came into power came the great crash in America—an event which caused heavy drawings on Japan's free gold market, while the sudden disappearance of American prosperity cut off the flow of gold from America in exchange for silk. The world was in economic chaos. The gospels by which countries scared of Bolshevism were to find prosperity again were not without echoes in Japan, and the Peers demanded the abandonment of Hamaguchi's "no loan" policy. But Hamaguchi declared there could be no financial health without sound finance, and he balanced his last budget at 1,440,000,000 yen—a figure soon to be looked back upon as characteristic of simpler and perhaps happier days. The "Home Goods" campaign assisted in the promotion of a Spartan outlook. As Home Minister, Adachi heard a good deal about the sufferings of the poor; but, as one whose political reputation was founded on murder, he had a mind above economics, and advised a more diligent worship of the Gods, and all would be well. "Lion" Hamaguchi did not care to invoke religious sanctions, but perhaps the pious exhortations of Adachi helped in the great endeavour to which he had devoted his life.

But the days were drawing to a close when the counsels of the nation could be directed by upright principle and high endeavour, and a reign of violence was coming. As yet, however, violence was not organised to seize the control of the State, but expressed itself in terms of brainless patriotism. On November 14, 1930, the Premier was at Tokyo station on one of his frequent propaganda tours, when a young man named Sagoya Tomeo stepped out of the crowd and shot him in the abdomen. Almost exactly nine years before, on the same spot, Hara Takashi, the Seiyukai Premier, had been similarly murdered. The pistol proved less efficient than the dagger, however, and the Premier was carried quickly to the hospital, where it was reported that he might recover.

His assailant, a young man of 23, belonged to the Aiko-kusha (Patriots' Society) the chief of which, Iwata Ainosuke, who was accused along with Sagoya, had been implicated in the murder of Mr. Abe, of the Foreign Office, in 1913.

Though hopes were held out of the Premier's recovery, it was obvious that he would be unable to fulfil his duties for some time, and there was a hurried meeting of such members of the Cabinet as were in Tokyo to decide on a substitute pending his recovery. Mr. Egi, the Railway Minister, took the lead in the discussion. General Ugaki, Minister for War, was the senior Cabineteer, but he had been ill for a long time, and was about to resign. Baron Shidehara came next, and was appointed. The appointment should have been a mere formality, but there was an eager candidate in the person of Mr. Adachi Kenzo, the Home Minister, who at the time of the shooting was in attendance on the Emperor at the autumn manœuvres. He hurried back to Tokyo but was too late. Probably none of his colleagues wished to have him as Acting Premier, but had be been on the spot it might have been difficult to resist his claim to the post, as the holder of the most important portfolio in the Cabinet. His henchmen loudly declared that Shidehara was unfit for the premiership ; but Mr. Egi's suggestion that Adachi should become President of the Minseito did not elicit any comment that suggested that the "king of elections" was regarded as a statesman. This arch-patriot not only missed the boat on which he desired to stand at the helm of State, but had the misfortune to be accused of lack of respect to the Imperial House. In his hurry to become Premier he deserted the Emperor on the field of mimic battle. He never quite lived it down.

The Seiyukai expressed a formal sympathy with the Premier, but indulged in such continous uproar in the House that it was almost impossible to do business. In one affray in the lobby three Government members were stabbed, and Baron Shidehara had narrow escapes of personal violence in the Chamber itself. There was a constant demand that the Premier either resign or attend in person. He attended accordingly on March 10th, but seemed only like the ghost of the old "Lion." Promptly the next day a henchman of Adachi's called on Baron Wakatsuki to press on him the necessity for a new Premier—not, of course, Shidehara. Mr. Miki Sukichi, a very outspoken member of the Diet, then called on Adachi, and told him that this sort of party work was not done. The two gentlemen had words.

On March 13th and 18th the Premier again attended the Diet and was heckled without mercy, and on the 20th he was little better treated in the House of Peers. Thereafter he took to his bed. Operations were performed on April 5th and 9th in the desperate hope of saving him. Acknowledging defeat at last, he resigned on April 11th, and Baron Wakatsuki, his predecessor as Minseito Premier, again took up the burden. Hamaguchi died on August 26th, and a month later all that he had striven for was flung to the winds, and all that he had saved was squandered.

"Lion" Hamaguchi was not born under the old régime like his predecessors, but yet in circumstances and amidst ideas so remote from those of to-day that his biographers write of him that, when he saw the light in Kochi, in 1870, as the third son of a minor forestry official, it had almost been decided to expose him, for a minor official had a very small salary and could not afford too large a family. Birth control was not practised in those days, but population control was. Seeing what a proper babe he was, however, the parents determined to keep him, though it would be hard to provide. He maintained the promise of his babyhood, and a neighbouring family named Hamaguchi, who lacked sons to carry on the name, adopted him, and, when he was nineteen, married him to their sixteen-year-old daughter. An official career was his choice, and he gave early signs of conspicuous ability. At one time he was offered a directorship of the South Manchuria Railway, and if he had accepted it the probabilities would have been against his reaching the Premiership. Yet it is unlikely that any such ambition was the reason for his refusal. Japanese Government Finance was his life interest, and he never departed further from its main arteries than the Communications Department, in which he became Vice-Minister in 1912. He was able and honest, but hardly brilliant, and had a firm will and a clear idea of what he wanted. That his financial theories were always sound only a devoted partisan would maintain, especially in view of the fact that when he died all the accepted ideas were being questioned and rejected, but the man was sound, his finance was sound, and his theories were at least simple and honest. His nickname "Lion" seems to have been given to him because of something forbidding and leonine in his aspect, coupled with a certain vehemence of which he was capable when speaking on any subject that he had much at heart. But he certainly roared very gently, and was most patient and courteous to all with whom he had dealings. His personal tastes were simple—and indeed, limited—but his steadfastness and courage entitle him to be ranked among Japan's greatest men. Few realised when he died that great political principles, so far as this generation in Japan is concerned, died with him.

CHAPTER VII

THE MANCHURIAN BACKGROUND

BEFORE considering the military action which thrust Japan back into the Middle Ages and re-established the soldier as the ruler of Japan, we must make a brief survey of the field chosen for the military power's assertion of supremacy. In the war of 1904–5 Japan had "saved Manchuria from Russia," whose rights she took over as far as Changchun; and Japan always lauded her own altruism in this act when she wished to justify a claim to some advantage as justly due to her. Where development by Russia had been a crime, development by Japan was a high virtue, and the Japanese propagandists were very fond of exhibiting photographs showing how much further Japan had gone than Russia. A new railway line from Antung, on the Korean border, connected with the Korean railway by a bridge, was constructed, but this was strategic rather than economic so far as Manchuria was concerned. Coal and iron mining, salt working, iron smelting, distillation of shale oil, created large industrial interests. Above all, the cultivation of the soya bean brought prosperity. But though one enterprise succeeded another and the South Manchuria Railway continually put out fresh tentacles, it was always "the blood and treasure poured out on the plains of Manchuria" that was invoked as creating Japan's indefeasible claims to whatever she might require in that region. Invested capital riveted her position, but the sentimental claim always came first. In the hands of numerous propagandists, not a few of them foreign hirelings, Japan's claims were continually flourished in the face of the world. The main points were:

Manchuria is a No Man's Land and never was part of China.

Strategically, Manchuria in the hands of a potential enemy threatens Japan's existence.

Economically, Manchuria is necessary to Japan's existence.

Only by Japan's action was Manchuria saved from annexation by Russia.

Japan's sacrifices of blood and treasure give her rights in controlling the destinies of Manchuria such as no other country possesses.

Japan's economic interests and investments in Manchuria cannot be allowed to be jeopardised by her own inaction or her neighbours' hostility.

There were supplementary claims:

Manchuria is one of the world's great highways and the security of transit must be preserved.

In Manchuria since the Japanese succession to the Russian leases there has been peace and progress, with freedom from civil war and from bandits. Manchuria has more railways than all the rest of China, the result of Japanese enterprise.

The most entirely false, though the most sedulously propagated of all these claims, was that Manchuria was not really part of China. The fact that China was expected to be infinitely grateful because Japan had saved it "for China" was a little discrepancy that was never noticed. For a hundred times that it appeared in the Press it was only contradicted once; yet there was no more favourite method among Japanese propagandists than to declare that the Chinese were superlative propagandists, while they themselves were but plain blunt men, sons of the samurai, all honour but no eloquence. Regarding the declaration that Manchuria was peaceful and progressive as a result of the Japanese presence, that is one of those half-truths which it would be wearisome to analyse. Briefly it might be said that Japanese prosperity was due to the South Manchuria Railway, which enjoyed all the advantages of a monopoly in a country naturally rich; the rest was due to Marshal Chang Tso-lin and to the muscles of the laborious Chinese.

The Japanese being quite aware that it was to Russia's

internal troubles rather than to Japan's military victories that they owed their success, always had some fear of revenge; but when the battle of Tannenberg showed that that was not to be feared for many years, they presented the Twenty-one Demands to China. Most of these had to be abandoned, but they clung to the Manchurian clauses.

The four years' intervention in Siberia, from 1918 to 1922, were so entirely discreditable to Japan that she was unable to turn to account her use and abuse of the Chinese Eastern Railway during that period, though at one time Japan had over a hundred thousand troops in Manchuria, sent by way of fulfilling the terms of a treaty of mutual defence forced on China in 1918.

In the years that followed, "issues" between the Japanese and Chinese multiplied. It has been mentioned how the South Manchuria Railway constructed for Chang Tso-lin a railway from Chengchiatun to Tsitsihar, despite the protests of the Russians, from whose railway it diverted a good deal of traffic. The line was a magnificent feeder for the South Manchuria Railway, and very profitable to the Japanese. As the Chinese received half the profits from the Chinese Eastern Railway, damage to that line was felt by them, so it was clear that it was Japan rather than China that disregarded the Russian protest. Later, however, the Chinese constructed a short chord line between Paiyintala and Tahushan, on the Peking–Mukden line, which made it possible to rail goods from Tsitsihar down to Peking without touching the South Manchuria Railway at all. There was immense indignation, the Japanese claiming a "treaty right" to object to parallel lines. Unfortunately there was no definition of what constituted a parallel line. The Chinese maintained that a line at an average distance of a hundred miles and running through a country whose population had increased enormously since the treaties were made, could not be regarded as injurious, and that to circumvent its construction would be economic strangulation.

The tide of indignation rose higher still when a contract

was made with a firm of Dutch engineers for the construction of a port at Hulutao, a place with considerable natural advantages within a very short distace of Lienshan, on the Peking–Mukden line. A port had been badly needed there for years, the lack of it being a serious handicap to the development of the Peking–Mukden line and all its northern hinterland. When the contract was placed, the same people who had insisted that Dairen was insufficient and that Manchuria must have another outlet through Korea, rose in their wrath and denounced the attempt at Hulutao to ruin Dairen.

(These outlandish names were heard of again when the Japanese took action to maintain their "rights" in Manchuria.)

Nor was this the sum-total of Chinese major offences in Manchuria. They had also constructed a railway from Kirin to Mukden in the face of the protests of Japan—protests which rose to their height over the question of linking up at Kirin with the Kirin–Changchun line and at Mukden with the Peking–Mukden line. The Japanese saw in this a plan to rail produce on Chinese lines right across the Japanese line for eventual export from Hulutao. But the linking of two railway termini about a mile apart is so obvious an action that no effective obstruction could be offered. Here was an attempt on the part of the Chinese to take a hand in the development of Manchuria on both sides of the South Manchuria Railway. Nobody could say that the lines were redundant, for the population and the agricultural production had so increased that the existing lines were badly congested, as the Japanese themselves complained. It has often been said of Asiatic immigrants in "white" countries that their virtues make them more unpopular than their faults. Similarly the enterprise and increasing capacity of the Chinese was much more disliked by the Japanese than the venality of their generals or the prevalence of bandits.

For the time being the Nationalist Government at Nanking

had not succeeded in unifying China: there was trouble both with the Canton faction and the Communists; but Marshal Chang Hsueh-liang had received his appointment from Nanking and had declared himself Nanking's staunch adherent. That, combined with the growing enterprise of the Chinese in Manchuria, made it seem desirable to the Japanese army to strike without further delay.

But before we come to the dramatic events of September 1931, there is another aspect of the Manchurian background to consider. There was the "persecution" of the Koreans. This was an instrument for promoting the forward policy that came into Japanese hands fortuitously, for the Japanese are hardly clever enough to conceive such a plan in advance: it would need an almost diabolical subtlety. For over a century there had been a slow drift of Koreans over the northern border into the Chientao region, a rather uninviting place, but capable of cultivation. At the time of the annexation of Korea in 1911 there was a great trek on the part of those who had resisted the Japanese. The climate is severe and their sufferings were terrible, but they cleared new land and settled down on it. They were bitterly hostile to Japan, cultivated hatred, and dreamed of revenge. Some would make border forays, others tried to study military arts in the hope of making a more serious invasion. The Japanese followed them "for their protection." They set up consulates with armed guards in the towns, where Japanese police were conspicuous, while Chinese hardly existed. The Japanese point of view was that this was the best way of controlling these recalcitrant and dangerous subjects.

But as time went on a new phase developed. Koreans who got into disputes with Chinese officials were not slow to discover that as Japanese subjects they were able to get very powerful backing. As a natural result of this, the Chinese, who had hitherto regarded the influx with indifference, or even with benevolence, began to change their opinion. So little had the Chinese regarded the Koreans as foreigners that they had freely allowed them to hold land, but when some began to defy Chinese orders it was very clear that a change of attitude was necessary. The holding of land by foreigners was not only against the law, but there was a strong prejudice against it. It is true, the treaty of 1915 (known as the Twenty-one Demands Treaty) specified that Japanese might hold land in Manchuria, and it followed that other nations enjoying "most favoured nation" treatment would share this right. But permission for Japanese to hold land did not impose on Chinese owners any obligation to assist in the exercise of this right, and Japanese complained that they could never acquire land. It was easy enough to get it transferred from a Korean holder, however, so the Chinese extended their prejudices to Koreans. The more firmly the Japanese established themselves in Chientao for the protection of Japanese subjects the more was heard of Koreans being persecuted. Nor were persecutions confined to this particular region. In April 1927 sixty Koreans were persecuted by the Chinese police at Shihchiatzu, on the Antung–Mukden line, and similar complaints arose wherever the Japanese employed Koreans as a mask for Japanese penetration. Actually in some places large tracts were hired by Japanese, where a Chinese owner had been complaisant, but complaints increased of the "refusal to lease land according to treaty" as the relations became more tense.

Although Japan claimed a "special position" in Manchuria, this was not specifically mentioned in the treaties as conferring on Japanese subjects rights denied to the citizens of other Powers; and, the question being raised whether Japan had any preferential right to supply advisers in Manchuria, Mr. Hanzawa, the editor of the *Diplomatic Review*, set forth the thesis, afterwards to become very fashionable, that the Chinese themselves had no special rights in Manchuria and Mongolia, which were not originally a part of China. "Issues" multiplied in Manchuria, and came before different people for settlement.

The Governor-General of the Kwantung Leased Territory, the Commander-in-Chief of the Kwantung Army, the President of the South Manchuria Railway, and the Japanese Consul-General at Mukden were all very important persons, but as their decisions might overlap or even disagree, and so embarrass the forward movement, a demand emerged (voiced in the *Chuo Koron* in August 1927) for the appointment of a single authority instead of "three-headed" or "four-headed" control.

The first sign that the Japanese propaganda about "persecution" was having effect was a disturbance in Korea, where, in December 1927, a number of Chinese shops were wrecked and plundered. Many Chinese flocked into Seoul, where better order was kept, and fifteen hundred fled into China. Newspapers throughout Japan and Korea were warned not to report anything that would disturb the public mind.

More reports of persecution followed. Japanese complaints were made to the Chinese authorities. The Governor of Kirin replied that the men on whose behalf complaint was made were undesirables, such as gave Japan herself much trouble; but he offered them naturalisation, so that they should not become the subjects of diplomatic dispute. Consul-General Kawagoe (later transferred to Tientsin and thence promoted to the Ambassadorship) objected, on the ground that undesirability had not been proved. The Koreans themselves held a mass meeting and decided to become Chinese, "as the Japanese did nothing for them." The discussion raged, the military men being mostly against allowing China to naturalise Koreans, and a Korean newspaper was suspended for saying that if the Koreans were being persecuted in China they were suffering for Japan's sins.

At this period Chinese were pouring into Manchuria in great numbers, which the Japanese regarded with benevolence, since they were good workers and increased the wealth of the South Manchuria Railway, but those who loved always to tax the Chinese with some fresh wickedness found evidence of it here, for, they said, Koreans were the proper immigrants for Manchuria—an argument which gained some favour because of the large number of Koreans who had invaded the Japanese labour market.

A Kirin man, Mr. Wang, was appointed Vice-Minister for Foreign Affairs at Nanking, but the fact of the Chinese Foreign Office being well informed on Manchurian affairs only embittered the disputes instead of helping to solve them. Mr. Wang, among other things, told the Japanese that some Koreans were indeed persecuted—pedlars of Japanese morphia and cocaine.

CHAPTER VIII

THE GATHERING OF THE CLOUDS

In the autumn of 1930 it began to be certain that the army was out for mischief in Manchuria. Disputes increased in number and in bitterness, Koreans were egged on to physical encounters with the Chinese, and the army was compiling lists of unsettled matters in dispute, ranging from large questions of railway policy to the latest bout between soldiers and labourers. Dr. Sengoku, Hamaguchi's president of the South Manchuria Railway, resigned, owing to ill-health, and on the recommendation of Prince Saionji, Count Uchida, a diplomatist and former Foreign Minister, was appointed. The Prince, no doubt, regarded him as a steadying influence, but the more common idea was that so important a man would dominate policy more effectively and help the forward movement.

By the time the Diet opened in January 1931, Baron Shidehara was feeling keenly the pressure of the forward movement, but he continued steadily on his way. Reaffirming that his policy towards China was a friendly one, he assured his critics that this did not mean the giving away of Japan's rights and privileges. He pointed out that though the situation in May and June 1930 in Shantung had been disquieting, no Japanese lives had been lost. He generously refrained from contrasting this with the preposterous military expeditions sent by Baron Tanaka in 1927 and 1928 which did cause a loss of Japanese lives which would otherwise have been safe. He extolled the constructive work done by General Chiang Kai-shek, President and Commander-in-Chief in China, who had (for the time being, at least) suppressed the Communist-bandits, and was creating a new China, following the same path that Japan had taken years before when she, in a similar way, emerged from an inferior status to take her place among the Great Powers.

Emphasising in a practical manner the Government's sympathy with China, the First Class Order of the Rising Sun was conferred on Marshal Chang Hsueh-liang, Consul-General Hayashi in Mukden handing over the insignia on January 31, 1931. But a spirit of disorder was abroad. A Seiyukai member attacked Shidehara in a long speech full of venom but empty of scruple, and when Shidehara rose to reply the Seiyukai howled him down. In the House of Peers Mr. Kawamura Takeji wrathfully declared that Japan was losing Manchuria through Shidehara's spineless diplomacy. Mr. Honda, a former ambassador, at a public meeting at the Tokyo Kaikan, denounced Shidehara for a solid hour, and, though there were many counts in his indictment, it was always Manchuria, Manchuria, Manchuria that was the subject of complaint. This and the jingoism of the Peers were more serious matters than the howling of the Seiyukai.

The defence forces were getting restive. The Government found it difficult enough to reduce departmental expenditure in the civil departments, but almost impossible in the case of the army and the navy. Consequently, when the Finance Department let it be known that its new plans for the budget assigned half the total reductions to the defence forces—fifteen million yen to come off the army estimates and thirteen million off the navy—the army decided that it was time to do something about it. The Military System Inquiry Commission presented its report, pointing out how impossible it was to reduce the army expenditure in view of the army's need of mechanisation. Nor was this the only fresh expenditure required. General Kanaya, Chief of the General Staff, pointed out the necessity of adding a division to the Korean garrison, especially as General Ugaki's presence in Korea, where he had been appointed Governor-General, facilitated such a movement. Most direct and most ominous of all was the warm support given to the proposal by General Minami, Minister for War, who said that in case of war in Manchuria and Mongolia, soldiers already in Korea could be sent to the front "without exciting the feelings of the Powers so greatly as would the dispatch of troopships from Japan proper."

Nobody argued seriously that Japan's land forces were inadequate for home defence. The military demands were obviously for adventures on the mainland. A new regiment and a battery of field artillery were demanded for Formosa, not because there was the least need for them, but because anti-Japanese sentiments were frequently aired on the mainland. Indeed, a situation was growing up in Fukien not altogether unlike that in Manchuria. The Formosan Chinese, under Japanese rule, had improved in economic condition, as the Koreans had; but, like the Koreans, they hated their masters and all their ways. Those who had Fukien connections, however, and had business on the mainland, were quick enough to discover the advantage of being Japanese subjects, the chief being that they could defy law and authority in Fukien with impunity. So there was "persecution" there too, and the Fukienese began to feel the same sentiments towards the Formosans as those felt by the Manchurians towards the Koreans, which contributed so much to the unrest in Manchuria.

It never struck General Minami, when he enlarged on the advantages of being able to rail troops straight into Manchuria, that he was giving the very highest endorsement to the objections that the Chinese raised to the completion of the railway from Tunhua to the Korean border.

The army could keep its incidents in hand, ready to produce for the inflammation of public opinion at the right moment. Their choicest was the murder, which took place in June 1931, of a Captain Nakamura, who, with a sergeant and two guides, one Russian and one Chinese, and a passport describing him as a student, was doing intelligence work on the Manchu–Mongolian border. The party was captured by a company of Chinese soldiers and shot for spies. For the time being the news was kept out of the newspapers.

Enough excitement was caused by another affair. Some twenty miles north-east of Changchun, at a place called Wanpaoshan, was one of the tracts of land acquired by Japanese capitalists and worked by Koreans. The Koreans for a long time had been at work on an irrigation ditch a couple of miles in length, and as the work progressed, so did the misgivings of the Chinese in the neighbourhood, for a flood, they said, would put one hundred and thirty Chinese families in jeopardy. The Japanese denied it. Threats to interrupt the work brought Japanese police on the scene, though it was far from the railway zone; but on July 1, 1931, there was a free fight: the Chinese farmers destroyed the work, many blows were exchanged, and there was even pistol-firing, but fortunately without fatal effect.

The affair was widely advertised as a culmination of the persecution of Koreans by the Chinese, and it had a tragic sequel. Demonstrations by Koreans against Chinese residents took place in Chemulpo and other places in Korea, in which Chinese were murdered, and on July 5th there was an organised raid on the Chinese in Pyongyang, the chief town in North Korea, no great distance from the border. The work was savage and thorough, over a hundred Chinese being killed, houses looted and burnt, and belongings demolished, the police doing nothing to curb the violence until it had exhausted itself. The long course of anti-Chinese propaganda, together with the demonstrations made in other places, should have been sufficient to put the Japanese authorities on their guard. The Press in Korea is under such strict control that the anti-Chinese propaganda may be regarded as having official approval, if it was not actually supplied by the Japanese.

In all these cross-currents of disturbance there was one man who held persistently on his course, working for peace and understanding. Baron Shidehara, the Foreign Minister, constantly kept before him the fact that a friendly neighbour is a better customer than one who is hostile, and continued the policy which he began in 1924, and continued even through the trying days of the beginning of 1927, of relying on friendly persuasion, however perverse at times the Chinese might seem, rather than on the high-handed methods that the military men favoured. He always deprecated the wild exaggeration of "incidents" by which many politicians and nearly all the Press constantly tried to inflame feeling against China. In this case he immediately recognised the wrong done, and offered compensation. Dr. C. T. Wang, the Chinese Foreign Minister, however, with a rankling memory of much larger compensation that China had had to pay on much smaller occasions, and of greater offences against Chinese where compensation had been contumeliously refused, demanded a completer apology and more generous terms.

It happened the very day before the Wanpaoshan farmers' battle that the Minseito, the Government party, in reply to attacks made on it, and especially on Baron Shidehara's "weak" foreign policy, issued a manifesto, which began thus:

Soon after the Minseito Cabinet was formed, the boycott of Japanese goods in China, which had been general, subsided. In May last year the reciprocal Customs Agreement was concluded between the two countries. Moreover, the way is now open for the resumption of negotiations for the settlement of many problems relating to the South Manchuria Railway which had long been at a deadlock. In short, Sino-Japanese relations, which at one time were on the brink of rupture owing to the military diplomacy pursued by the Tanaka Cabinet, bid fair to be restored to the former state of friendliness.

This was no more than the truth, but the work was undone by those who organised the Pyongyang massacre, after which the boycott movement flared up again. Soon Manchurian affairs were to be taken out of the hands of the Foreign Office even more completely than when the military intervened with independent action at the end of 1925.[1]

[1] See the present writer's *Japan in Recent Times*, p. 334. On the earlier occasion Baron Shidehara had decided that military action was

That the military party, supported by the Seiyukai, was determined to carry out its own plans in Manchuria, few people doubted; and so little, despite its manifesto, could the Minseito be described as a party devoted to peace and non-intervention that it offered no effective counterpoise. That the war party chose its time is certain, but why it chose the particular moment at which it struck is a problem which admits of a good deal of speculation. Fundamentally there was megalomania—a passion for empire, bred of previous successes, the self-conviction brought by long repetition that Manchuria was Japan's, bought by blood and treasure. Then there was the growing solidarity of China. There were still sharp internal quarrels, but China was unmistakably progressing towards unity, especially the alarming unity of the Three Eastern Provinces with Nanking. It was formerly easy to exact indemnities, to obtain concessions, to foist advisers; now it had become impossible and every day China was seeking to throw off the older bonds. She openly declared that she did not consider treaties imposed by force binding. She was pressing with a constancy which presaged success, slow though actual progress might be, for Customs autonomy, abolition of extraterritoriality, and the control of the settlements in the treaty ports. There was some danger of losing ground rather than gaining it. Worse was the fact that a friendly diplomacy seemed to be succeeding where the military men would much rather see their own energetic methods as the instrument of success. More than this, the army was losing credit in Japan; it was less popular and less respected; the weight of the shield was irksome and its usefulness was doubted. Should the Government succeed in cutting down its budget, it might have as little prestige as the army had in England or America. It was necessary, before the next Disarmament

---

unnecessary—but it was taken in spite of him. Later, when he declared in the Diet that Japan had no desire to interfere with Manchuria's internal affairs, he was sharply attacked by the supporters of the military for saying such a thing.

Conference, to give such a demonstration as would convince the public that only the army could advance the national fortunes.

A Government less devoted to sound finance and less determined to have it, notwithstanding the difficulties in the way, might have looked with favour on adventures in China: diversions abroad are an ancient and well-tried remedy for dissatisfaction at home; and dissatisfaction was constantly seeking self-expression. The masses felt the pressure of hardships and privations which they could not explain, and of which, as a consequence, they were inclined to accept the Socialist explanation. Neither party was prepared for this, and whichever was in power, the political heresy hunt went on unabated. It was kept as quiet as possible, and the fact of arrests was seldom allowed to be published; but from time to time there would be a big raid that was hailed as the final extirpation of Communism; and one could be pretty sure of a Cabinet Minister, a short time after, regretfully confessing in a speech that dangerous thoughts were as rife as ever.

The punishment of crimes of violence, robbery or fraud, was seldom severe, but offences against the Peace Preservation Law—which meant membership of a Communist Society or merely the study of Communism—were sternly dealt with. Yet among students, among workmen, in the army itself, the doctrine was constantly propagated that Japan was not free and that the fruits of the labours of the people enriched a corrupt caste which arrogated to itself an authority which it pretended only High Treason would dare dispute. How far this counted in the calculation of the time for making a military demonstration it is impossible to say. It counted for a good deal with that sinister reactionary Adachi Kenzo, the Home Minister, with a Queen's blood on his hands, during whose term of office the Press was gagged and thought enchained to a degree before unknown.

In China unprecedented floods in the Yangtse valley

paralysed the Government organisation over large and wealthy areas; England had suffered a severe reverse in a financial war and had abandoned the gold standard; the United States had millions of unemployed and vast sums of money in jeopardy abroad. The moment was auspicious.

CHAPTER IX

THE BREAKING OF THE STORM

So steadily did Baron Shidehara keep to his course that to the last it seemed as though he might steer safely to a peaceful settlement, and the fact that he did not was due to open mutiny on the part of the heads of the army. The army was publishing its lists of "unsettled issues," and exploiting the killing of the spy Captain Nakamura, but the country at large remained calm, so the army decided to act without any mandate. On August 4th, addressing a meeting of divisional commanders, General Minami, Minister for War, expatiated on the growing gravity of the situation in Manchuria and Mongolia. He warned them that it was not a passing phase, but due to a decline in Japan's prestige and to the Chinese mania for the "recovery of rights." The army, he said, must have a stronger sense of loyalty and public service. He went on to deride the ignorance of the pacifists who were promoting the Disarmament Conference at Geneva.

The meeting, of course, was a private one, but General Minami took care that it was fully reported in the Press, and the best papers, like the *Jiji* and *Asahi*, reproved him sharply. The *Asahi* said his object was to prevent the reduction of the army budget allotments, and that that was why he was making the public believe that war was imminent. Japan, it said, was in no danger of being attacked by any foreign Power, and as for the protection of rights in Manchuria and Mongolia, military men would do well to remember that neither in the Ruhr nor in Tsinan had the presence of foreign troops been particularly serviceable for this purpose. It concluded that Japan's military men were incurably antiquated in their ideas. In 1919 when the *Asahi* protested against the intervention in Siberia,

its staff was terrorised by bullies and its aged proprietor beaten; now again handbills appeared on the
streets calling on the populace to annihilate the paper.
The army had its revenge later as the populace did not
respond.

Baron Shidehara himself mildly remonstrated with his
bellicose colleague. An exhortation to the cultivation of the
martial spirit, he said, was all very well from an officer to
his juniors, but publishing it in the Press was not a desirable procedure. General Minami replied haughtily that he
thought it would do the public good.

In the first week of September there was a big Seiyukai
meeting at which Mr. Mori, a party leader, solemnly said,
"We are meeting on the eve of war." And he spoke of the
position in Manchuria in a manner that must have been
gratifying to the Minister for War.

On September 14th that stormy petrel Colonel Doihara,
"head of the special military organ at Mukden," visited
Baron Wakatsuki, the Premier, and Baron Shidehara, the
Foreign Minister, to communicate to them the army's ideas
on the Manchurian question. He told the waiting reporters
that he could not divulge the attitude of the Government
towards the military requirements—which could only mean
that it was not favourable. But when he got back to Mukden,
he said, he was going to take the negotiations over the
Nakamura murder out of the hands of the Consul-General
and treat direct with the Chinese military authorities. On
the 16th, Baron Shidehara appealed to Baron Wakatsuki for
support in settling the matter in the regular way, which
the Chinese were anxious to do and which would be to the
advantage of both countries. But Baron Wakatsuki, though
not lacking in courage, no longer had the energy or force
of character to stand up against the army. The murder of
Hamaguchi and the illness of General Ugaki had left the
army without control. The *Mainichi* stated that the permanent officials at the Foreign Office were on the side of the
army.

Lieutenant-General Honjo,[1] commander of the Japanese army in Kwantung province (the leased territory), in these last days visited all military posts in Manchuria, expatiating on the prevalence of bandits, the duty of protecting Japanese lives and interests, by drastic measures if need be, and the importance of fostering the military spirit. When he returned to Mukden on the evening of September 15th, orders were issued for mobilisation on a war footing, and on the 17th morning this same operation was carried out wherever there were Japanese troops in Manchuria.

Thus all was in readiness. At 10.30 on the night of September 18th, a Japanese military patrol was marching along the main line of the South Manchuria Railway at Peitaying. Presently, according to the official statements, they heard an explosion behind them, and, hurrying back, found that a bomb had damaged a couple of sleepers and dislodged a length of rail. Some Chinese soldiers were seen near the spot (there were Chinese barracks close by), and the patrol fired at these men, killing three of them.

Events followed with a celerity which is a tribute to the Japanese staff work. A company turned out on the spot and captured the Chinese barracks. By 2.20 a.m. troops with a couple of armoured cars were approaching the walled city. The spot where the Peking–Mukden line crosses the South Manchuria Railway (the strategic point where Chang Tso-lin had been murdered three years before), and the famous Mukden Arsenal were occupied in force. The aerodrome and the whole flying equipment were captured. At 4.30 the wireless station was taken, and Japanese sentries were posted round Chang Hsueh-liang's mansion. Before dawn the whole Chinese city of Mukden was in the hands of the Japanese, whose cavalry were posted at every gate and entrance. Every Chinese bank was occupied.

[1] Honjo took a very prominent part in the subsequent operations and was rewarded by being made an *aide-de-camp* to the Emperor. He had been a military adviser to the Chinese, and, like other such advisers (General Matsui, for instance), seems to have used his post for the patriotic purpose of conspiring against his employers.

During the 19th the headquarters of the Kwantung Army was transferred from Port Arthur to Mukden, a division of troops was on its way from Korea, and the air force from Pyongyang (north Korea) was ordered to Mukden. Wherever there were Japanese residents in any number the Japanese troops were strengthened. Chinese garrisons were taken by surprise and disarmed. The Young Marshal had warned them, in case of the Japanese making a *coup*, not on any account to resist; but the Japanese did their utmost to provoke incidents, and where they thought it advisable to do so, they bombarded and burnt the barracks. Marshal Chang Hsueh-liang had thought that non-resistance would prove the shamelessness of the *coup* and leave the Japanese no option but to withdraw. He was mistaken. The Japanese were prepared not merely to the last gaiter-button but to the last prevarication.

The newspapers reported that when the news was taken to Baron Shidehara, his face turned grey. At ten o'clock in the morning a Cabinet Council was held in Tokyo, at which General Minami explained that the difference between the present situation and previous outrages was that on former occasions the trouble had always been caused by bandits, but on this occasion the line had been blown up by regular troops. The military authorities, he said, hoped to settle the trouble quickly, as they were anxious that the Japanese residents all over China should not be exposed to peril. The Cabinet made public the announcement of its decision, which concluded: "The Government has decided on the policy of making every effort to prevent further serious developments of the situation. The Minister for War has issued instructions to the Commander of the Japanese Garrison in Kwantung province in the same sense."

Whatever the Minister may have done, the Press reported, without contradiction, that General Kanaya, Chief of the General Staff, had wired instructions to General Honjo to annihilate the Mukden army and chastise the arrogant

Mukden Administration. The Mukden barracks had already
been bombarded, several hundred of the Chinese troops
being killed, and the rest scattered, some simply fleeing
without definite objective, those retaining some traces of
formation making off along the Peking–Mukden line for
Chinchow. There was some fighting at the bridge where
Chang Tso-lin had been murdered, but a large body got
away without annihilation. With them fled a considerable
number of the civil officials. The Young Marshal was not
with them. He had been in the Rockefeller Hospital at
Peiping, suffering from typhoid fever, and was making a
slow recovery. There were rumours that he had been
poisoned.

At the Cabinet Council Baron Shidehara confirmed the
news that the Chinese troops had orders not to offer resistance, he acknowledged the impossibility of foretelling what
would happen, but said he hoped the incident would soon
be closed. What his fears were he did not say; the destinies
of the country had been taken out of his hands overnight.

The fears of the Chinese were apparent. Their newspapers declared that the railway had been damaged by the
Japanese themselves in order to provide them with an
excuse for fulfilling their carefully prepared *coup*. They did
not fail to observe that Colonel Doihara (later known as
the Lawrence of Manchuria) had just returned from a visit
to headquarters at Tokyo; and certainly his part seemed to
be mapped out for him, for the very next day we find him
installed as Mayor of Mukden, and enrolling a new Chinese
police force of several hundred men to keep peace and
order in the city and show that the Chinese were engaged
in a self-determination movement. It was significant that
the first of the many embargoes imposed in Japan on the
publication of news of Manchurian developments was one
which prohibited any mention of Japanese backing for
Chinese independence movements in Manchuria. Baron
Shidehara, faced with the painful alternative of leaving
everything to the military by resignation or making out as

good a case as possible in defence of the very people who had flouted him so insolently, accepted the role of advocate. But he drew the line at Doihara as Mayor. So a Chinese puppet was put in his place. Japanese military administrations were put in control of the Chinese communes at Antung, Yinkow (Newchwang), Changchun and several other cities, and in all of these a Chinese camouflage was soon devised. Thus was initiated the policy of turning Manchuria into a vast puppet show. The Foreign Office had its hands full. Every ambassador and minister stationed in Tokyo was making inquiries on behalf of his Government, and on the 20th the Chinese Government appealed to the League of Nations for aid against Japanese aggression.

The Cabinet Council held on September 22nd gave the keynote for the whole campaign that was to follow. General Minami laid before his colleagues a plan agreed upon between himself, the Chief of the General Staff, and the Inspector-General of Military Education (the triumvirate which ruled the army), for the dispatch of troops to Manchuria and for measures to be taken to secure the safety of Japanese lives and interests. General Honjo, commanding the Kwantung Army, had, said the Minister for War, appealed for such aid as this plan would provide, and the situation in Changchun, the northern terminus of the South Manchuria Railway, and in Chientao, the Korean colony in Manchuria, was so menacing as to demand the dispatch of reinforcements. There was a heated debate. Baron Shidehara dwelt on the foreign complications arising out of the fact that the treaties made it impossible for Japan to do just as she pleased without regard to the other Powers, while Mr. Inoue, the Finance Minister, feeling his plans for financial reconstruction falling about his ears, protested strongly against the waste of money on military adventures.

General Minami's reply was that he had presented the plan to the Cabinet only as a matter of courtesy; that it was quite within the rights of the military authorities to dispatch troops, since the full number permitted by treaty was not there, and that there was a state of emergency. He proposed, moreover, that the opportunity be taken to settle all outstanding disputes with China. Baron Shidehara said he could neither consent to a dispatch of troops which bore the likeness of a military expedition, nor to the proposed means of deciding all Sino-Japanese issues, but the Minister for War was not to be moved. Hardly had the Cabinet Council dispersed when General Minami called on the Premier to inform him that General Hayashi, in command of the troops in Korea, had, on his own responsibility, in view of the state of emergency, dispatched an expedition to Manchuria. Baron Wakatsuki expressed strong disapproval, but Minami said that when he was in command in Korea he had done an exactly similar thing, on a lesser emergency, without seeking instructions. With that the Premier had to be content. General Minami proposed settling the Manchurian business out of hand with Marshal Chang Hsueh-liang, but the Foreign Minister and the rest of the Cabinet considered that it was a matter for negotiating with Nanking, and the General did not press the point.

Meanwhile the military adventure went ahead according to plan. So swiftly and so uniformly were the operations carried out that it was impossible to believe that scattered military posts all acted uniformly by spontaneous military genius. It may be argued, of course, that they only carried out the instructions which had been prepared in case of emergency; but everywhere the Japanese made the first move.

Little resistance was met with anywhere. At Changchun, where the South Manchuria line ends and the Chinese Eastern Railway begins, a more considerable opposition was put up than anywhere else. This was an important Chinese military post protecting the terminus of the Russian railway—for the Russians did not exercise their disputable right of guarding the line, but left that to the Chinese, who performed it efficiently. They were not efficient enough to combat the Japanese army, however: their barracks were bombarded and burnt, and they were driven out after heavy casualties had been suffered. The Japanese themselves had 142 casualties in this engagement. At Kirin a similar occupation was effected without much bloodshed. The Chinese troops were not inclined to submit but were overawed and disarmed, and then left to fend for themselves. At Tunhua it was the same. The termini of every railway in which Japan had a financial interest were occupied by Japanese troops.

The prearranged plan completed and every strategic point in Manchuria seized overnight, other developments followed. Chinese in Mukden fled south along the Peking–Mukden railway; Japanese inhabitants of that region fled north to Mukden. During the three weeks that followed the first outbreak on September 18th, not only had every terminal in which Japan was interested been captured, but every purely Chinese junction and terminal had had bombs dropped on it by Japanese planes; on the Mukden–Hailung line, specially objectionable because of its "paralleling" the Kirin–Changchun Railway, Japanese airmen destroyed both station and barracks, killing and wounding hundreds of Chinese. Numerous reports appeared in the Japanese Press of massacres of Koreans, of Chinese firing on the Red Cross and from under the white flag, without any care for accuracy of statement. Chinese reports told of Japanese attacks on a passenger train on the Peking–Mukden Railway. The Japanese promptly denied them. But there happened to be European passengers on the train. It was significant that their testimony was accepted as irrefragable—a tacit acknowledgment that there is a geographical element in the comparative value of testimony.

The military authorities, while they had determined to flout their own Government and to disregard the League of Nations, were at the same time quite aware of the value of a "good Press." They had no trouble with the Japanese newspapers. They were so well trained in the obligations of patriotism that even the *Asahi*, which, on the eve of the outbreak, had been telling some plain truths about the military men, immediately came out as their staunchest defender. The military throughout were indulgent towards Japanese reporters. A week after the explosion at Mukden they conducted a party of them over the scene of the outrage. Three Chinese corpses in uniform were still lying in appropriate positions, with bullets through their backs, and though the line was intact, a length of rail and a damaged sleeper were on view to be photographed. Scepticism, had there been any, would have hidden its head ashamed.

A little anxiety was felt as to whether the plan had worked perfectly in more remote points. At Taonan the Chinese general showed that he understood the situation: he proclaimed the independence of Heilungkiang (the great Amur Province), and marched off with his troops to capture the capital, Tsitsihar, and make ready for the reception of his Japanese friends. He was heard of later, as will be recorded.

The culminating point of these operations was the attack on Chinchow. This was an ancient Chinese city which had once had some notoriety in Europe but had been forgotten again. Its brief spell of fame was when some Western capitalists, chiefly American, undertook to construct on behalf of the Chinese Government a railway from Chinchow to Aigun, on the Amur, almost opposite Blagoveschensk. The contract was given to a British firm, Messrs. Pauling & Co., but, owing to Japanese and Russian objections, the scheme fell through. Chinchow came into prominence again, as a provisional seat of government, when the Japanese drove Chinese authority out of Mukden on September 18, 1931. On October 8th, the Japanese troops, who had advanced along the Peking–Mukden Railway, made a bomb attack on Chinchow. The planes first flew over the the city, distributing handbills, reading:

Chang Hsueh-liang has already completely forfeited the confidence of the people of the North-Eastern Provinces, and has lost his former stronghold. He is, however, still impenitent, and has established a provisional Liaoning (Mukden) Government at

Chinchow, plotting to disturb peace in the districts where people are living in security under the rule of the Japanese army. The Japanese army, which is devoted to the protection of Japanese rights and interests, and of the populace, for the sake of justice, does not for a moment recognise General Chang's provisional Government, and is now compelled to take positive action with a view to destroying its base. Let all citizens confide in the Japanese army and resist the establishment of General Chang's Government. Otherwise the Japanese army will regard Chinchow as hostile to it and proceed to destroy it completely.

No time to ponder over these weighty words was given. The planes proceeded to drop about seventy bombs on the town, but the army was not ready to follow up this destructive work, and after the planes had discharged their deadly loads the city was left in peace for a season.

Seldom has an event so far off the main currents of the world's affairs produced such an instant reaction over a large part of the civilised world. Hitherto the Japanese had kept the world quiet with assurances of peaceful intent and early evacuation, accompanied by the usual phrases about the integrity of China and Japan's innocence of territorial ambitions. Now there was a feeling that Japan had taken steps that it was impossible to explain away but must be acknowledged as aggression of the most wanton and barbarous kind. But the world was yet to understand Japan's mastery of the art of explaining away.

The military men were not perturbed in the least. Their explanation was that planes were indeed reconnoitring over Chinchow to discover the dispositions of the Mukden troops which were believed to be there, and that, as these planes were fired on, they had to drop bombs in self-defence. It was not pretended that any of the planes were damaged. So self-defence was stretched in its meaning to cover not merely the seizure of every strategic point in a country twice the size of France and the disarming of troops and their expulsion from all accessible barracks, but it included the dropping of seventy bombs on an entirely undefended city far from the South Manchuria Railway zone, and in a part of the country whence the very few Japanese residents had already withdrawn.

The military authorities denied the preliminary dropping of handbills, though they had furnished copies to the Japanese Press, while the Chinese Press published English translations in which the expressions used regarding Marshal Chang Hsueh-liang were vulgarly abusive. These may have been an artistic touch added by the translator, but are quite as likely to have been discreetly suppressed by the Japanese newspapers. For the time being the military denial had to be accepted, and as the bombs were so much more effective than the handbills, it hardly seemed worth while to discuss the scraps of paper. However, within a week the Minister for War was summoned to the Privy Council to explain the situation to that august body, and, while insisting that the dropping of the bombs was a pure act of self-defence, General Minami admitted the handbills without hesitation.

All military announcements emphasised the fact that the Chinese people enjoyed great benefits from the activities of the Japanese armies—except, of course, the bandits. Benevolent sentiments, however, do not preclude necessary severity. We may take one incident from "the districts where the people were living in security under the rule of the Japanese army." It was reported in the *Manchuria Daily News*, an English daily published in Dairen in the Japanese interest:

Hsiao Kung-tien, an 18-year-old Chinese, within the walls of Kaiyuan, was caught by the Japanese troops for tearing off over 30 slips of paper bearing the proclamation of Commander-in-Chief Honjo of the Kwantung Army, within the walls of Kaiyuan (on the S.M.R. main line) during the night of September 28th, while daubing the other placards with anti-Japanese inscriptions.

The young man having owned up to the guilt, he was shot at the parade ground at 7 a.m. on the 5th instant under the order of Captain Iida. The body was handed over to Prefect Tung at 9 a.m. Chin Meng-chou and four others suspected of being implicated were handed over to the same prefect under bond of good behaviour.

On the 3rd instant, with Captain Iida's permission, the young prisoner wrote a letter to his parents, saying in part:

"I was drawn against my will into the International Relations League by Tsai Chi-min, who went to Kirin since. I feel that I played to his tune, but too late. The Japanese soldiers have been treating me considerately, and my lasting sorrow is that I have not served you as I ought to have."

Such are the incidents of self-defence—a self-defence which developed later into the holy mission of enabling the Chinese people in Manchuria to realise their long-cherished desire for independent self-government. Japanese apologists continually tell us that the Chinese are past masters at propaganda, but the fact is that the Chinese know their business so ill that an incident like this went unnoticed. A military execution for an offence which, even had there been an acknowledged state of war, would have been more appropriately met with a "swift kick in the pants" seems rather excessive.

It has already been mentioned that some resistance was put up at Changchun: even the burning of the barracks and the driving out of the troops did not completely restore tranquillity. Accordingly, on October 6th, Lieutenant-General Tamon, in command of the army division which had occupied Changchun, issued the following proclamation:

The North-Eastern troops, which challenged the Japanese troops, have already been defeated and scattered in all directions. I am now devoting my whole attention to the maintenance of peace and order, for the promotion of the security and happiness of the people at large. Order is being gradually restored and the security of the people being enhanced. It is therefore very regrettable to note that many evil-disposed persons have found their way into many places in Manchuria of late, and have been attempting to incite anti-Japanese feelings and to disturb the peace, acting in collusion with similarly refractory persons in Manchuria. I regard Chinese who help anti-Japanese acts, or who act in a manner disturbing to peace and order, and those who fail to inform the Japanese troops against such evil-doers as themselves guilty of hostile acts against the Japanese troops, and will mete out severe punishment to them under military law. Special rewards will, on the other hand, be given those who have quickly informed the Japanese troops and facilitated the arrest of the offenders for their contribution to the maintenance of public peace and order. Let all people, officials and private individuals, co-operate closely for the restoration of complete security and peace, and so promote their own happiness.

These proclamations indicate that, though a state of war had been expressly denied in the Japanese Government's communications to other Powers, the military men, even of the highest rank, did not act as though that distinction made any material difference.

CHAPTER X

THE TAKING OF MANCHURIA

HISTORY consisting so largely of a record of the crimes and follies of mankind, no explanation is necessary for devoting so large a part of this chronicle to Japan's continental doings. The bombing of towns, the desolation of countrysides, and the overriding of civil authority by military invaders were regarded rather academically in the West as tests of the efficacy of the League of Nations, the Nine Power Treaty of Washington, and the Treaty of Paris known as the Kellogg Pact. A long course of propaganda had accustomed the Japanese mind to the idea of energetic action in Manchuria. Baron Shidehara had tried to avoid it, but he took up the thankless task of counsel for the defence.

The discussions at Geneva, followed with breathless interest at the time, are useful to-day only to students of international relations. The Council of the League of Nations met on September 22nd, less than four days after the alleged explosion on the railway, and advised both parties to withdraw their troops. Mr. Yoshizawa, the Japanese delegate, objected on two grounds. One was the venerable and overworked excuse that public opinion throughout Japan would be exacerbated; the other was that issues between China and Japan must be settled without the intervention of a third party. This was the most tenaciously held of all Japan's political doctrines. First enunciated before the presentation of the Twenty-one Demands in 1915, the failure to make it effective on that occasion had only increased Japanese determination to make it good in future. At Washington in 1922 there was effective intervention, but Japan gained her point in so far as the formal negotiations were concerned, which took place between the Chinese and Japanese delegates alone.

Dr. Alfred Sze, the Chinese delegate, said that negotiation was impossible with Japanese troops in occupation. Yoshizawa said that Nanking had proposed them. Sze denied it flatly. Thus at the outset the Chinese and Japanese were directly at variance over questions of fact, and so they remained, except when the Japanese delegate declared that he had not been informed and must wait till he heard from his Government. In reply to the League's pronouncement that both sides should withdraw their troops (though it was rather a novel doctrine that the aggrieved country should withdraw its troops from its own territory) the Japanese Cabinet decided that Japanese troops could not be withdrawn until all the hundreds of "issues" had been settled, which was another way of saying that they must all be decided in Japan's favour. This was said in plain words in a message from Nanking, and on these grounds China appealed for a verdict from the League. Japan gave a promise to withdraw her troops as soon as she could, upon which the League asked China to try and settle the quarrel by direct negotiation.

In military circles in Japan the intrusion of the Council of the League was sharply resented, and it was reported that General Minami had advocated ignoring it. Actually the army did ignore it, carrying out its plans undisturbed. More headstrong officers demanded immediate withdrawal from the League and refusal to participate in the Disarmament Conference.

Japan made promises of withdrawal, but regarded the Chinese attitude as sufficient reason for not fulfilling them. While the Council was drawing up a resolution that hoped for a satisfactory settlement by October 14th, General Honjo sent a summons to Marshal Chang Hsueh-liang to come to Mukden and make a settlement acceptable to Japan. This, of course, was the policy of "effecting local settlements" by which Japan constantly tried to undermine the Central authority in China. Moreover, it was on a very similar order that the Old Marshal had made his last journey to Mukden, and his son did not desire a similar end. He replied that negotiations could be held only by the Nanking Government. General Honjo sent him an insulting message asking what he wanted done with his father's body—which, as often happens in China, was still awaiting final sepulture a long time after death. Another message asked him where he wanted his belongings to be sent; and they were put on a train and sent to Peking without waiting for an answer. So was the promise fulfilled that private property should be held inviolable.

Mr. Stimson, the American Secretary of State, expressed in a Note to Japan the opinion that the military were acting without orders, which was true so far as the Foreign Office was concerned, but the whole procedure of the seizing of Manchuria was timed so beautifully and carried out so perfectly that the Staff orders must have been very perfect indeed. At Geneva Japanese officials gave private assurances that the military were indeed acting on their own authority, and promised that, if Japan were only allowed to save face, the civil power would regain control and do the right thing. It was an old Japanese diplomatic gambit, but perhaps the officials themselves did not realise how completely the initiative had passed out of civil control in Japan, apparently for ever.

On October 9th, the day after Chinchow was bombed, the Japanese Minister handed to the Chinese Foreign Office a Note which he had received from his Government. The whole trouble, the Note said, was caused through deep-rooted anti-Japanese feeling in China—a feeling which culminated in the recent challenge to the Japanese troops, which compelled them to take measures of self-defence. As evidence of this anti-Japonism the Note cited the boycott which had been China's retort to the Manchurian seizure! The boycott, said the Note, was conducted by the Kuomintang, or Nationalist party, and was therefore an instrument of national policy and was tantamount to war!

Considering the seventy bombs and the handbills on

Chinchow the previous day, there was a touch of humour when the protest went on to say that both the Chinese and Japanese representatives had assured the Council of the League at Geneva that their respective countries would do nothing to aggravate the situation—yet the boycott was becoming worse.

An extremely threatening protest was handed to the Chinese Mayor of Shanghai by Mr. Murai, the Japanese Consul-General, in which, after describing the sufferings of the Japanese as though they were some hunted and persecuted sect, he demanded that the boycott cease forthwith. The fact that on June 30th, little more than three months earlier, the Minseito party in Japan had affirmed that, thanks to Baron Shidehara's conciliatory policy boycotts had disappeared, was completely overlooked.

Japanese merchants in Shanghai were only very indirectly responsible for military doings in Manchuria, and they had good reason to feel aggrieved, for the boycotters developed a technique which was exasperating and even alarming, though the Chinese merchants dealing in Japanese goods were always the chief sufferers. Boycotting appealed to the gangster spirit, and opened a way for making money out of patriotism—which, after all, was a popular occupation in Japan. The Japanese Government, at a later date, insisted that the Manchurian and Shanghai troubles were entirely different things; but this distinction was maintained for diplomatic purposes. The boycott was essentially a response to the rape of Manchuria.

There were signs that the navy felt some jealousy at the army getting all the glory and getting it so cheaply. As the boycott flared up so rapidly and widely, a Naval Council was held at Tokyo on October 7th, at which Admiral Abo, Minister for the Navy, announced that the squadrons at Sasebo and Kure had been ordered to hold themselves in readiness for service, and the assembled admirals agreed that if Japan's protests against the boycott were ineffective, Japan should proceed to decisive action without delay—so evidently the navy as well as the army considered that it had the right to make war when it chose.

The boycott spread to the South, and in Canton the Chinese police shot a number of anti-Japanese demonstrators. This was taken in Japan as an earnest of Mr. Eugene Chen's readiness to fall in with the Japanese ideas of how Manchuria should become an appanage of Japan without disturbing the territorial integrity of China. The Chinese President, General Chiang Kai-shek, saw in the Japanese attacks the possibility of a realisation of his greatest hope—the unification of China. There was bitter hostility between the "rebel government" in Canton and the "Soong Dynasty" in Nanking, but the President thought that the Chinchow outrage must surely close the ranks, and he began to talk of declaring war on Japan. Mr. Eugene Chen sent a long telegram to Baron Shidehara which had the appearance of being an indignant protest against Japan's violation of the principles professed by the Japanese Foreign Minister during Mr. Chen's visit earlier in the summer, but which, when more carefully examined, could be read as renewing the offer made at that time by the Canton Foreign Minister. The *Jiji* reported that both the Foreign Office and the military authorities were ready to negotiate with Canton, having decided that it was useless to do so with Nanking and intolerable to have anything to do with the Young Marshal. At the same time, the three chief Canton leaders—Wang Ching-wei, the veteran revolutionist; Sun Fo, son of Sun Yat-sen, and Eugene Chen—sailed for Shanghai with the object of amalgamating with or supplanting the Nanking Government. Less notice was taken of the fact that some Canton troops were transferred to Shanghai—an action which was to have momentous consequences.

Abroad the propaganda was sedulously spread, and was swallowed uncritically by the Press, that the trouble was entirely due to military hotheads, that the Japanese Government and people were opposed to it, and that the best thing was to leave it alone and presently the better minds would get control again.

In Japan itself there were no signs that this was the case. The military authorities intimated that if the Canton Government wanted recognition it must look sharp, or there might be a second or even a third Chinchow (which had been bombed in self-defence).

As for Manchuria, said the military spokesman, Tokyo would negotiate with its provincial governments if no government emerged which could negotiate on behalf of the provinces as a whole. This was the first public suggestion of the setting up of a puppet government, Manchurian governments having hitherto been a prohibited subject. The indignation expressed abroad seemed, indeed, to have the effect of silencing all voices except the military or those who spoke for them. But they would have been silenced in any case. It is a good line in the Diet, when peace broods over the world, to rail against the country's "spineless diplomacy," but when anything is actually doing, criticism disappears. To a great extent opinions actually change, which was an experience so common in England and America when those countries entered upon the Great War, as to need no explanation. Those whose opinions do not change do their best to avoid being beaten up by patriotic societies. The civilian members of the Wakatsuki Cabinet, however, did not feel that the bomb of September 18th should have blown them all to bits, and they proposed that General Oshima, a former Minister for War, and Dr. Yamakawa, a noted scholar who had long served the Government, should go to Manchuria and try to bring about an understanding between the Foreign Office and the military leaders. The War Office and General Staff opposed this vehemently. They were ready enough to say that untoward things like the bombing of undefended towns were contrary to orders, but they resented even the proposal of remedial measures—a military device so successful on this occasion that its exploitation on a much larger scale in the future was inevitable.

So far as the people at large were concerned, there was nothing to raise a doubt as to the righteousness of the cause. Not only were the newspapers on the side of the army without a dissentient voice, but the broadcasting stations, which were under the direction of the Department of Communications, became sources of endless Manchuria propaganda. Sometimes gallant officers would broadcast addresses in which they did not spare the League of Nations, England in particular coming in for their castigations. Foreign criticisms were the only disturbing element, and when some European or American newspaper took the Japanese side the gratitude with which this advocacy was quoted was almost pathetic.

It was insisted upon that at Geneva nobody but the Japanese delegates understood the facts of the case, and the constant reiteration that everything was done in self-defence, that nobody was more anxious for Japan to withdraw than was Japan herself and that all provocation came from the Chinese side, had different effects on differing temperaments. Some of those to whom the Japanese statements appeared to be wide of the facts began to wonder whether, after all, they had not been seriously mistaken, and that Japan was really labouring under an intolerable grievance. Others only became the more exasperated as the Japanese Notes outdid themselves in cynical persiflage and in insulting attempts to divest plain English and French words of their obvious meanings. Not that Japan broke entirely new ground. At the outbreak of the Great War all protested that they were acting in self-defence; since then they had all undertaken not to resort to war as a national policy, so there was no alternative but to say that this was not war. The statesmen at Geneva were all indurated by war propaganda, but even so, Japan's declarations that, where she was concerned, words had no meaning except such as she chose to invest them with, rather took away their breath.

The Council met on October 13th, and there was much unfruitful verbosity, Mr. Yoshizawa reading a dreary historical essay which went back to 1894, when Dr. Sze said, "While we have been sitting quietly here, Japanese aeroplanes have continued to drop bombs on undefended cities. Five bombs were dropped on Takushan, and this morning, at the very moment when we were discussing the situation here, three Japanese planes bombed Kontangtse."

Never was the contrast between Dr. Sze and Mr. Yoshizawa more marked than on this occasion. As an advocate Dr. Sze was far superior in appearance, manner, and speech. The difference was so great that Japanese advocates turned it to account. It is always effective to praise the oratory of one's opponent, and Mr. Yoshizawa's manner was described as that of the samurai, unused to words, who could only make a plain statement of the facts, and leave that to prevail, if it would. But some of the Japanese delegate's own countrymen were less flattering. They criticised his hard, cruel mouth, his ungracious manner, his unreadiness of wit. Only when it was realised that the League would never resort to force did these critics discover that the rest of the Council had found Yoshizawa's arguments so irresistibly weighty that they could do nothing against them.

While in Geneva Japanese delegates were declaring that none was so anxious to withdraw as Japan, but were discovering a multitude of reasons why that desideratum could not be attained, all the propaganda in Japan was against withdrawal, and work was started on the Kirin–Keinei line connecting Changchun with the North Korean railways, to which China had so strenuously objected. The Press in Japan was forbidden to mention it.

There had been two full-dress debates in the Council of the League without any effect on the position, except that some of the members began to wish that China would agree with Japan somehow, and on October 23rd General Minami was the chief speaker at a banquet at the Kinsui restaurant in Tokyo, exalted army officers, high officials of the South Manchuria Railway, and secretaries of the Foreign Office being present. He was very emphatic on the theme that the present opportunity must be taken for the fundamental settlement of all China problems. Count Uchida, President of the South Manchuria Railway, agreed with him, and said he could answer for the agreement of Prince Saionji, upon whom he had called. It would appear that at this meeting Baron Shidehara made a last bid for peaceful methods. The more bombastic speeches were communicated to the Press at considerable length, but all that was vouchsafed regarding Baron Shidehara was that he described the impression made abroad by the affair, especially in the League of Nations, and explained in detail the point of view that international law would take of the military action in Manchuria. It was also stated that he had a prolonged *tête-à-tête* with General Minami, who was emphatic on the necessity of resisting all interference from the League.

The Foreign Office was tied to the chariot-wheels, and issued a communiqué in which it was said that Japan was opposed to all plans of the League of Nations for withdrawal prior to settlement, and reaffirming that the Chinese boycott was as much against the treaties to which China had appealed as an appeal to arms would be—an argument which it would be rather difficult to sustain, but which nobody in Japan was concerned to contradict. Japan, it was subtly implied, had not made an appeal to arms, but would be no worse than China if she did.

With such a good lead as that of General Minami, and that of General Suzuki, President of the Ex-Soldiers' Society, who, in a belligerent address at Himeji, denounced China's right to construct ports or railways, to object to any Japanese construction, to impose a tariff, or to resist Japanese wishes, it was natural that patriotism should become more vocal than ever. The League of Nations was solemnly warned in the Press and severely scolded. Yet popular enthusiasm was not so great as might have been expected with such powerful propaganda. On the other hand, there was no opposition except a whisper or two from Labour parties, which found no echo in the Press, and represented no large number of workers.

Quite apart from the question whether it really would be unsafe for the Japanese subjects in Manchuria if the Japanese troops were withdrawn, there were excellent reasons against such withdrawal which were not enlarged upon at Geneva. The chief of these was that the Japanese troops were fully occupied in hunting down the Chinese armies which they had disarmed. In Europe there was some talk of the bandit plague, and the impression was carefully conveyed that this was an old state of affairs, and one of the causes, in fact, that made it imperative for Japan to go in and clean up. The fact was that, while there always had been bandits, they were few in number and had generally levied blackmail on villages off the beaten track. When a quarter of a million soldiers were turned adrift, besides a large number of agriculturists whose families had been murdered and their homes destroyed, banditry became a large-scale occupation.

Such remnants of the Young Marshal's army as retained some formation had gone southwards but were discouraged by bomb-dropping on Chinchow, while every railway junction that could contribute to such a concentration was bombed. From time to time the Japanese Press published estimates of the numbers of thousands of bandits in each district and spoke of the need for suppression. The *Manchuria Daily News*, so obscure from the Japanese point of view as often to escape the notice of the censor, was almost alone in shedding any real light on the situation. By its reports on bandit suppression, sometimes with a panegyric on the Napoleonic strategy with which bands of these wretched men were surrounded and exterminated, it quite unintentionally gave its few readers an idea of the ruthless man-hunt that was going on over a large part of Manchuria.

Yet the territory was so vast that in the remoter parts Chinese military formations were not altogether destroyed. Some of the Kirin troops kept together in Harbin, and much more important was the existence of the extensive province of Heilungkiang, with its capital on the north side of the Chinese Eastern Railway, and its Governor still on good terms with Marshal Chang Hsueh-liang. The necessity of Manchuria being independent of China so that Japan could negotiate with its government or governments was constantly harped upon, and, considering that the Japanese strenuously denied all connection with any independence movements in Manchuria, they were very industrious in seeking for independent Governors with whom they might negotiate. On October 22nd, General Minami was ready with a list, and proposed direct negotiations with:

Yuan Chin-kai in Mukden;
Chang Ching-huei in Harbin;
Hsi Chia in Kirin;
Chang Hai-peng in Heilungkiang; and
Tang Yu-lin in Jehol.

The Cabinet Council, to whom this list was submitted, cautiously said that it might be advisable to deal with Nanking first.

General Minami had not waited for his colleagues' approval, for a week before he presented his list it was announced that the Heilungkiang troops had declared their allegiance to General Chang Hai-peng, and would shortly march into Tsitsihar and take charge there. General Chang Hai-peng was an elderly but active soldier who was in charge of the southern part of the province, with his headquarters at Taonan. The official head of the province was General Wan Fu-lin, whose capital was Tsitsihar; but he was away from his capital in ill-health, and appointed General Ma Chan-shan, in command at Taheiho, almost opposite Blagoveschensk, to act for him. The announcement from the Japanese side, therefore, that Chang Hai-peng was a good friend of Japan and would occupy Tsitsihar was rather ominous. So also was the simultaneous announcement that Marshal Chang Hsueh-liang and General Chang

Tso-hsiang (Governor of Kirin Province) had agreed to set up a provisional government for Kirin Province at Harbin, seeing that the generals in Kirin and Harbin respectively, with whose goodwill General Minami had declared himself satisfied, were Chang Ching-heui and Hsi Chia, and that the Young Marshal took an early opportunity of publicly denouncing Hsi Chia, while Hsi Chia, for his part, denounced Chang Tso-hsiang, whose position he had usurped.

General Chang Hai-peng began his advance on Tsitsihar —an operation the successful achievement of which, Mr. Edo of the Foreign Office informed the Press, would solve the difficulty about the leasing of land to Japanese in Heilungkiang province; but General Ma, having come down hotfoot from Taheiho to Tsitsihar, crossed the Chinese Eastern Railway and penetrated many miles along the Taonan Railway. At the Nonni River it was found that Chang Hai-peng's men were approaching, and as it was known that the power of Japan was behind this advance, Ma, preferring strategy to bloodshed, blew up the Nonni bridge, and retired a little way to await events.

The Japanese were swift to take strong measures. They announced that they could not allow the railway to be put out of action in this way, as it was a line in which Japan had a financial interest, and that it would be repaired on November 4th. Orders were given to both Chang and Ma (according to the Japanese reports) to retire ten kilometres from the bridge. On the 3rd there were already Japanese detachments north of the river, and these, without much parley, came into collision with Ma's troops. Each side, of course, blamed the other for starting the fight, and there was the usual Japanese story of the violation of the white flag by the Chinese. Apparently the Japanese never expected the Chinese to offer resistance and took it for granted that they could advance at will. There was some sharp fighting. It was, in fact, the best fight that the Japanese had had since operations started on September 18th, and a Japanese report declared that General Ma, in his enthusiasm, telegraphed to the Young Marshal and to General Wan Fu-lin declaring that he would wipe out the Japanese, against whom, according to another alleged proclamation, he was going to "fight to the last man."

For the time being the Japanese had suffered a reverse. The Japanese official version had it that Ma had committed an act of bad faith in attacking the Japanese, who beat him and could easily have followed up their victory but refrained, thus allowing Ma to commit another act of bad faith by taking up a fresh position and getting reinforcements. General Ma Chan-shan delivered yet another attack on the 16th and 17th, and in the small hours of the 18th destroyed another bridge at Sanlin. Though the Japanese losses in these operations were much smaller than the Chinese, they were quite serious enough, and there was rejoicing in China. So long as the "last man" was ready to fight the Chinese could give the Japanese all the Pyrrhic victories thay wanted.

However, even Ma was turned to account. General Honjo sent him an ultimatum, and while his unsatisfactory reply was on its way, Ma attacked again vigorously. By some abstruse mathematical feat Japan had maintained hitherto that her troops in Manchuria did not exceed the number permitted by treaty; in the face of General Ma's hostility it was declared that treaty limitations were no longer binding!

The War Office declared that it had no desire to occupy Tsitsihar. Having prepared the way with bombing planes, the Japanese troops occupied it on November 18th. Chang Hai-peng, Japan's friend who was to have captured Tsitsihar and set up a provincial government there, having remained in the background from the time that General Ma Chan-shan appeared on the scene, General Chang Ching-huei, who was to have set up a pro-Japanese government for Kirin province, was hurriedly brought from Harbin to become head of an independent government in Tsitsihar, and General Minami announced that as soon as the proper arrangements had been completed with him, the Japanese troops would be withdrawn to Chenchiatung—which was far enough outside the South Manchuria Railway Zone, but nearer than Tsitsihar, less bleak, and involving less danger of collisions with the Russians. Unfortunately for the new independence movement, General Chang Ching-huei announced after a couple of days that he was willing neither to be Governor of Heilungkiang nor Governor of Kirin. Doubtless he knew that the last had not yet been heard of Ma Chan-shan and other Manchurian Herewards, though the Japanese did not yet realise this fact.

The spread of hostilities into the Amur province alarmed both Geneva and Washington, for it became apparent that none of the tentative dates by which, "if possible," the Japanese troops were to be withdrawn, were possible. The appearance of "independent" governments increased the need for Japanese troops rather than diminished it, for unless well protected these puppet organisations would be immediately extirpated. General Minami and General Shirakawa (a former Minister for War) were both beating the war drum vigorously, demanding more and more troops. There was vigorous bidding for Chinese generals, who, in the north, were rather like chieftains of free companies, and some of them seemed to be friends and enemies on alternate days. The Press sought consolation in vigorous denunciations of Britain, whose delegates at Geneva had been very unkind in their criticisms, and some fantastic speculations were put forward as to the reason for this, it being quite beyond understanding that Japan's acts should be objected to merely because they were wrong.

The Russian menace was made the most of in Japan. It might have been supposed that it would be wiser to culti-vate Russia's friendship at such a moment; but the certainty that Russia wanted to keep out of the business made it safe enough to use this means of eliciting sympathy in "capitalist" countries. That Russia was corrupting China was always a good line to take, notwithstanding the disastrous end of the Borodin mission. Besides, the check on the Nonni was such an unpleasant surprise that a Russian explanation was useful. It was immediately announced that Russia had supplied arms to the Heilungkiang troops, nor were such statements made only by irresponsible journalists. Mr. Edo, of the Foreign Office, on October 27th, stated without qualification that General Ma Chan-shan had Russian support—a statement the repetition of which was not prevented by Mr. Karahan's denial in Moscow two days later, nor its assertion as an "incontrovertible fact" by General Shirakawa on November 5th, on his return from a Manchurian excursion. The air was thick with stories of Soviet machinations.

On November 14th Mr. Litvinoff, the Soviet Foreign Minister, invited Mr. Hirota, the Japanese ambassador, to his office and presented him with a statement for communication to his government. This expressed regret that in spite of Mr. Karahan's clear statement, the anti-Soviet campaign in Japan showed no signs of abatement, but was being carried on by Mr. Nakano, Japanese Consul in Harbin, and by Japanese military men in Manchuria, and this at a time when the Japanese army was preparing to cross the Chinese Eastern Railway to Tsitsihar, thus paralysing the railway and causing serious loss to the Soviet Republic.

Baron Shidehara replied with a reassuring note, promising every possible precaution against damage or interruption of the railway, and asking for reciprocity in the avoidance of incidents. Mr. Litvinoff responded in friendly fashion, expressing satisfaction that Japan did not suspect Russia of hostile intrigue. But it is difficult to please everybody. Russia's inactivity during the period of the Tsitsihar campaign only caused suspicions in the United States that she must have a secret understanding with Japan.

On the night of November 8th there was an outbreak of shooting in Tientsin, Japanese and Chinese charging one another with beginning it. Its object was hardly clear enough to facilitate a choice between contradictions. Some Japanese warships were rushed to the spot. On the 11th the now grown-up "Boy Emperor," who had been staying on the Japanese Concession since his flight from Peking, suddenly left by a Japanese steamer for Dairen. On the 18th the Chinese delegate informed the Council of the League that should Mr. Henry Pu Yi (as he was generally called) become head of a spurious Government in Manchuria the Chinese Government would not recognise any such organisation. On November 20th the Japanese delegate informed the Council that Mr. Henry Pu Yi's departure was without the knowledge and against the advice of Japan. Nobody believed or was expected to believe this, and on March 1st the new régime was proclaimed with the former Emperor as Chief Executive. But much was to happen before this.

CHAPTER XI

JAPAN ACTS WHILE THE COUNCIL TALKS

In the early days of the invasion of Manchuria Japan gave assurances of early withdrawal, sometimes declaring that this was actually in progress. If there were any movements which could be called a withdrawal, they were dictated by the need for protecting the railway from bandit attacks, which were catalogued with minute care for future use. Actually the campaign developed steadily. General Minami still had a dislike to the publicity which the sailing of troopships received in Europe, and the Press was strictly forbidden to mention departures; but the local secretaries of the Ex-Soldiers' Association were notified of the time of the passing of troop trains and ordered to see that there was a good turn-out, with flags, to cheer as they went by.

Ingenious pretexts were advanced for ignoring the most solemn undertakings. The Japanese delegate to Geneva pointed out, for instance, that China had shown signs of disputing the validity of treaties signed under duress, and until Japan and China had come to a clear understanding that those treaties would not be disputed, the safety of Japanese subjects after withdrawal could not be assured.

The Council met in Paris in November. Sir John Simon, from whose presence and legal intelligence much had been hoped, discovered reasons why nothing could be done. When Dr. Sze proposed the invocation of Article XV. of the Covenant, Sir John supported Japan in opposing such a move, and pointed out that the benefits which Article XI. guaranteed, though even now non-existent in practice, would no longer exist even in theory if Article XV. were invoked. In the enormous volume of discussion which the League of Nations devoted to the Sino-Japanese dispute, this was really the crisis. Up to this point action had been possible; after the acceptance of this casuistry, the League only went through the motions of being alive, without any hope of potency. Sir John was lauded in Japan as possessing a great legal mind.

The conquest went on, and excuses never failed. One thing that the Western statesmen never really understood was that the Japanese had an entirely different conception of the truth to that which existed in Christendom. The Japanese have never been interested in philosophy, and having no difficulty in believing in incompatible things, do not see that incompatible statements create a difficulty. When they gave definite promises, such as that Chinchow should not be bombed again and that Tsitsihar should not be occupied, and these promises were immediately broken, they were the least embarrassed of any at Geneva. Similarly, when the Council proposed an armistice, the Japanese delegate said that Japan was already pledged to do nothing to aggravate the situation, and an armistice would aggravate it immeasurably; and when he was asked to put it to his Government that it should order the military men positively to stay their hands, he replied that only the Emperor could give such orders—knowing well that the Emperor has less initiative that the meanest of his subjects.

At length it was agreed that a commission of inquiry should be sent out. Dr. Sze pointed out that to send such a commission while Japan still remained in military occupation of Manchuria merely enabled Japan to complete her plans at leisure and to present the League with *un fait accompli.* While they had debated, he said, irreparable damage had been done and suffering was increasing.

A fierce propaganda campaign was raging against the Young Marshal. Everything was his fault, and the implacable demands for his destruction made the Council rather suspicious of the easy assurances that no more violence would be committed before the Commission of Inquiry arrived or during its visit. "Self-defence" explained everything—even such actions as the capture of Tsitsihar, contrary to specific promises and hundreds of miles from all Japanese interests.

Baron Shidehara tried to reassure the Council. On November 23rd, he visited General Minami, and pointed out how greatly shocked the Powers had been by broken promises. Minami replied that he would tell General Kanaya, the Chief of Staff, and later in the day Kanaya telephoned to Baron Shidehara that there would be no more fighting unless the Chinese provoked it. Shidehara knew what this meant, and begged the Council to see that the concentration of Chinese troops towards Chinchow ceased. On November 26th, the Premier and Foreign Minister summoned the Minister for War and asked him what was happening in Chinchow. Nothing, said General Minami, but the Japanese army must defend itself. Next day it defended itself by dropping more bombs, and there was more fighting in Tientsin. The army tried to get the fact of the bombing suppressed and said they had given no positive promise. Mr. Stimson, the American Secretary of State, said that every time Baron Shidehara had promised there would be no more attacks, attack immediately followed. At this the Japanese military were very indignant and declared they had never given such pledges, and that Baron Shidehara was guilty of violating military secrets. The Foreign Office in its turn said that Mr. Stimson had violated a secrecy he had himself asked for.

Although Japan presented the edifying spectacle of a united front to the world, there were some fierce quarrels at home—mainly due to the Foreign Office trying to act in an honourable and humane manner. The Seiyukai, ever ready in its role of Opposition, to discover improprieties in the conduct of Ministers of State, denounced Baron Shidehara for promising, when the troops were actually advancing, that there should be no attack; and when, mainly because of the difficulties of the position and the onset of winter, there was a withdrawal from Tsitsihar, there were Seiyukai hints that Baron Wakatsuki, the Premier, and Baron Shide-hara, the Foreign Minister, had taken upon themselves to advise the Throne upon a military matter. But perhaps it was General Kanaya, the Chief of Staff, whom they persuaded, for indignation now began to be expressed at his friendly relations with the Foreign Minister, and prophecies began to be uttered that he would soon resign. They were fulfilled.

The League Council had come to a point where it despaired of doing anything, and could think of nothing better than to compose a resolution so toothless that all delegates, including the Chinese and Japanese, could agree to it. To the fact that plans for the declaration of the independence of Manchuria were well on their way, with the puppets at the head of each province already installed, the Council shut its eyes. But China demanded that Japan should give an undertaking to the Council that between the passing of the resolution and the handling of the report of the Commission of Inquiry, Japan should not promote any independence movement or other disturbing change. Both Dr. Sze and Mr. Wellington Koo, the Chinese Foreign Minister, handed in their resignations to emphasise the necessity of this guarantee. There was consternation in the Council, and they were persuaded to carry on. Japan replied that the Young Marshal's troops were concentrating—which was by this time understood as a threat that Japan would attack whenever she thought fit. The resolution provided for the dispatch of the Commission of Inquiry, but nothing more.

The Council apparently forgot Chinchow; but just as it adjourned it was informed that petitions in the names of ten millions of the inhabitants had been handed in to the provincial and municipal governments in Manchuria. The number seemed rather excessive, and the fact that their chief prayer was for the overthrow of the civil government at Chinchow—the last civil government left that had not been called into being by the Japanese—was only credible on the supposition that the ten millions were all far-sighted politicians, whereas the main strand in the Japanese argument was that the Chinese were a simple people who only desired peace and protection and would welcome anyone who gave it to them.

CHAPTER XII

THE END OF DEMOCRACY IN JAPAN

In describing events which overlap one another in time, closely interlocked though they may be in their relations to one another, it is impossible to keep to a strict chronology. The political and financial crisis in England in August 1931 played its part in deciding when the blow should be struck in Manchuria; but for the time being its greater interest in Japan, except to the military conspirators, lay in its forcing on the attention of the public the question whether it would not be better to reimpose the embargo on the export of gold and to re-establish at a convenient moment a standard in which the gold content of the yen should be considerably reduced.

The explosion at Mukden on September 18th, even if we take it at its face value, only dislodged one sleeper; but it blew two years' hard work of the Government sky-high. The people had suffered keenly in the effort to counteract the effects of previous extravagances; but the country's finances had been put in order; great efforts had been made to promote manufacture of every sort, and a remarkable increase had been shown in skill and adaptability. There seemed to be every reason to believe that another year would see manufacture, trade, and finance all on a sound basis and with a prosperous outlook. In a single night all was swept away, and the financial reconstruction was all squandered on finding the means for making war. The irony of the situation was that without this effort on the part of peace-seeking statesmen, the war-mongers would have found it far more difficult to carry out their plans.

Confronted by action on the part of the army which was contrary to every effort of the past two years, the Cabinet might well have resigned, but there were other considerations.

In what was represented by the army as a crisis in which the nation was defending itself, the Government would have been regarded as deserting the nation in time of danger—and charges like this are more dreaded in Japan than in most countries. Besides, it seemed to the Government itself that resignation, at its best, would be surrender, and that it was its duty to stand by its guns and save what it could. Had not Mr. Ramsay MacDonald just made a similar decision in England?

The English example bulked rather largely. The sinister Adachi thought once more that he might attain his ambition of heading a Cabinet. Generally he was one of those who fulminated against following foreign examples and demanded that Japan should act entirely on her own initiative; but suddenly he found great virtue in the British idea of a National Government, and began to recommend one for Japan. He put out feelers, and found that it was doubtful whether he would get the support that was necessary. He was not the sort of man to appeal to the taste of Prince Saionji, who had a deciding voice. So for a time he dropped his project; but it was clear that the Minseito, though still commanding a big majority in the House of Representatives, was defeated for a long time to come, and Adachi again began to consider the patriotic necessity of a National Government.

A Defence Minister could wreck a Cabinet by the simple process of resigning. If the army or navy refused to allow a new Minister to be appointed, a general resignation was the only alternative, but a civilian Minister could not prevent a successor to himself being found. So Adachi adopted the method of absenting himself from Cabinet meetings. The Premier sent for him and reasoned with him. Surely he could co-operate with his colleagues as before? He regretted his inability to do so. Then the only decent course was to resign. No, he refused to do that; and if his refusal either to resign or to carry on his ministerial duties forced the whole Cabinet into resignation, that was their affair. Such was the loyalty of a professional loyalist.

When a Cabinet is smashed by one of its own members, and the succeeding Cabinet immediately reverses one of the most important of its. policies, his motives are naturally suspect. It is probable that Japan would have been forced off gold in any case, and it may be that Mr. Inoue knew this. The rumour most generally current was that Mitsui's had fixed the exchange for payment of huge bills for cotton ordered from America, and would have been in a serious fix if Japan had stayed on gold. The firm certainly made great profits by selling for depreciated yen what it had bought at the gold rate, but that it profited by the fall of the Government has been strenuously denied by responsible members of the firm. The rumour was also current that Mr. Inoue was not at all unwilling that the firm should receive a severe blow, since it was too powerful for the Government's comfort. There was a widespread belief that Mr. Adachi received a couple of million yen out of the transaction; it is certain that Japanese statesmen do, lacking means of their own, accept the patronage of wealthy business houses, but Mr. Adachi had among his followers a reputation for financial integrity, and the new party—the Kokumin Domei—which he started, never gave any indication of that vigour which it is said that only a couple of million yen can infuse. The fact remains that when Mr. Inukai, president of the Seiyukai, took office the day following Baron Wakatsuki's resignation, the new Government's first act was to reimpose the embargo on the export of gold and to let the yen drop. The peace and stability for which Hamaguchi and Wakatsuki had striven were replaced by war and inflation.

Reference is made elsewhere to the manner in which the radio was used for Manchurian propaganda. Hitherto there had been strict moderation in the use of the radio for political purposes, though Cabinet Ministers had to be allowed a certain amount of freedom of the air. While Mr. Inoue was still in office as Finance Minister, a lecture on the disastrous consequences to be expected from going off gold was prepared for broadcasting. The Government fell and Japan went off gold immediately, but the lecture was duly delivered on the date arranged. It was unfortunate, but staff work is not always perfect even in Japan. The lecture may have reminded philosophic listeners that fundamental principles are not reversed even by a change in the Government.

It is difficult to say what the new Premier stood for in the way of political principles. He was a strong protectionist and at times rather a Chauvinist—but those are qualities that are found in nearly all Japanese politicians. He was democratic in the sense that he was of undistinguished origin, had earned his own living, and had been a member of the Imperial Diet ever since that institution was founded. He was supposed to be a Chinese scholar, had been a journalist in his young days, and a war correspondent at the time of the Satsuma rebellion in 1877. He was a disciple of Fukuzawa, the great educational reformer and modernist at Keio, the university that he founded. He lived in some style and was supposed to have been well rewarded for some service that he had done the Mitsubishi firm. He was also supposed to be under the patronage of Mitsui, but there was nothing singular in this, for the great firms had become patrons of politics and politicians irrespective of party.

Inukai's party affiliations were somewhat mutable. For some time he headed a party of his own, the Kokuminto; and in 1916 he joined hands with the Kenseikai (afterwards Minseito) to fight the Government headed by General Count Terauchi. He favoured political dare-to-dies rather than soldiers, and was an advocate of the Defence Ministries being open to civilians. He had the reputation of being a scrupulously honest and high-minded statesman, but in so regarding him it is necessary to remember that Oriental and Occidental standards differ. That Inukai was on very friendly terms with such men as Viscount Miura and Toyama Mitsuru and that his popularity was increased thereby is as much as need be said on this point.

Hara, who, when Terauchi's Government fell, in 1918,

headed a Seiyukai Government, was rather afraid of this fiery and indefatigable little man, and got him to accept a seat on the Diplomatic Advisory Council, a position which silenced a good deal of the criticism which he would otherwise have directed against Hara's headlong administration. With all his energy, his popularity, his reputation as a "God of the Constitution," and his Machiavellian skill in political manipulation, he seemed always to miss the prizes of the political life, until, when General Baron Tanaka died in 1929, he was chosen to succeed him as president of the Seiyukai. Former affiliations and past criticisms were washed out by the simple process of declaring that the Seiyukai's principles were those which he had always supported.

At first Mr. Inukai held the portfolio of Foreign Affairs in addition to the Premiership. It was usual for a Minister for War to pass from one Cabinet to another, as he belonged to no party, but General Minami resigned: in the troubled waters that he had created in Manchuria were other fish for his frying: and General Araki, who, whatever his military talents may have been, certainly had a genius for publicity, became Minister for War. It is said that when, at a preliminary Cabinet meeting, somebody asked Inukai who was to be his Foreign Minister, he pointed a finger at General Araki, whose vanity was flattered, though he wondered just what this little man meant. Actually Mr. Inukai sent for his son-in-law, Mr. Yoshizawa, whose undoubted merits had been obscured by the impossible task he had undertaken at Geneva of defending Japan's actions in Manchuria.

So this "God of the Constitution," at the age of 75, became Premier, a fact which disguised for a while the disappearance of even the shadow of democracy from Japan. His administration was short and inglorious, and when it had passed away a Labour member in the House of Representatives referred to it bitterly as the Militarists' Robot.

The demoralising effects of subordinating the civil power to force were soon seen, in a series of murders which were excessive even for Japan. The cult of loyalty and patriotism in Japan, being entirely divorced from reason and morality, manifests itself fundamentally in a readiness to be killed—and to kill. Murder, so long as it is committed for any other purpose than that of robbery, commands the greatest admiration, and when violence is let loose and glorified it is natural that the thoughts of men brought up on tales of homicide should turn to bloodshed. The murders of Mr. Hamaguchi and of a Labour member of the Diet, Mr. Yamamoto, had been in a tradition that to kill a statesman is an indication of a deep conviction that the State is not being well served and that he who kills a Socialist does God service (God, of course, being the Emperor). There had been some notable murders in the previous reign, but the Showa era will go down to history as the bloodiest in Japan's chronicles both in public and private slaughter.

As the fanatical quality of patriotism and Emperor-worship was sedulously fostered, the inclination to commit murder for the sake of glory inevitably increased. Being directed against the system of civil government, the murderers naturally sought justification in charges of civil corruption. That there was civil corruption was true, but the victims were the men least guilty; and that the Defence Services had any higher standard it would need a bold champion to affirm.

The first of these typically patriotic acts was the shooting of Mr. Inoue Jonnosuke, on February 9, 1932. The society who sent one of its youngest members to do this deed professed to disapprove of Inoue's economic policy—but that had been radically changed when the Wakatsuki Cabinet resigned nearly two months before. On March 5th followed the murder of Baron Dan, the Chief Director in the Mitsui firm. As it was popularly believed that Mitsui's had profited largely by the frustration of Inoue's policy, it was difficult to see on what principle they should both be murdered. There had been propaganda against both. A number of influential people who were anxious, for their own advantage, that Japan should go off gold, had complained loudly that Inoue's policy was ruining not them but the country. Mitsui's also had many enemies: the firm had a reputation for ruthlessness in profit-making, and some of the army economists would talk at times like good Marxists. So both murders passed muster as patriotic.

Inoue, indeed, had not gone into eclipse with his resignation. When the Diet met (only to be dissolved so that a new House with a Seiyukai majority might be elected) he had made a weighty interpellation. The British example, he said, had led to some speculation on the part of those who believed that Japan must follow suit; but this had been stopped by October 25th by the raising of the bank rate. By imposing the embargo on December 14th the Government had put two hundred million yen into the pockets of the capitalists—and where was the business prosperity that was supposed to result? He was still fighting for the democratic principle in politics. He was one of the strong group, of whom Hamaguchi was centre, and with his chief's powerful support had contested army estimates, until it appeared that the civil power might really get the mastery. He refused to give up the fight merely because the military men had broken loose, but campaigned for his party and principles. It was when he stepped out of a car to enter a school which had been hired for an election meeting that his murderer shot him. He had been warned: a bomb had been thrown at his house and he had received a short sword by parcel post. He knew very well what risks he ran, but kept calmly on with his work. As usual it was the cowardly assassin and not the courageous statesman who became the national hero.

When Baron Dan Takuma was shot outside the Mitsui Bank it caused no little stir, for the Baron was a man not only of great wealth but of an imposing presence, and was well known abroad, having headed economic missions to Europe and America. Two days before he had made a speech of welcome to the League of Nations Commission, headed by the Earl of Lytton, who had come to investigate the Manchurian problem. The Premier, Mr. Inukai, in the course of an interview, said that the murder was unique in that the victim was not in a position of political authority. He also remarked that it appeared that Rightists could be as dangerous as Leftists, and this was a notable piece of understatement, because the Rightists had a monopoly of political murder, whereas the dangers to be apprehended from the Leftists were all in the region of "thought." They had no assassinations to their credit.

Baron Dan's murderer, a youth named Hishinuma Goro, had, like the murderer of Inoue Jonnosuke, been instigated by a man known as "Priest Nissho," or "Priest Inoue," one of the numerous men who combine political ruffianism, intrigue, patriotism, espionage, and a fanatical religiosity. For a week after the murder he was in hiding in the house of Toyama Mitsuru. The police knew he was there, but waited patiently rather than violate this patriotic sanctuary. Toyama ran no risks. Having demonstrated his greatness, he advised the murderer to give himself up.

As a precaution against criticism, General Kanaya, the Chief of the General Staff, resigned, and H.I.H. Prince Kanin was installed in his place. A Chief of Staff, after all, is not sacrosanct and is accessible to newspaper reporters, but an imperial highness cannot be dealt with except in the terms of profound respect. There was some talk of Count Uchida, the President of the South Manchuria Railway, resigning, but General Araki, the Minister for War, said he was too valuable and that he could not allow him to resign. Like most of Araki's prophecies, this was falsified after no very great interval. It was said that Inukai came to an agreement with Araki, that the Manchurian and Mongolian affairs should be treated as local incidents and that the Nanking Government should be ignored, and this was regarded as a surrender to the War Ministry by the Foreign Office. The Nanking Government certainly never agreed to the severance, but that was not quite the same thing. General Araki was very well advertised throughout his holding of office. There were few days when his photograph did not appear in the newspapers, and he talked in terms of the most exaggerated nationalism.

In spite of the subject being taboo, there was a great deal of talk about the future of Manchuria, and Doihara, who, denied the Mayoralty of Mukden, became the "independent provincial government's" adviser, visited Japan and told everybody that Manchuria was to be a monarchy under Henry Pu Yi, who, meanwhile, was closely guarded by the Japanese chief of police in Mukden and not allowed to see visitors.

CHAPTER XIII

THE NEW STATE OF MANCHUKUO

EVIL had definitely gained the upper hand, and it is probable that in future histories the gallant struggle of the Hamaguchi-Wakatsuki Cabinet will be hardly mentioned, and we shall read of the eating up of China as though it were a huge but orderly meal. While these things are still recent, however, it is right to interrupt the narrative to tell of these domestic events. We may also with advantage glance at matters that have since become almost irrelevant; for while the Mukden railway incident and the seizure of the strategic points were all carefully planned, there was no very definite plan as to what was to happen after that, except that throughout Manchuria Japan was to rule and that Manchurian resources should enrich Japan. The spiriting away of Henry Pu Yi from Tientsin to Mukden pointed to a definite idea not merely of creating a new State with a puppet ruler, but also to the possibility of eventually placing that ruler on the throne of his ancestors at Peking. The latter consummation has not been attained at the time of writing and may be abandoned; but if events had shown that it was impracticable to install the heir of the Manchus as ruler of Manchuria, the earlier plan would also have been thrown aside, along with the puppet. There were many schemes, among which opportunity made its selection.

In Europe, attention was concentrated on a point which in Japan was regarded as of no importance—whether Japan would keep her word, which she had given, not to attack Chinchow. The attack might become important, but the promise was gossamer—its keeping depended entirely on questions of military necessity of which Japan was sole judge. At that date Europe did not realise this, though M. Briand had emphasised the fact that the League could believe nothing that was not vouched for by its own observers, or other neutral witnesses. Accordingly, Colonel Badham-Thornhill, British Military Attaché in Peiping, with the American and French attachés, went to Chinchow, whence they proceeded to Mukden and reported that there was nothing that could be called a concentration of troops in Chinchow, or any preparation for hostilities. As Japanese military officers had been telling the Japanese Press exactly the opposite, this aroused great anger, and elaborate stories were invented of the manner in which the Chinese had hoodwinked the attachés.

The Government, in view of what it intended to do, issued a public statement reviewing the Manchurian affair. Its keynote was the Chinese failure in civil administration. Wherever the Japanese army had driven out the intolerable soldiery of Marshal Chang Hsueh-liang, the local authorities, much to the Japanese regret, had always fled, leaving the inhabitants a prey to anarchy, whereas they clearly ought to have stayed and co-operated with the Japanese. Humanity forbade that the inhabitants be left in this plight, so the Japanese military authorities, at great sacrifice, shouldered a duty which they had no desire to assume and no right to evade. Bandits, including many officers and men "discharged" from the Chinese forces, had increased their activities since the beginning of November, and had made 1,529 raids in forty days. The statement proceeded to contradict the military attachés flatly. The Chinese in Chinchow were undoubtedly making preparation for attack. Marshal Chang Hsueh-liang had agreed on December 7th to withdraw, but showed no signs of doing so. So long as the Chinese, simulating a peaceful attitude, remained in Chinchow to inspire bandit raids throughout the country, the Japanese would have to take proper precautions. In deference to their promises and the feelings of the League, they had acted with the greatest restraint, but further toleration of hostility was impossible, and the Government was sure that the world would recognise Japan's patient forbearance.

To give the foreign military attachés the lie, and to fill the newspapers with accusations that Sir Miles Lampson, the British Minister in Peiping, was conspiring with the Young Marshal against Japan, did not help to make the manifesto any more convincing. On December 24th, the British, American and French Ambassadors visited Mr. Inukai, and told him of the anxiety of their Governments regarding Chinchow. Mr. Inukai assured them that the Japanese forces had not the least intention of attacking the city. The *Asahi* said that the Chinchow civil government and troops might withdraw or be thrown out, whichever they chose, but that withdrawal was not enough, their organisation must be broken up. Many announcements were made regarding a "cleaning-up" campaign, and it was true that a man-hunt was going on throughout Manchuria, though seldom far from the railway, and that Chinese were dying of cold, hunger, and wounds everywhere.

After all, the Chinese withdrew: there were so few soldiers that a train-load on three successive days saw the last of them on their way to the Great Wall. When the Japanese aeroplanes reported that all was clear the Japanese troops marched in. It was not the line of action which Geneva had been given to understand they would take, but they repeated what they had said in the manifesto— that humanity compelled them to save the city from anarchy, and that Chinchow was a base of organised banditry. A military communiqué ungraciously found in the withdrawal another cunning trick of the Young Marshal, who knew he could not resist, and therefore took this means of convincing the League of the genuineness of his non-resistance policy.

Whatever the League may have thought about the Japanese disregard for the truth, there was great rejoicing in Japan. The Press expatiated on the conclusion of the campaign and the ushering in of the constructive stage. General Muto began a proclamation with, "Now that Japan has completely exterminated the bandits——" Plans for emigration, banking, and industry were discussed; and on

January 7th, 1932, a new report stated that the whole of the South Manchuria Railway zone was infested with bandits.

Though independence movements were not allowed to be mentioned in the Japanese Press, it was one of those prohibitions that faded out without express revocation. As early as November 22, 1931, it was announced on "good authority" that there would be an early formation of a republic with the era name of Tatung, or Great Harmony. If the name seemed ironical that was only because the Japanese conceive that to call black white is more that half the process of making it so. General Chang Ching-huei, who, in spite of his timidity both at Tsitsihar and Harbin (or perhaps because of it), was well in Japan's good graces, asked General Tang Yu-lin, Governor of Jehol, to join the band of "independent" provincial governors; and General Yuan Chin-kai of Mukden announced that there would be no Manchurian army in the new republic, but a police force trained by Japanese instructors. There was also plentiful discussion over the need for a centralised Japanese authority. The extent, the form of government and the method of Japanese control were all still in the air, unless we adopt the supposition that the Japanese plan definitely for years in advance, and that the army leaves everybody guessing until the moment comes for giving effect to the plan. In the case of Jehol, it is possible that its annexation may have been decided upon from the beginning, but that as it had in the meanwhile to be conquered, this part of the plan was deferred, in order that the new State might be presented to the Lytton Commission as an accomplished fact.

The democratic camouflage still had its uses. At a party meeting on January 20, 1932, Premier Inukai said that the solution of the Manchurian and Mongolian problems rested with the Seiyukai, and that self-determination was the order of the day. The three Manchurian provinces had already declared their independence, but this was all done again more formally, and by various deliberate stages the State of Manchukuo was brought into being on March 1st, with

Henry Pu Yi as Chief Executive. The Powers were notified on March 12th. Japan withheld formal recognition for a time. The League of Nations Commission of Inquiry was in the land, and it would have looked rather like a defiance of the League to take such a step; for recognition on Japan's part could only have meant a readiness to protect the new State against any who might dispute its sovereignty.

CHAPTER XIV

THE HIGHEST FORM OF PATRIOTISM

EVENTS in Japan are the chief concern of this chronicle, though the doings of Japanese abroad occupy so much of its space, and Tokyo claims our attention again. The Seiyukai Premier found it impracticable to carry on even the pretence of representative government with a large majority of the Opposition party in the Diet. The Diet was dissolved so that one more amenable might be elected; and as the usual precautions were taken, including a wholesale eviction of Minseito prefectural governors and their replacement by Seiyukai men, the desired result was achieved without difficulty. The Diet that was dissolved had included 247 Minseito members and 171 Seiyukai; the new one assembled with 303 Seiyukai members and 144 Minseito. Since the dissolution there had occurred the murders of Mr. Inoue and Baron Dan, and it was one of the customs of the Diet to fasten the responsibility for any untoward events on the Government, so the Opposition began the good work at the first meeting of the Diet. But Premier Inukai declared that the murders had been shown to have been committed by the Ketsumeidan, or Blood Brotherhood, a society that existed before his Government came into being, so that it was clear that it was the previous Cabinet which was responsible for the deterioration in public morals. This so enraged some of the members that there was a rush for the rostrum, and they had to be dragged back by the officials appointed to keep order. The Premier also spoke of plans for the control of foreigners—not that there had been any foreigners connected even in the remotest way with the murders, but it was always a safe line to take. The Seiyukai did their best for the army, but could not do enough. A Premier who believed in representative government and even in the supremacy of the civil power went in jeopardy every day, and when Inukai went for a short walk by himself on March 31st, having given his bodyguard the slip, there was the greatest anxiety.

Concentration on loyalty as the only virtue and disloyalty as the only crime has its effect on the course of justice. In the midst of this excitement, one Hirose Daikichi received a sentence of eight months' imprisonment (which he did not have to serve, as stay of execution of sentence was granted simultaneously), for a swindle in which he profited to the extent of 2¾ million yen (a quarter of a million sterling), and at the same time a man who was convicted of having sought membership of a proscribed radical party was sentenced to a long term of real imprisonment. On the other hand, the disconcerting readiness of young men to shoot statesmen was given as a reason for sentencing Mr. Hamaguchi's murderer to death; but that was only a gesture. He did not hang, and remained no long time in prison. Murder is too much admired for the murderer to be harshly dealt with.

The acts of violence in Japan somewhat diminished the horror that was felt when, on April 29th, at a Japanese Imperial birthday parade in Shanghai, a Korean threw a bomb at an assembly of Japanese notables. Mr. Shigemitsu, Minister to China, lost a leg; Mr. Kawabata, President of the Shanghai Residents' Association, was killed; General Shirakawa, General Ueda, and Admiral Nomura were injured (Shirakawa dying on May 25th). Major-General Nagata, one of Manchuria's conquerors, visited the wounded notables, and then informed the Press that it would take a decade to purge Manchuria of subversive elements. Less than four years of this decade had passed when Nagata was himself murdered by a colonel at his desk in the War Office: he had been unaware of the subversive elements nearer home.

Early in May, Premier Inukai made a speech on the necessity of political purity, and was reminded by the Press that his own party had won power by bribery—a fact which was enlarged upon later. The Lytton Commission were not in Japan to be horrified by the next murder, but were in China, being instructed by Japanese guides on the degeneracy of Chinese civilisation. On May 15th, a group of young officers invaded the official residence of the Premier, cutting down policemen and servants who tried to stop them. The Premier, though he guessed their errand, was undismayed, and demanded to know what they wanted. Their reply was to fire a dozen or more bullets into him, and leave the house with the Premier lying dead. At the same time other gangs tried to capture the city's power stations, or rather to destroy them; but they proved very inefficient, and their bombing exploits did little damage. The murderers gave themselves up, and the men who had attacked the power stations were rounded up by the police.

Most of the men concerned in these crimes were either young army and navy officers or men from the town of Mito. Some towns, like Kumamoto in the south and Mito in the north, are famous for inhabitants who are careless of mortality and desperately mortal. The headquarters of fanatical patriotism was the Aikyojuku, or "Native-Land-Loving School," of which the head was one Tachibana Kozaburo, always known as The Master. He was forty years of age. In youth he gave signs of becoming a brilliant scholar, but suffered a nervous breakdown which probably altered the course of his life. In a somewhat Tolstoyan manner he took to the preaching and practice of salvation through agricultural labour, and gathered a pretty large following, whom he imbued with a sense of the sacredness of the soil and the high duty of working on it. There was little of the Tolstoyan spirit, however, and Mr. Tokutomi, the Japanese historian, appropriately compares Tachibana with Yoshida Shoin.

The murderers of Mr. Inoue and Baron Dan were Mito men, but not members of the Aikyojuku; the raiders who tried to destroy the power houses as well as the civilians who shared in the Premier's murder were members, and so were those who, not long before, had made destructive raids on the Premier's and Lord Chamberlain's houses, the Metropolitan Police Board, and the Seiyukai headquarters. To be a Mito man at all was auto-suggestive of murder. It was seventeen Mito men who killed Ii Naosuke in 1860; and as this noble was a really great man, Mito gained a lasting kudos, and the citizens regard themselves as the makers of the Meiji Restoration. The flood of loose patriotic talk about a Showa Restoration was a large factor in producing the crimes that stained Japan's domestic history in the spring of 1932.

After the murder of the Premier, Tachibana fled to Manchuria, and the Press was forbidden to mention his name, though it was permitted to speak of the Master and to extol him as one of the shining lights of loyalty. For two months he was in hiding, not, as was afterwards explained, because he wished to escape, but in order that, before going to prison, he might write his Gospel of Salvation. This work being completed, he surrendered, and was brought back under guard to Tokyo. His guards paid him a respect which can only be compared with that accorded to a captured monarch, and, at the principal stations, vied with civilian admirers in offering him refreshment.

CHAPTER XV

THE HORROR OF SHANGHAI

For diplomatic purposes Japan maintained, after the Shanghai adventure that must now be related, that it must be regarded as something entirely separate from the Manchurian affair, while the Chinese insisted that it was all a part of the same monstrous aggression. Nobody recording the events of this period can regard them as separate except in so far as they require a separate description. That they were happening simultaneously was the least of their connections. They had common causes and their effects cannot be entirely separated. Japan's stipulations, when asked what were her terms for peace in Manchuria, included a better observance of the treaties, the prohibition of the boycott, and the abolition of anti-Japanese movements and anti-foreign education. The offences thus indicated were later given as the leading causes for the trouble in Shanghai, where, indeed, they were more in evidence than in Manchuria.

A few days before Captain Nakamura's espionage excursion ended fatally for himself, Mr. Shigemitsu, the Japanese *chargé d'affaires* (later appointed Minister), was authorised to discuss with the Chinese Foreign Minister, Mr. C. T. Wang, the question of abolishing extraterritoriality—on conditions, of course. On October 14, 1931, the Canton leaders, who had been trying to make terms on which they should participate in the government, but whose plans, so far as relations with Japan were concerned, had been completely upset by the Manchurian outbreak, proceeded to Shanghai, which had become a political centre as important as Nanking: diplomatic pronouncements proceeded from the republican capital, but plans for the active countering of Japanese encroachments were formed in the commercial centre.

On October 16th, the Japanese Embassy in London issued

a statement regarding the intolerable character of the boycott, especially in Shanghai, and simultaneously the complaint
came that three Japanese had been assaulted in the streets
of Shanghai on the 15th. There was much agitation and a
loud demand for the landing of Japanese troops, but Baron
Shidehara was able to prevail on the military men to be
more moderate, and it was announced that the intention
to land troops had been abandoned. This did not give
general satisfaction, and Admiral Shiosawa, Commander of
the First Overseas Squadron, gave the first public intimation
that the navy was anxious to share in the glories that the
army was monopolising, by announcing in respect of the
situation in Shanghai and the reported fortification of
Nanking, that he would take decisive action if Japanese
interests were threatened.

Before launching any attack on Shanghai, the Japanese
were very insistent that the boycott, of which they chiefly
complained, had nothing to do with Manchuria. That
hostile feeling elsewhere for what had happened in Manchuria was justifiable or natural was never admitted. Marshal
Chang Hsueh-liang resigned his position as Superintendent
of the Four North-Eastern Provinces, and was reinstated by
the Nanking Government. After that it was only by constant
repetition that the Japanese were able to convince even
themselves that the Marshal was merely an independent
robber chief and that neither he nor his territory really
had any connection with China. The evidences of China's
hostility spread wider. Japanese residents in Canton thought
it wise to move to a safer place, and there were reports of
hostility expressed chiefly in boycott along the Yangtse and
in Amoy. Consul-General Murai's report from Shanghai that
Japanese trade had come to a standstill was somewhat
minimised by the fact that the Japanese factories in China
were still working.

A political boycott, of course, always enables a number
of people to demonstrate their patriotism at somebody else's
expense, and China was not free from this weakness. The

Shanghai boycott had become a "racket." On November 5, 1931, the Nanking Government ordered a cessation of all anti-Japanese activities, being moved thereto partly by the determination of the Japanese to find in them excuses for further attacks, and partly by the complaints of Chinese chambers of commerce that the boycott was developing into a system of gangster blackmail, but in spite of Nanking's order the boycott continued. The feeling against Japanese aggression was so bitter that it could not be otherwise. Nor was this China's only offence. A Japanese correspondent in Shanghai complained:

China, with all her avowed trust in the League of Nations and America for the solution of the Manchurian conflict, is feverishly at work on fortifications at strategically important places along the Yangtse valley, apparently obsessed with a nightmare of attacks by Japanese warships. In Nanking, the capital, trenches have been constructed and forts on Sutseshan Hill reconstructed. Forts at Woosung, Kiangyin, Shaosan, and Kiukiang have also been repaired or reconstructed.

Cet animal est très méchant: quand on l'attaque il se défend.

Nanking's exhortation was effective, however, in so far that there was a lull in the complaints of gangster methods. Mr. Kurata, one of the Japanese cotton magnates of Shanghai, said that British goods were making steady headway in China, and that the monopoly which Japan had secured in Manchuria was very poor compensation, but this could not be put down to the boycott. Britain had just gone off gold and was reaping the transient benefits of depreciation.

To understand what happened at Shanghai, we should do well to take note first of an incident in Tsingtao a few days before. In reporting an outrage at Tokyo on January 8th, when a Korean threw an ineffective bomb at the Imperial procession, a correspondent of the Kuomin news agency wrote, that "unfortunately he threw it at the wrong carriage." The news appeared thus in the *Minkuo Jihpao* of Tsingtao, a paper of the same name in Shanghai, and the *Ching Chao* in Foochow—all Kuomintang, or Government party papers. In Tsingtao the Japanese had things very much their own way, there being no International Settlement, as at Shanghai, to exercise a restraining influence. When the ineptly worded reference to the bomb outrage appeared, the Japanese Residents' Association held an indignation meeting. When they had worked up their feelings sufficiently, they marched, a thousand strong, to the newspaper office and wrecked it. Next they went to the local Kuomintang headquarters, which was situated on the fifth floor of an eight-story building. They smashed their way in and set fire to the contents. Soon the whole building was ablaze, and the Japanese mob, now very ferocious, would not allow the fire brigade to approach.

But the ordained blow was not to be struck in this place or at this time. The Mayor of Tsingtao called on the Japanese Consul-General and apologised for the offence so violently resented; but the Residents' Association demanded that the Mayor eat humble pie in their presence, that the Kuomintang be dissolved, and that the *Minkuo Jihpao* be permanently suppressed. The Japanese naval authorities landed bluejackets for the protection of their nationals, and they also warned their belligerent countrymen that if they did not behave themselves they would be severely dealt with. Some of the Chinese wanted to publish their own account of what had happened, so that the world might know the truth, but the more cautious among them dissuaded the others even from this mild course. The Mayor called on the Consul-General to discuss questions of arrest, punishment, and damages, but the Consul-General refused to see him. Later it was announced that Mr. Tanimura, Japanese Consul in Nanking, had protested to the Nanking Government against the disrespect for the Emperor of Japan shown by the three Kuomintang papers. It showed a lack of control over the Press, he said.

Critics wise after the event are always ready to say what should have been done; but it is seldom that we are provided with a demonstration in advance. If the Japanese admiral at Shanghai had possessed the same wisdom and moderation as his subordinate officer at Tsingtao, Japan would have been spared a very black stain on her history. Shanghai was naturally the storm-centre of Chinese indignation about the doings in Manchuria, and discretion should have prompted the Japanese to comport themselves with dignity and restraint. That was never their way, however. On January 18, 1932, when feeling was more bitter than ever on account of the news of the last Chinese administration being flung out of Manchuria and of Chinchow being occupied, five Japanese priests of the Nichiren sect, notorious for the din with which they conduct their devotions, came swaggering down a street in Shanghai banging their drums. It was not a novel sight: such people take more liberties in China than custom allows them at home: but in the existing state of feeling, it led to a collision with a group of Chinese workmen. The priests were badly beaten. Two took to their heels and the other three were rescued by the Chinese police, but not till one had received injuries from which he died next day.

The Japanese simmered for a day before they boiled over: then a band of fifty gathered at the place where the priests had been attacked, stormed a small factory from which the assailants had emerged, and set fire to it and to adjacent buildings. Running amok through the town, they came into collision with the Chinese police, one of whom they killed, while one of their own number was shot dead by a Chinese policeman.

This happened in the small hours: later in the day the Japanese held an indignation meeting, marched to the Consul-General's office to demand strong measures, and from there to the headquarters of the Japanese naval squadron. Consul-General Murai had already protested against the "disparaging" remarks in the *Minkuo Jihpao*, and the same newspaper now had a visit from a Japanese naval party demanding formal apologies on the largest scale for having reported that the navy had supported the attack on the factory. The report was evidently erroneous, for Admiral Shiosawa, in an interview with an *Asahi* representative, said that the mob attack had injured Japan's cause. He also told the correspondent that he was expecting naval reinforcements on the 23rd and 24th, and would then take reprisals, though he could give no details of the plan, as that was a naval secret. The Admiral's reprisals were far more damaging to Japan's "cause" (if the "cause" was anything higher than predacity) than any mob demonstrations. Actually the mob was absolved of precipitating trouble, for it was quite clear from what happened both at Tsingtao and Shanghai that local disturbances had very little to do with Japan's making war on China. The aggressor chose his own time and his own place, and was not hurried into unforeseen combat by fortuitous outbreaks of mob violence.

Early on January 28th, Admiral Shiosawa gave notice to the authorities concerned that, if he had no satisfactory reply, he was going to start operations next morning. The Municipal Council met hurriedly and declared a state of emergency. General Wu Teh-chen, the Cantonese Mayor of Greater Shanghai, who had already dissolved the Anti-Japanese Society on the 26th, agreed to all demands regarding arrests and compensation, and Consul-General Murai declared that he was quite satisfied. The international Defence Committee, acting in good faith, played into the hands of the Japanese, whose regular forces, even at that late hour, they did not expect to act in bad faith. To the Japanese fell (at their own demand) the task of defending a large area where few foreigners except Japanese lived, besides a tract outside the International Settlement which had to be "protected" because a number of Japanese lived there. Here the Chinese were in force because it was believed that the Japanese desired to destroy the railway, which would greatly hinder Chinese defence. As the Japanese moved in to take up the protection of Chapei, from which the Chinese troops had been ordered to get out, the inevitable happened. Shots were fired. Each side accused the other of firing first, and the affray soon developed into a midnight battle. At 4 a.m., bombing planes from the airplane carrier *Notoro* began their work, attacking the railway station and other points till 7.30. They began again at 8.30, destroying neighbourhoods where the Chinese *franc-tireurs* were supposed to be located. Next morning in the early hours there was a sharp fight to put a Chinese armoured train out of action, from which something heavier than rifle-fire had been disturbing Japanese complacency. Foreign mediators, horrified at these doings, managed to arrange an armistice, but it did not last long; there was more firing on the 29th, whereupon the Japanese airplanes again bombarded the thickly populated Chinese quarter.

The War Council in Tokyo had declared on the 26th, that the Japanese navy would exercise the right of self-defence. On the 30th, it dispatched the airplane carriers *Kaga* and *Hosho* to Shanghai, besides many more warships. On the 29th, the nine Japanese cotton mills in Shanghai closed, throwing sixty thousand workers on the streets, "in order to co-operate with the Navy in suppressing the anti-Japanese policy." A few days later the Consular Body, reporting to Geneva, said that one of the dangerous elements in the port was the great horde of unemployed.

The bombing in a thickly populated area had frightful results. People lay mangled beneath the ruins of their houses, and a great exodus began. Everything with wheels that could be pressed into service was loaded up with the pitiful treasures of the humble or with those too feeble to walk, and those who could not even get a share in a wheelbarrow or rikisha carried whatever they could. Constant streams of innocent victims of naval self-defence poured over the bridges across the Soochow Creek into the safe part of the International Settlement, where the great firms had their offices and the well-to-do their houses. It was a time of no little anxiety to the guards, of several nationalities, who were protecting the different sectors. A wild and panic-stricken mob easily gets out of hand and does incalculable damage:

and at the best there were problems of food-supply and sanitation to consider.

His consular colleagues tried in vain to get Mr. Murai to consider questions of reason and humanity; ambassadors who approached Mr. Yoshizawa were told that they were deceived by propaganda. By the 1st of February, Japanese tanks were participating in self-defence in the streets of Shanghai and a general offensive had begun. Japanese warships also fired on the Nanking forts to try and divert the Government's attention from Shanghai. The wholesale murder of civilians and desolation of their dwelling-places being reported at Geneva, Mr. Sato, who had succeeded Mr. Yoshizawa as chief delegate there, had no better excuse to offer than that a Chinese newspaper caption had showed disrespect to the Emperor—evidently referring to the "wrong carriage" story.

An early piece of very complete destruction was that of the Commercial Press, an institution of which China was rightly proud. Besides its being a very successful commercial venture of an entirely exotic type, it was the most important agency of Chinese education, being the sole source of school books for a very large part of China. It also housed a library of Chinese books, ancient and modern, of inestimable value. It was not even suggested that the destruction was accidental: on the contrary, it was pointed out that the Chinese school-books were anti-foreign and particularly anti-Japanese. The Japanese fury was always directed specially against anything cultural or progressive in China ; for Chinese culture reminded them of a debt the consciousness of which had become irksome, and Chinese progress threatened them with a possibility the contemplation of which was terrifying. Japanese soldiers occupied what was left of the Commercial Press on February 5th.

From day to day reports of varying degrees of destruction were received; and the Japanese daily announced the complete destruction of the Woosung forts at the river-mouth, but every day found the indomitable gunners in action again. An incident throwing some light on the situation was the replacement of Japanese guards at the Toyoda Mill by British. The mill was far to the west of the sector "protected" by the Japanese, and became a danger to everybody in the vicinity. Mr. Takai, the Chairman of the Japanese Cotton Spinners' Association of China, acknowledged that the mills were safe except where they were protected by Japanese troops, and the change accordingly effected at the Toyoda was satisfactory to everybody.

Not the least shocking feature of the Shanghai fighting was the work done by "plain clothes men." The bearing of arms in Manchuria by Chinese not in military uniform was always referred to in terms of the greatest indignation, but independent accounts of the fighting in Shanghai ascribed many of the cruellest atrocities to armed Japanese civilians. These roamed about in bands, frequently "executing" prisoners in batches. Often the chief work of the Japanese military patrols was to dispose of the bodies of men, women and children which these *franc-tireurs* left in their wake. Nor, apparently, was any restraint exercised. Japanese newspapers published photographs taken by their own correspondents of groups of these civilians, and a staff correspondent of the *Mainichi* ingenuously described their night hunts when he and his friends, from behind sandbag barricades, would fire at everything they saw moving.

It became abundantly clear that the Chinese resistance was wholly unexpected. Japanese marines had often been landed before in Chinese ports, and it was taken for granted that when they did so they would immediately be acknowledged as masters of the situation. The destruction and slaughter were the result of rage at the unexpected resistance, and fear that superior numbers might overwhelm the attackers. The man responsible was obviously Admiral Shiosawa, so he was hurriedly replaced by Admiral Nomura, a man with level head, popular among American and British naval men, with whom he could talk familiarly and easily. There was a rumour that Shiosawa had committed suicide; but, on the contrary, the naval authorities arranged carefully to save his face.

Nomura arrived on the 8th, but proved to be as ferocious as Shiosawa. Unable to silence the Woosung forts, the Japanese destroyed instead the villages in the neighbourhood. The arrival of plentiful reinforcements calmed the Japanese frenzy, but only for as long as it took the new men to get into action. Nomura consented to a brief truce, during which nuns went into the ravaged area to assist the terrified women and children in getting away. The soothing effect of their presence was counteracted in no small degree by constant flights of Japanese planes overhead; but, brief and abortive though it was, the truce saved many lives. The people saved were in most cases distraught with terror and famished with hunger and thirst, through not having dared to leave even the most insecure shelter lest they be shot at sight.

The Japanese public, by every channel of propaganda, was fed on glory day and night, but invincibility was so slow in fructifying that the Press clamoured for a "decisive attack"—in self-defence, of course. The Consular Body in Shanghai strove to ameliorate conditions but in vain. The Japanese had had a taste of trying to land at Woosung and did not like it, so they continued to land at the wharves in the safety of the International Settlement, in spite of all protests, both Chinese and consular. From here they could take up their positions at their ease. They had not missed the lesson of the Great War, that the most dangerous of all military operations is to land on a hostile coast.

The Consular Body reported to Geneva that the initiative in aggression lay all the time with the Japanese; a Japanese naval communiqué accused them bluntly of lying. General Araki, Minister for War, in a statement issued in Tokyo, said that the Chinese outrages threatened to precipitate another Nikolaevsk or Nanking affair, and that such a contingency must be prevented. It is interesting to note that eighteen months later General Araki again harked back to the massacres of Nikolaevsk and Nanking as something that the Chinese must not be allowed to repeat, evidently forgetting that the Nikolaevsk massacre was perpetrated by Russians and that no Japanese at all were killed at Nanking, thanks to the courageous moderation of Baron Shidehara.

Japanese troops were poured into Shanghai, and preparations made for a mass attack. The representatives of the Powers warned Japan that for any untoward result she alone would be responsible, and preparations were made for evacuating the International Settlement if necessary, but the battle-front had moved northwards, into the marshy land, intersected with creeks, lying beyond Chapei. The Japanese, though they had had an unexpected taste of Chinese resistance, thought the general advance would be a triumphal march, but the resistance, mainly on the part of the 19th Route Army, a Cantonese force, was more stubborn than ever. The general advance began on the 21st of February, and on the 22nd and 23rd the Japanese were in retreat.

Something had to be done. On a sector, therefore, where there was much barbed wire but no movement, a heroic deed was staged. Three privates were asked whether they would make the necessary sacrifice. Of course, they consented. Versions of the story vary somewhat; but the one that is generally accepted is that the three were given a long cigar-shaped bomb, which was a load for all to carry. Bearing this, they advanced, and, when they arrived where the wire was thickest, the bomb exploded, and they were blown to pieces along with a certain amount of the wire. From the many stories afterwards told about their devotion to death, it was evident that they were expected to die in the execution of their task. They rather than the barbed wire were the objective of the bomb.

No military need dictated the action and no military advantage was gained; but the moral effect was tremendous, every newspaper in Japan displayed the news with enormous headlines. Extraordinary details were gathered of the three heroes, all Kyushu men. Prizes were offered for the best

songs and the best tunes to which to sing them. Uniformed
bands went on tour and marched through the streets of
towns playing "The Song of the Three Human Bombs."
Crowds gathered round gramophone shops to hear the
records. Lectures were given on platform and over radio,
and the nation was solemnly assured that the Great War
had produced no such heroic deed. Carrying the bomb
became a popular game for little boys, whose training in
the martial spirit begins when they leave the cradle. Eventually a statue was erected in their honour.

Not the least part of the national satisfaction in the exploit
of the Three Human Bombs seemed to lie in the fact that
they met their deaths in the tremendous detonation of their
own bomb rather than, as many of their comrades had done,
at the hands of men for whom they cultivated contempt.
The Chinese, on the other hand, experienced an unaccus-
tomed thrill of national pride in the fact that thousands of
their soldiers heroically faced certain death from superior
weapons. Strangely enough, they seemed to get their highest
emotional reaction from the exploit of a young American
airman named Short. The Chinese had a few planes, but
were so greatly outnumbered that it was hopeless to use
them—they lost them whenever they did, but one day, just
after the Human Bombs incident, young Short went up.
Several superior Japanese planes went after him, but he
killed a Japanese airman before his own fatal crash.

Admiral Nomura's presence at Shanghai did little good,
after all. A genial manner and fluent speech find some tasks
too great for them. Nor did the presence of Mr. Matsuoka
Yosuke help—a man still more fluent but less genial.
Japanese and Chinese commanders met on Admiral Kelly's
flagship *Kent*, but though they agreed in principle to a
simultaneous withdrawal, the Japanese added so many
conditions that it was almost stultified. A good deal of
irritation was felt in Japan, for the Lytton Commission had
arrived there on February 28th, and it had been hoped to
have things cleared up before their arrival; and the League

of Nations Assembly was just about to meet; moreover, Mr. Stimson had just spoken with great emphasis and very unfavourably towards Japan, and a boycott was threatened in America.

The continuation of gratuitous murder and senseless destruction in Shanghai was making the Powers impatient, and Japan and China definitely promised a "Cease Fire" at 2 p.m. on March 3rd, though Mr. Yoshizawa was cautious enough to reserve Japan's right to resort to self-defence. On the 4th, Dr. W. W. Yen at Geneva read to the Assembly three telegrams just received recording Japanese troop landings and attacks that very day, and Mr. Sato's endeavour to find an explanation was met with laughter.

As it was arranged that the Lytton Commission should visit Shanghai before Manchuria, there was some effort to clean up a little before their arrival. On the other hand, it rather precipitated the declaration of the independence of Manchukuo, which took place on March 1st, as it had become inconvenient to delay it longer. The Commission arrived in Shanghai on March 14th, and, though most of the corpses were hurried out of sight, the spectacle of a square mile of devastation was sufficiently horrible.

After the "Cease Fire" the discussion of terms for Japanese withdrawal went on for many weeks, and the campaign petered out rather than came to an end. The Japanese sent their troopships up the Yangtse and landed troops at a convenient undefended spot on the lower right bank. Under the double fire the Chinese had to retreat, but, after the Chinese had withdrawn, the Japanese had no valid excuse for staying. Naturally they claimed uncommon virtue in their withdrawal. Eighteen months later, little of Chapei had been rebuilt, but the completion ceremony was performed of an enormous fortified barrack at Hongkew Park, which went by the modest name of the Japanese Landing Party Headquarters. Opposite to it, and more significant, was built a handsome Shinto shrine, a sign that the Emperor of Japan, God Incarnate, had extended his hand over Shanghai.

Never did military operations on so large a scale have so little military purpose, but from the Japanese point of view the effort was not wasted, in that the spectacle of many mediators striving in vain for peace had lowered the prestige of Europe, and diminished European trade. Some acknowledgment was made of the misdeeds of Japanese civilians, which had contributed largely to the trouble. Sixty-seven were deported as undesirables, and there were even some farcical trials.

CHAPTER XVI

THE GALLANT FIGHT OF MA CHAN-SHAN

In the enormous province of Heilungkiang, General Chang Hai-peng, one of Japan's friends, had proved a failure, and Chang Ching-huei, brought over from Harbin, had excused himself of the responsibility of taking charge. The rightful Governor, General Wan Fu-lin, was in Peiping, where he had been ill, and whence it was difficult for him to get back to his province. The men whom Japan tried to place in authority were both afraid of General Ma Chan-shan, who had come down from Taheiho, on the Amur, and given the Japanese a good fight at the Battle of the Bridges on the Nonni River. The Japanese had occupied Tsitsihar, contrary to the diplomatic assurances that they would not.

With the onset of winter, the Japanese began to withdraw from Tsitsihar, however; having hurried thither from warmer latitudes, they found the Heilungkiang capital excessively uncomfortable, and there were many cases of frostbite. General Ma Chan-shan began a drive on Tsitsihar from Lientien, and his subordinate, General Hsu Pao-chen, began an advance from Koshan with the same objective. On this news reaching the Japanese, however, they immediately ordered a brigade to proceed from Mukden to Tsitsihar. They had hoped for a withdrawal for the winter from a climate so severe, but there was great indignation when it was found that the world at large regarded the first stages of this withdrawal as due to an exceedingly sharp note from U.S. Secretary of State Stimson. The War Office issued a very indignant communiqué stating that such an inference had "provoked high indignation among patriotic people. The Japanese army does not for a moment brook intervention or restraint on the part of a third Power. . . . In short, the Japanese army . . . is not amenable to interference or restraint of any kind, except that it acts under Imperial orders."

For the time, however, self-defence was not found necessary at Tsitsihar. The rather surprising news came from Harbin that General Ma Chan-shan had ordered General Hsu Pao-chen to stop his advance on Tsitsihar, and further that he had dismissed both General Hsu and General Tien Kuai-sheng, another of Governor Wan Fu-lin's henchmen. Lieutenant-General Ninomiya, Vice-Chief of the General Staff, returning from a tour in the north, was the first to bring the news that General Ma Chan-shan had signified his allegiance to Japan, but said that it was not to be reckoned on too confidently, as Heilungkiang was full of adherents of General Wan Fu-lin, who needed watching. General Ninomiya's story was confirmed, however. An enterprising Japanese journalist secured an interview with General Ma at Hailun, and the General was full of admiration for the Japanese and of regrets that they had misunderstood each other. He sent a secretary down to Harbin to interview General Chang Ching-huei, the Japanese nominee (who had returned thither after all), and to discuss terms of friendship.

There followed a rather remarkable transaction. The Japanese had taken all banks under their control, including Marshal Chang Hsueh-liang's Central Bank, in which they deposited under their own safe keeping four million dollars of salt revenue that they had seized. The Young Marshal sent an order on the Bank for this sum to General Ma, and the surprising news soon became known that the Bank had honoured the draft, which it could only do with express permission from the Kwantung Army, and that Ma had the money. It looked like a grim jest at the expense of the Young Marshal.

General Ma set out to recover Tsitsihar in the Japanese interest, but made such slow progress that there was some doubt about his new zeal even from the outset. But other new adherents of the Japanese cause also had their troubles, especially General Chang Hai-peng, in Taonan, who could hardly distinguish between his own army and the bandits whom it was supposed to be exterminating. With the new year there came the news that the Japanese had occupied Chinchow, and this apparently confirmed Ma's allegiance, which had been suspected of wavering; he informed General Chang Ching-huei that he had broken off all connection with the Young Marshal. There was a chaos of risings against the Japanese, described without any discrimination as "bandit raids." The remains of the old Kirin army, which had been ejected by the Japanese, and was now called the anti-Kirin army, was at war with the new levies raised and armed by Japan, and called the new Kirin army. General Ma won some regard by acting as mediator between the two and bringing about peace for the moment. But a disconcerting fact about Japan's attempts to create a new Manchukuo army was that the new troops, with an utter failure to appreciate Japan's might or to serve their own interests, constantly deserted and joined the bandits.

On February 16th General Ma Chan-shan flew from Tsitsihar, where he was now an "independent" Governor, to Mukden, where there was a reception at the Yamato Hotel, all the independent Governors (put in office by the Japanese) meeting General Honjo, Commander-in-Chief of the Kwantung Army, General Miyake, his Chief of Staff, and other Japanese notables. There was much mutual admiration. Ma returned thence to Tsitsihar, via Harbin, where somebody took a pot-shot at him just before he mounted his aeroplane. Harbin at that time was a good place to be out of; while its "independent" Governor had been thanking General Honjo for bringing peace and order to his province, chaos had come there, and the Japanese had to bring up aeroplanes and a large military force to save their nominee from the wrath of the remnants of the old Kirin army that they had driven out five months before.

Soon after General Ma Chan-shan got back to Tsitsihar, he let it be known that he had played a trick on the Japanese in order to gain time and money, and he and his compeers were tremendously pleased with its success. There was great anger in Japanese quarters at having been outwitted, but probably no more moral reprobation than in China. The idea of all being fair in war was traditionally carried out much more logically in the Far East than in Europe; and in Japanese history one reads of struggles in which changes of allegiance decide the issue of the day far oftener than prowess in arms.

Whatever one may think of Ma's strategy, there can only be admiration for the gallantry with which he fought for a cause which he knew was doomed. The Japanese soon drove him out of Tsitsihar, and the fighting moved further and further north, in a wild country. The seasons changed from the arctic cold of winter to the damp and torrid heat of summer, which is found trying even by the natives in North Manchuria. Ma was always on the move, as often attacking as attacked. But his enemy had unlimited resources, while Ma's own force was diminishing every day. Sickness and want decimated his men, but he fought doggedly on. At length the news came, in August, that Ma Chan-shan was dead. The Kwantung Army, which was liberal with its communiqués, published an account of Ma's end, in which it paid tribute to him as a gallant enemy:

The heroic death of Ma Chan-shan, near Hailar, in North Manchuria, was worthy of the soldier that he was. Under heavy skies from which drenching rain fell daily, Ma, with a bodyguard of eight hundred, fled eastwards, over the hilly country east of Hailun, closely pursued by the Japanese cavalry and some Heilungkiang troops. On July 27th, at 9 a.m., he crossed the Hailun river, not knowing that the Amakasu corps lay in wait entrenched on the north bank, cutting off his retreat. When Ma came within range, the Tanaka battalion, on the heights of the north bank, poured in a hot fire, killing 200 of the enemy, who, with their ranks badly depleted, abandoned a large quantity of machine-guns and rifles, and at an accelerated pace continued their flight eastward along the Hailun valley. Rain had hardly stopped for several days, and the valley was almost impassable, but in their desperation the remnant plodded on, with the

Tanaka battalion close at their heels. Ma Chan-shan had a raincoat over his uniform of lieutenant-general, and was wearing the First Military Order on his breast. He was immediately behind the vanguard and was encouraging his men to make the best pace possible. About 3 p.m. he was hit by a stray bullet and fell from his horse. Ma Chan-shan's horse had the Chinese character *chan* branded on his buttock, and carried a magnificent saddle with gold stirrups. A leather bag full of bullion and gold ornaments was fastened to the saddle. Riderless, the chief's charger galloped away eastward.

The rearguard, determined to carry away their chief's remains, stood on the defensive and put up a desperate resistance to the Japanese attack. But the furious onslaught of the Tanaka Battalion was too much for them. Seeing the sacred remains borne away on a stretcher, they took to flight. Near the spot where Ma Chan-shan fell, the bloodstained First Order and other decorations were found scattered on the ground.

A leather case, Ma's personal property, was also found, containing a code book and photographs, a letter from General Honjo, dated March 23rd, and another from Colonel Itagaki, dated December 29, 1931, and other important documents. The pursuing troops annihilated Ma's force to the last man, in the depths of the Hailun valley on July 29th, and also captured the leader's horse.

Alas for this heroic story. General Ma Chan-shan turned up again many months later. The whole company had not been annihilated after all, a remnant escaping into Soviet territory, where they were received with the usual proprieties. Ma Chan-shan went for a trip to Europe before returning to China; and then, according to the Japanese Press, the adventure that had been so admirable had a sequel only too characteristic. Large funds had been collected to support his cause, and when he was asked what he had done with them, he protested that only a small fraction of the sum collected had ever come to his hands. So the memory of a heroic struggle was beclouded by a squalid squabble over cash.

But it was also brightened by the comment of a Chinese journalist in Shanghai. The death of General Ma was duly reported to the Emperor of Japan, and there must have been some embarrassment when it was found that the report was incorrect. In fact, as the journalist put it, the incident raised a very delicate question—can God be misinformed?

When Japan laid a heavy hand on Shanghai it was believed that a crushing blow at the centre of Chinese activity would bring Manchurian resistance to a swift end. The fight put up by the Nineteenth Route Army, however, proved to be the chief inspiration of General Ma Chan-shan, and galvanised countless groups of the old Manchurian army into action. Nor was Ma's the last effort to withstand the Japanese invasion. Ill armed, scattered, and without possibility of replenishment, the army which, when taken by surprise on September 18, 1931, had seemed so helpless, kept up the fight for years.[1]

[1] In 1937 some two hundred and fifty Japanese soldiers were killed in Manchukuo in the course of actions against bandits.

CHAPTER XVII

THE ART OF RECOGNITION

BY prohibiting all mention of Japanese encouragement of independence movements in Manchuria, Japan endeavoured to create an illusion of there being a spontaneous movement among the inhabitants, and it was in the hope of the declaration of independence being taken at its face value that recognition was delayed. There was no lack of demand for immediate recognition: many people thought it only logical that Japan should recognise the State that she had created, and the army was specially insistent. To the army, indeed, Manchuria was a military colony, and it was determined that none of the divided authority that had existed in South Manchuria should continue in the new State, but that it should be a military dictatorship.

General Araki, the Minister for War, made the first of a series of slips in this matter. He declared that he could not allow Count Uchida to resign the Presidency of the South Manchuria Railway, and as Count Uchida was far from being so strong a character as he was commonly supposed to be, perhaps Araki was right in thinking that he would serve as a convenient mask for a military dictatorship. The military men as a whole, however, were of opinion that if the supreme military head of the new State was not to include in his multiple offices the presidency of the railway, the president was at least to be subordinate to him; and a former Foreign Minister could hardly be expected to subordinate himself to a military ambassador. A way out was found by appointing Uchida Foreign Minister in the new Government that had to be formed after Premier Inukai was murdered. It was stated that Uchida accepted the appointment only on condition that Manchukuo be immediately recognised, but events did not endorse this belief.

There were many speculations as to whether the visit of the Lytton Commission had any effect upon the date chosen for recognition. It was certainly hoped that the Commission would be converted to the Japanese point of view, and no effort was spared. All the best talkers gathered round and did their utmost. There are no people in the world so gifted as the Japanese with the power of persuasion, and even the "old Japan hand" succumbs when a full battery is turned on him. Charming ladies in lovely clothes overwhelmed the Commission with their innocent smiles; and as for hospitality, there is nothing like it in the world. But even in the Japanese garden everything was not lovely. At New York the Commission heard of the murder of Mr. Inoue; in Tokyo they were welcomed by Baron Dan one day and shocked to hear of his murder the next. They saw a square mile of wanton devastation in Shanghai. At Harbin they heard of the murder of Mr. Inukai. All this "patriotic" work counteracted much of the favourable impression created by earnest gentlemen and smiling ladies. "Imponderables" often count for much.

As the time approached for the publication of the Commission's report, hope that it would be favourable to Japan vanished. There was no thrilling uncertainty as to whether a lady or a tiger would emerge from the Commission's door. To recognise Manchukuo in the face of an unfavourable report would have a more defiant air than Japan desired to assume, so it was decided to take this step just before publication. Count Uchida, therefore, speaking at the opening of a special session of the Diet on August 23, 1932, said:

Those who seek to place upon Japan the responsibility for the Manchurian revolution by tracing the independence of Manchukuo directly to our military operations, simply labour under an ignorance of the facts, and their opinions altogether miss the point. Again, as regards those who fancy they detect a secret connection of some sort on the part of Japan with the foundation of the new State, basing their suspicions on the fact that there are a number of Japanese in the employ of the Manchukuo Government, I need only point to the existence of many precedents for the enlistment by a young Government or a newly founded State of the services of foreigners. Our own Government, since the Meiji Restoration, have employed many foreigners as advisers or as regular officials: their number, for instance, in the year 1875 or thereabouts exceeded five hundred. Those who misconstrue the presence of Japanese in the Manchukuo Government in the fashion alluded to, are placing the responsibility where it does not belong.

Manchukuo has come into being as a result of separatist movements in China herself. Consequently, the view expressed in certain quarters that the recognition by Japan of the new State, thus created, would constitute a violation of the stipulations of the Nine-Power Treaty is in my opinion incomprehensible. The Nine-Power Treaty does not forbid all separatist movements in China, or debar the Chinese in any part of the country from setting up of their own free will an independent State. Hence, should Japan extend recognition to the existing Government of Manchukuo, founded by the will of the people of Manchuria, she would not thereby, as a signatory Power to the Nine-Power Treaty, violate in any way the stipulations of that treaty. Of course, it would be a different matter if we assumed that Japan was seeking to annex Manchuria or otherwise to satisfy a hunger for land. But I hardly need waste words on once more disclaiming, at this juncture, any territorial designs on our part in Manchuria or anywhere else.

This could hardly be described as a plain statement of fact, for there was hardly an important official in Manchukuo without his Japanese adviser or "vice." Hardly an order was given that was not given in Japanese; and, in spite of the fervent assurances of the spontaneity of the creation of the new State, it would have been difficult to discover any real evidence of a desire for separation from China. Even the new Manchukuo official hierarchy, the creatures of the Kwantung Army, were passive rather than active upholders of the new régime.

The legal aspects and the practical importance of recognition naturally received much attention, for it was very unusual for a new State to be brought into existence entirely through foreign intervention, with no effort whatever on its own part, but with considerable opposition, and with strenuous objections on the part of the State thus forcibly partitioned. From an English source the Japanese desires received at this time some effective encouragement. Since about 1913 the Japanese Foreign Office had retained as its adviser Dr. Thomas Baty, a gentleman with a European reputation in international law. We find him as early as November 1928, in the course of an article on the work of a brother jurist, objecting to the hypothesis that "recognition" is necessary in order to confer on a new State an international status.

A moment's reflection will show how inconvenient this would be. That a State should simultaneously exist and not exist— should exist so far as France was concerned, and have no existence *quoad* Italy—would lead to the most awkward and embarrassing complications. Fortunately the law is not so feeble as that.[1] The fact of statehood depends on a clear objective test. The fact that a government is in supreme control in a given territory, whilst no serious attempt is being made by a former ruler to reduce it to submission, is conclusive that a new State has arisen there. Its existence does not depend on the taste and fancy, or on the interests, of established nations; and its rights and duties flow, not from their "recognition," but from its existence.

Was there anything prophetic in this utterance? It was expanded in due course into an argument for the existence of the State of Manchukuo. A Government was, it is true, in supreme control in the given territory, but it was the Government of Japan. Early in August 1932, while the world was awaiting the publication of the Lytton Report, Dr. Baty published an article in the Japanese Press, in which he advanced his argument that the existence of a

[1] Unfortunately the law is a great deal feebler "than that." The very serious attempt being made (1938) by Republican Spain to reduce Francospania to submission has not prevented Italy from "recognising" the rebel government, and there are indeed "most awkward and embarrassing complications." The League of Nations tried to create international law out of the spurious science which went by that name, but international law is still whatever a strong Power can get away with, and will remain so while such doctrines as that quoted above prevail.

new State was proved by the fact that no serious attempt was being made by the former ruler to reduce it to submission—which, in the circumstances, seemed an unworthy gibe against China in her distress, especially as China had laid her case before the League of Nations and was careful to authorise no hostilities against Japan in Manchuria. Dr. Baty declared that the Manchukuo Government was worthy of recognition, that it was "organised by the Manchurian people voluntarily and firmly," and that if Japan extended recognition there would be no room for criticising this action as a breach of the Nine-Power Treaty.

Dr. Baty's article could hardly have been published at a more unfortunate time. All the evidence was against the new State being "organised by the Manchurian people voluntarily and firmly." The public had been exhorted in the name of the Chief Executive (the newspapers had been forbidden to call him Mr. Pu Yi any more) to cultivate the spirit of Wang Tao—generally translated The Kingly Way. The boundaries of the new State were still so uncertain that nobody knew what was going to be done about the great province of Jehol. General Kobayashi interviewed in Peiping on July 22nd, had declared that Jehol was already part of Manchukuo, though he admitted that it would have to be conquered by the Japanese—a notable endorsement of Dr. Baty's pronouncements on the worthiness of the Manchukuo Government.

But the most striking commentary on the gibe against China for not making energetic attempts to recover dominion was found in the fact that thousands were making a gallant though unacknowledged bid, while not a Manchurian was lifting a finger to defend the independent State to which in theory thirty millions were so passionately devoted. Attacks were actually made on Mukden in August, and a number of aeroplanes were destroyed while the attackers made off with others. The Japanese army was so much annoyed that it threatened punishment of those who mentioned them— they were "serious attempts made by a former ruler"—at least the army declared that the Young Marshal was behind them.

From end to end Manchuria was in turmoil with the "bandits," who wrecked trains and even attacked considerable cities like Kirin. Two of Japan's Occidental propagandists, Messrs. H. W. Kinney and J. N. Penlington, off to Geneva with a "refutation" of the Lytton Report, were on one of the unlucky trains, and lost their clothes as well as the typescript that was to convert Geneva. Near Antung, on the Korean border, attacks on trains were particularly frequent; and at Newchwang, on September 7th, Mr. Corkran, of the Asiatic Petroleum Company, and Mrs. Pawley, a young girl newly married, were kidnapped in broad daylight and kept prisoners for forty-four days. Their release was effected by a Japanese civilian, a member of one of the patriotic societies interested in encroachments on China. He went up to the bandits' lair with *carte blanche* by way of settlement. Nothing was allowed to be published regarding the terms, but the report generally credited had it that the ransom included a considerable quantity of arms and ammunition besides gold watches and other fancy articles.

The most notable attempt of all to recover "independent" territory began on September 28, 1932. Like General Ma Chan-shan, General Su Ping-wen, unable to gain his ends otherwise, took service under the Manchukuo Government ("voluntarily and firmly organised"), and was in command of the troops whose duty it was to protect the western part of the Chinese Eastern Railway. On September 28th he revolted, with all his men, and took possession of the border town of Manchuli, where people change from the Chinese Eastern Railway to the Trans-Siberian line General Araki contemptuously dismissed the report as simply the usual trouble caused in Chinese armies by the commanding officer robbing his men of their pay. General Wan Fu-lin, the Governor of Heilungkiang (the one who had been ill in Peiping), who also had been parleying with the Japanese, threw in his lot with Su Ping-wen, while at the same time it was reported that General Su Shu-men, with eighty thousand men, had attacked Harbin, and in Kirin a massacre of Koreans, the "spearheads" of Japan, was reported.

There were many Japanese in Manchuli, and a Japanese plane dropped letters for Su Ping-wen, promising a pardon if he would return to his Manchukuoan allegiance. This he rejected, but after negotiations he passed a hundred and twenty Japanese women and children into Russian territory. The men he kept as a safeguard against a Japanese bombardment. General Su held the line nearly as far as Tsitsihar, and it was at that time as peaceful as any part of the railway in Manchuria, for there were attacks everywhere—so much so that "Kirin Train Reaches Hsinking Safely" was thought worthy of a big newspaper headline. A General Headquarters for a punitive force against Manchuli was organised at Tsitsihar, and, after deliberate preparations, the expedition started out on November 29th. Chaluntun and Hailar were bombed, and various outposts of Su Ping-wen's army disposed of. Anticipating that they would have to fight all the way if they went by rail, the Japanese assembled a large number of motor lorries, and, considering the bitter cold, made the crossing of the Khingan range in excellent time and with very few casualties.

Su Ping-wen did not wait for Manchuli to be blown about his ears. Like many of his countrymen, he had espoused a cause that he knew was lost, and held on with great tenacity; but he avoided a useless martyrdom, and, after liberating his prisoners, he crossed the border with his men, who were disarmed and interned. There followed a somewhat undignified discussion with Moscow, Mr. Amau, the *chargé d'affaires*, being instructed to demand the surrender of the refugees, which Mr. Karahan naturally refused.

Before returning to Europe the Lytton Commission again visited Japan for farewell courtesies. General Araki lectured the Commission on Japan's sacred mission, but did not go so far as when he had a Japanese audience, for then he talked of the extirpation of white influence east of Suez. A radio announcer almost simultaneously told the Empire's listeners that the Commission had been to China to get a big bribe.

On the same day when Count Uchida prevaricated so valiantly about Manchurian independence being an entirely spontaneous movement of the people themselves, Mr. Mori Kaku, a Seiyukai leader, declared that he regarded recognition as much more than the exercise of a legal right. It should, he said, be a proclamation of Japan's attitude towards all Asiatic problems. Japan must cast off the Western civilisation that had obsessed her too long. This might lead to more Shanghais: was the nation prepared? Count Uchida said that Japan would see this thing through though utter ruin might be the consequence.

But though Japan had not yet "recognised" Manchukuo, she had already determined the framework and functions of its governance. On August 8, 1932, General Muto Nobuyoshi, former Inspector-General of Military Education, was appointed Minister Plenipotentiary to Manchukuo, Commander-in-Chief of the Kwantung Army, and Governor-General of the Kwantung Leased Territory. The great dispute as to who should be President of the South Manchuria Railway suddenly ended. The Kwantung Army had been very insistent on the railway coming under its control; but it was not deemed expedient to make the new Plenipotentiary a complete Pooh Bah, so the railway presidency was retained as a civil post, but subordinate to the Military Ambassador. General Muto was, in short, dictator over all Manchukuo, civil and military, Chinese and Japanese.

The military victory was complete, but the proprieties had still to be observed. A Japanese civilian, Mr. Komai Takuzo, came to Tokyo as the envoy of the Chief Executive, Pu Yi, and asked the Japanese Government for the speedy recognition of Manchukuo. He also repeated what had already been hinted in notes from Hsinking—that for those who recognised Manchukuo the door would be open, a doctrine which did much to reconcile Japan to the idea of other countries not extending recognition.

Muto had a big send-off on August 20th. Japan notified the League that he was much more than an ordinary ambassador. Yes, indeed, said Mr. Lo Wen-kan, the Chinese Foreign Minister, he was more than an ambassador, he was a harbinger of annexation. General Honjo, the conqueror of Manchuria, was now superseded, but his services were recognised in his promotion to a post in attendance on the Emperor.

The Ministers of the new State—though their names are but a matter of historical curiosity—were:

Chief Executive—Henry Pu Yi.
Prime Minister and President of the Council of State—Cheng Hsiao-Hsu.
Foreign Minister—Hsieh Chieh-shih.
Foreign Vice-Minister—Ohashi Chuichi (Japanese).
Secretary-General—Komai Takuzo (Japanese).
Minister of Communications—Ting Chien-hsiu.
Minister of Justice—Feng Hang-ching.
President of the Privy Council—Chang Ching-huei.
Minister of Finance—Hsi Hsia.
Minister of Industries—Chang Yen-ching.
Home Minister—Tsang Shih-yi.

Every Minister had a Japanese Vice-Minister who wielded all real authority. Only the name of Mr. Ohashi is given in the above list, for he was the most prominent. Judging by the reports of his activities he made no pretence whatever of consulting Mr. Hsieh Chieh-shih, but delivered his own pronouncements in a masterful manner. Perhaps the Ministers found it embarrassing to meet one another, for after five years the farce of pretending that there was a Cabinet was given up, and the Ministers became puppet heads of Departments under a Puppet Emperor.

General Muto having proceeded to Hsinking ("New Capital," as Changchun had been renamed), signed on September 15th a treaty whereby Japan formally recognised Manchukuo and undertook to defend it against attack from without. Mr. Hsieh Chieh-shih, the Foreign Minister, for once acting ostensibly in his own person, telegraphed to the Assembly of the League of Nations that corruption was now stamped out, and that the new State had just laws, efficiently administered. But the Japanese official report stated that bandit raids averaged four a day and that there were 117,000 bandits in the field.

People not so far distant as Geneva found that the paradisal picture drawn by Mr. Hsieh Chieh-shih smelt of mortality. The bringing back of the ashes of deceased heroes caused irritation rather than a holy joy. They were landed at Kobe from each weekly steamer and taken through the streets in procession in taxicabs, motor-cycle police riding by the cortège and shouting to the populace to remove their hats. But the insistence on respect being shown sometimes failed sadly, and in October 1932 there was something like an uproar because some of the neat white boxes which contained the ashes were sent to the relatives by parcel post; but this, no doubt, was through pressure of business, for, in spite of the bandits having been exterminated several times during the year, a larger consignment of ashes than ever had just arrived.

No sooner was Manchukuo recognised than it started on a career of conquest—in self-defence. The Japanese War Office publicity bureau is liberal in communiqués. One of these, published on Christmas Day, 1932, declared that at a meeting of the Kuomintang Central Executive at Nanking, it had been resolved to rescue Jehol from the Japanese menace and to recover Manchuria, also to cultivate amicable relations with Russia and America, and to purchase war-planes and munitions. The Young Marshal was chiefly blamed for all this, but his "liquidation" had so often been demanded that something fresh was needed, and the communiqué now demanded the liquidation of the Kuomintang, whose cultivation of friendly relations with foreign Powers was described as "China's old trick of playing off one Power against another." This communiqué is worthy of record because it marks the next step towards the destruction of China, definitely decided upon even before the first was complete.

It may be supposed that when men like Generals Wan Fu-lin, Ma Chan-shan, Su Ping-wen and others took their places as makers of the new State at the outset, they thought that they were holding their own as best they could. It is hardly likely that from the outset they were inspired by a deep but patriotic duplicity. At the outset, they were not greatly different from Yuan Chin-kai, Chang Ching-huei, Hsi Chia, and Chang Hai-peng, except in so far as they were all better soldiers and had hitherto been comparatively free from having to deal with Japan. But when they realised that to be "independent" was merely a euphemism for taking service under the Japanese, they came out and fought for their liberty.

Jehol was a special instance of this hesitation on the verge of a false independence. When the independence of Manchukuo was declared in March 1932, Jehol was included. It had only lately been placed by the Nanking Government under the control of Marshal Chang Hsueh-liang, and the propagandist fiction that Manchuria was never a part of China could not be stretched to cover Jehol, which was the "Imperial Province" *par excellence*. Nor up to this time had any attempt been made by the Japanese to occupy it. General Tang Yu-lin, who had for some years been Governor of Jehol Province, and had a good reputation, had at first apparently been prepared to consider acknowledging Hsinking as the fount of authority, but refused to have anything to do with the new State when he discovered that it was only a Japanese counterfeit. The Japanese industriously warring against bandits in the Three Provinces left the fourth alone. Frequently they chased the enemies of the new régime across the border, but seldom pursued them, and they referred contemptuously to Jehol as "the Mecca of bandits."

Refugee recruits joined him in such numbers that Tang

Yu-lin found them an embarrassment rather than a source of strength. Their appetites were good but their fighting power was dubious. Tang put an embargo on exports of foodstuffs, and taxed the people in every way he could think of in his straits for money. Japanese critics could find nothing bad enough to say of him, and they said that he even put a tax on the birth of babies. He was jeered at as master of an opium province; his moral turpitude was proved when he remitted the opium revenue to Marshal Chang Hsueh-liang; and words failed his critics when it was reported that he was receiving help from the Marshal.

The Mongols of Jehol presented a petition to the League of Nations to save them from Chinese tyranny, so in preparing to add Jehol to the other provinces, Japan was almost doing the work of the League—except for the trifling fact that the Manchukuo officials were all Chinese tyrants themselves. But under Japanese tuition they wore their rue with a difference. The Mongol petition doubtless was intended to show Geneva how little the North liked Nanking; but the uncertainty as to the status of Jehol, notwithstanding the original declaration of independence, gave point to Lord Lytton's remark on the difficulties of recognising a State of which even the Japanese officials admitted that they were far from certain as to the location of the boundaries.

There was a pretence of great indignation in Japan when Jehol, so far from seeking to know the wishes of Hsinking, declared that it intended to have nothing to do with Japan. On December 12, 1932, there were clear indications that the Japanese were preparing for an attack, but the League of Nations had not yet come to a decision on the whole question of Manchuria, and nominally everything was at a standstill. Manchukuo called upon her ally Japan to lend assistance in bringing this rebellious province to heel.

After the worst had happened at Geneva, an ultimatum was delivered to Jehol by the Hsinking Government on February 22, 1933. For a month past there had been sporadic bombings of Mongolian towns by Japanese planes from Chinchow and Tungliao. Accounts from Chinese sources described these raids as terribly destructive, and declared that large numbers of incendiary bombs were used; but the Japanese reports declared that the population of every town greatly rejoiced at the arrival of the Japanese, and blessed them for delivery from the tyranny and exactions of native rule. When the Japanese march on Jehol began, it was swift. Japanese reports described desperate resistance on the part of the Chinese. The fall of one town after another was recorded, but when at last the expeditionary force reached Jehol, held by a motley horde lacking food and arms alike, it met with little resistance. It was useless to resist when the slaughter of the populace and the destruction of the city would be the only possible results. All along the road from Chinchow there had been slaughter and ruin, but the Japanese had lost only one man killed and thirty injured. So the defenders, who had done little but eat up the provisions, fled from the Imperial city and left it to be incorporated into Manchukuo by the Japanese, who took possession on March 4th.

The campaign was advertised as the swiftest on record, the mechanised army advancing as much as fifty miles a day despite a rough road and cruel weather. On March 5th it was announced that Japanese waitresses had arrived in the wake of the army, to be installed in numerous little cafés, where they ministered to the needs of their countrymen.

The Japanese pursued the fugitives to the Great Wall and even beyond it. Chinese regular troops and volunteers marched up to defend the Wall, and there was some dreadful slaughter. But the fact that badly armed and untrained men stood up to the mechanised army of Japan contrasted sharply with the utter unreliability of the new Manchukuo troops, who apparently enlisted only to get the equipment, with which they straightway deserted.

On the eve of the lightning rush to Jehol, Count Uchida, the Foreign Minister, announced in the Diet that Chinese regular troops had invaded Jehol, a province of Manchukuo, wherefore Japan was called upon to exercise her fundamental duty of maintaining the peace of the Far East and of the world.

Thus was completed the creation of Manchukuo; but it took years to make railway travel as safe as it had been before the "incident." A legend grew up, however, that that was the condition from which Manchuria had had to be rescued, and this was instilled into every foreign visitor.

CHAPTER XVIII

THE MANCHURIAN AFTERMATH

More than Manchuria was lost on September 18, 1931. It is doubtful whether the bomb even dislodged a railway sleeper, but it did irreparable damage to the League of Nations. The League being a by-product of the Great War, it may have been unreasonable to expect it to work for peace, and there may also have been something fundamentally unsound in the conception. For it looked to the gaining of moral ends by force and by economic pressure. It may be that moral ends cannot be served that way, but the manner in which the Manchurian problem was handled left a feeling that the helpless had been tricked by clever people who could have saved them but thought the expense too great.

Something was gained, however, in the Report of the Lytton Commission. National histories being all so hopelessly biased, Mr. G. B. Shaw once suggested that they should all be rewritten by neutral committees of the League of Nations, and that only the volumes thus produced should be used for instruction in school. Here was a happy example of what could be done by such means. The Lytton Report was an excellent piece of history. When an advance copy arrived in Japan it was immediately reprinted and had an enormous sale. But it will never be used as a text-book in Japanese schools: every patriot devoted himself to the task of "refuting" it.

Mr. Matsuoka Yosuke was sent to Geneva as Refuter-in-Chief. He lacked a pleasing or diplomatic manner, but he was undeniably able, and great hopes were based on the power of his advocacy. He did his best, but Japan's actions had been indefensible, and her attempts at justification only annoyed everybody by their shameless subterfuges. Mr.

Matsuoka was to change all this. Geneva was busy with the Manchurian question when the Diet met in January 1933, and Dr. Ashida, formerly of the Foreign Office, who had been elected in the Seiyukai interest, made a long inter-pellation on the great question of the day. The burden of Dr. Ashida's complaint was that though a co-ordination of the whole national policy was the one thing needful now that they had undertaken this responsibility for Manchukuo, the fact was that Manchukuo was a monopoly of the militarists, and that there was not an important office in the State not occupied by an officer or protégé of the army, and he asked whether the Minister for War had any inten-tion of receding from the assumption that the army was everything.

Reuter sent a scrupulously fair summary of this inter-pellation to Geneva, whereupon Mr. Matsuoka made a grieved protest to Dr. Suzuki, President of the Seiyukai. Dr. Suzuki without hesitating telegraphed a denial that any such interpellation had been made—notwithstanding its appearance verbatim in the Official Gazette. It was a little unfortunate that Dr. Ashida had lately become presi-dent of the *Japan Times*, in which he had printed the interpellation in full in his own excellent English. But no harm was done. Refutations by mail arrived too late to do any good. Dr. Ashida argued powerfully that the presen-tation of a clear plan for administering Manchuria for the benefit of the Manchurians would make far more impression on the League than the verbal juggleries hitherto depended upon. But it was left to Mr. Matsuoka to impress the League, and he impressed it very badly. The climax of mendacity was reached in a message published in the Japanese papers as from the Nippon Dempo Tsushinsha stating that the correspondents at Geneva were astonished at the great difference between Reuter's message and the text of Dr. Ashida's interpellation—which they had not seen. But that was good enough for the Japanese public, whose intelligence is always rated by the journalists at a very low level.

Whatever ideas the Japanese authorities may have had of benefiting the Manchurians, it soon became clear that the only instrumentality they could imagine was that by which everything had been done hitherto—the South Manchuria Railway. An issue of new capital was announced in February 1933, and at the same time all coal and iron mines and all new railway development were committed to its charge. Mr. Pao Kuen-chen, the Manchukuo representative in Tokyo, issued a statement to the Press explaining how, because there was no co-ordination between the working of the various railways in Manchukuo, and because they owed large sums for construction, equipment, and management to the South Manchuria Railway, it had been found best for this company to take over the whole Manchurian railway system, including contracts for all new lines. For the most urgent of these, the Tunhua-Tumen, the Lafa-Harbin, and the Taitung-Hailun lines, the public was invited to subscribe 100 million yen new capital, with a guaranteed divided of 4 per cent. The new issue was made on March 1st, the anniversary of the proclamation of Manchukuo.

In the course of the long discussions by the League of Nations over the Manchurian affair, there were several occasions when, despite Occidental inability to understand the situation, the Japanese expressed great satisfaction. For instance, by way of implementing a League resolution, the British Government put an embargo on the export of arms to China and Japan alike. It was so obvious that, while this might embarrass China, it made no difference whatever to Japan, that Japanese critics thought that they were bestowing the highest praise on Sir John Simon when they saw in this embargo a wily device for helping Japan. But the embargo, like the idea that it would force Japan's hand to cut off credits and loans (which was put forward in high quarters in England), merely indicated that there were British statesmen who were still living mentally in the period when England was the world's workshop and the world's banker.

It being manifestly impossible that Mr. Matsuoka Yosuke should convince the world that when Japan made war she was really keeping the peace, and that when she broke treaties she was only transferring their integrity to a higher plane, it was very fortunate for him that his failure was total. No half-victory would have satisfied his countrymen. For patriotism had become such a morbid and irritable growth that a negotiator who secured less than a conqueror's terms for Japan was in danger of his life. Prince Saionji, returning from Paris with the spoils of war in 1919, was threatened with assassination; Admiral Takarabe, having won advantages for Japan in the London Naval Treaty, was presented with a dagger on his return. When Admiral Nagano, having failed to convince a later naval conference that Japan's claims were anything but ridiculous, came home, he was given a rousing reception; and Mr. Matsuoka, returning empty-handed from Geneva, became a national hero. The national spirit had risen to such heights that agreement on equal terms had become a derogation of dignity.

Japan had forcibly torn from China four great provinces, had fired on the capital, had devastated a square mile of her greatest port, and had erected there a great fortified barracks and a Shinto shrine to symbolise Japanese dominion, but the army was still far from satisfied. Some attempt was made to continue the war in North China. Posts on the Great Wall were taken and the Chinese troops driven far from that ancient barrier. But these performances only demonstrated again that, though the Chinese were not yet equal to the Japanese in their equipment for scientific war, they realised in a new manner that they were fighting for their country's cause. At Shanghai the 19th Route Army had shown a valour equal to anything that Japan could display; and in the retreat from the Great Wall, they showed other admirable qualities. The Japanese Press described the beaten forces as a disorderly rabble whose demand for quarters caused further distress to the impoverished population of the ancient Capital. Actually they behaved finely. The wounded were brought in by an insufficient supply of motor trucks, and distributed among the crowded hospitals. The soldiers, hungry, ragged, and defeated, plodded doggedly after them. Arrived in Peiping, they sat quietly by the roadside, while their officers found quarters; and in the houses where they were quartered they gave as little trouble as possible and cleaned up before they left. Restraint was preserved even when several hundred Japanese troops were railed in from Tientsin and added to the Legation guard, who swaggered in the streets where Japanese lived, "to protect them," though the residents showed so little sense of needing protection that Japanese women and children went about on foot as usual. For several days Japanese bombing planes, fully loaded, flew over the city.

The Japanese army had already, in its communiqués, declared its intention of destroying the Nanking Government; but there was some fear of measures more energetic than the moral condemnation of the whole League, so the war against China was called off till a more propitious moment, and the Occident returned to the well-fostered delusion that the civil power had the upper hand and that the army would henceforth behave itself—except for such little things as murdering Japanese statesmen.

A military agreement was made, providing for a demilitarised zone south of the Wall, and was signed at Tangku, at the mouth of the river below Tientsin, on May 31, 1933. Its effect was to hand over power to the Japanese, but peace of a sort was preserved until the abuses which it protected brought about new crises.

In launching the Manchurian campaign the army looked for a victory at home as well as abroad. It was due largely to its own heavy military expenditure in peace-time that the Government had found it difficult to make ends meet, and had been compelled to cut off the subsidies from industries that it was anxious to foster, to postpone public works, and to deny departmental expenditure on every possible occasion; but this only increased unemployment; there was bitter discontent; trade unions were militant, yet almost inactive for want of funds; and poverty suicides were frequently reported. Military pamphlets encouraged the discontent by sympathising with the poor, especially with the farmers, but never forgot to emphasise that defence was the first need. This was a counterblast to the demands for a reduction in military expenditure, and a campaign by soldiers and patriots was carried on against democratic government, which was threatening to put the civil above the military power.

The blow that was struck on September 18, 1931, was as much against constitutional government as it was against the Chinese. A wave of patriotism swamped the country. The needs of the campaign stimulated industry and put an end to the rigid economy which, after all, had made the present extravagance possible. Naturally, the first instinct was to ask for higher wages when work increased, but all such talk as this was silenced by the inculcation of the patriotic need of standing together against a hostile world. Foreign exchange being allowed to collapse, there was a sudden stimulation of exports, but wages were cut down. To have expected immediate relief would hardly have been reasonable, and in the north of the Main Island there was terrible hardship in 1932, owing to a local failure of crops —and of banks. The Press was forbidden to mention bank failures or financial crises, and, while the nation at large was being fed with glory, there was hunger in a considerable section.

The trade unions allowed themselves to be swept off their feet and converted into patriotic societies for the promotion of overwork and underpay. More important politically were such bodies as the Great Asia Society, promoted by General Matsui for the subjugation of China under the name of liberation; the Kokuhonsha, the mouthpiece of Baron Hiranuma's senile fanaticism; and numerous others that played their part in creating intolerance and destroying democracy.

The murders of 1932 were the direct result of the Manchurian venture, which glorified militarism and violence. The murderers, civilian and military alike, wanted a military Government and even administration by martial law. But the army was as full of jealousies as a girls' school, and there were other difficulties. The Imperial Diet still existed and could not be altogether ignored. Mr. Takahashi, the Finance Minister, became Premier temporarily, as he had done eleven years before when his chief Hara Takashi was murdered; but he was unwilling to accept a formal appointment. Dr. Suzuki, president of the Seiyukai, with a large majority in the Diet, was very willing to run the risks for the sake of the honour of the premiership, and the Minseito would rather see an opponent in office than a man "above party." On the other hand, the Minister for War was talking at large of the murders being a public testimony of the nation's disgust with party corruption. If there were to be a military premier, then General Ugaki had the best claims and was willing; but he had been so reasonable as to consent to the reduction of the army, and the fire-eaters hated him. Next came General Minami. But Araki was uneasily conscious that the same Cabinet could never hold himself and his immediate predecessor. The right to advise the Emperor on the subject lay, in any case, with Prince Saionji. So Araki rushed off to the Prince's villa at Okitsu to advise Saionji to nominate his friend Baron Hiranuma.

Saionji had little liking for soldiers, but he had still less for such patriots as Baron Hiranuma and refused flatly to take Araki's advice. Suzuki, a consummate political wire-puller but no statesman, was another type that Saionji disliked; and to nominate a Minseito man was to risk political confusion and more murders. So the Prince chose Admiral Saito, a statesman well proved for imperturbable courage and sobriety of judgment.

The Premier's choice of Ministers is limited. The army and navy appoint their own, who frequently continue in office when Cabinets change. But there is a tradition that when there is some serious breach of discipline, whether in the military or civil services, the Minister concerned should resign "to show his sense of responsibility." Naval and military officers had partaken in the Premier's murder, and Admiral Osumi resigned. General Araki was enjoying his post with tremendous zest and did not want to resign. Having made his arrangements, he gave out to the Press that General Masaki, Vice-Chief of the General Staff, General Hata, in command of the Gendarmerie, General Koiso, Vice-Minister for War, and General Muto, Inspector-General of Military Education, all wanted him. He then made the expected gesture, and resigned. Viscount Saito offered it to General Hayashi, and the newspapers came out with panegyrics on the mighty deeds of the Korean garrison in the conquest of Manchuria; but Hayashi declined on the understanding that he would come next, and Araki continued in office. Muto resigned in anticipation of the Manchukuo dictatorship and Hayashi succeeded him, so he did not even have to wait for promotion. Minami also, who had done so much in preparation for the Manchurian *coup*, had a special post made for him in Manchukuo. The appointment of H.I.H. Admiral Prince Fushimi as Chief of the Naval General Staff and of H.I.H. General Prince Kanin as Chief of the Army General Staff contributed much towards raising the Services above the shafts of criticism.

Not that there were many of these shafts. Among newspapers the *Miyako*, of Tokyo, alone definitely condemned the lack of discipline in the army, and some time afterwards the army endeavoured to get a clause added to the Peace Preservation Law making it as definitely a crime to criticise the army as it was to criticise the Emperor. This was more than the legislators found practicable, but the warning was enough.

Even if the Press were gagged, there remained one outlet

—the one that the army hated most of all. The House of Representatives was still a place of privilege, though it took courage to be critical even there, as one might be beaten or even stabbed in the lobby. And when the Diet met in special session on June 3rd, after the new Cabinet had been sworn in, Mr. Sugiyama Motojiro, a Labour member, lashed out vigorously at Governments so subservient to the army as those of Inukai and Saito. The farmers' debts, he said, were mounting, and what was the Minister for War going to do when the men came back from the front to find that their farms had been sold up? He proceeded to read a manifesto given out by Inukai's murderers, and this so alarmed the House that it passed a motion that it should not be included in the stenographic report. The Minister for War, replying, protested against an insinuation of his own complicity in the murders. He shared the murderers' patriotism, he said, but not their misdeeds, and his constant care was to avert such deplorable incidents.

The Premier deplored the assassinations and said he was convinced that the naval and military authorities would restore discipline. He did not know that they were already contemplating his own murder. Instead of improvement there was deterioration. It could not be otherwise when every device was used for the promotion of sympathy with the murderers. The murders were regarded not as crimes but as a political problem. The Minister for Justice, Dr. Koyama, gave a big dinner for high officials of his own Department and his colleagues in the Cabinet, at which the company discussed the proper attitude of the judiciary towards the trials. Self-mutilation is supposed to prove sincerity in Japan, and General Araki received from Niigata perfecture alone nine little fingers cut off to prove the vehemence of their owners' desire for pardon for the murderers. It may be noted that the same prefecture sold 4,962 girls into prostitution in the first half of 1932.

Nor was a favourable verdict the only concern of sympathisers. Less than two months after Inukai's murder complaints appeared that the murderers were suffering in health through their confinement, and the fact appeared to be regarded as a great scandal. In contrast to this was the appearance in court at that time of two hundred of the men arrested early in 1928 on charges of Communism— unaccompanied by murder or any other crime. They had been under arrest for more than four years, and the conditions of confinement are such that few emerge without permanently impaired health, and all but those naturally immune suffering from tuberculosis.

No nostrum for the cure of bodily ills is so firmly believed in as murder is in Japan for all ills of the body politic. Soon after Admiral Viscount Saito had taken office, it occurred to Dr. Imamaki, a well-known patriot, that the Spirit of the Foundation of the Empire was still unawakened and that Japan's glory was not made manifest. So he engaged a *gorotsuki* (a ruffian who commits unlawful violence for hire) to murder Saito for a hundred yen, which he paid in advance. The *gorotsuki* spent the money on a week-end spree in a licensed brothel and left the Premier alone. His patron wrote him a reproachful letter, which he straightway used as an instrument of blackmail. Dr. Imamaki gave him a thousand yen (about £70) to keep him quiet, but the extortion continued, and the elderly reactionary was so sure that his patriotism would be taken into account that he denounced the blackmailer to the police. He did not misjudge the efficacy of his reputation. His trial and that of the *gorotsuki* dragged on for some months. They both pleaded patriotism. Dr. Imamaki, pointing out that he wielded no weapons himself, said that his interest in assassination was purely academic: he regarded it merely as a possible instrumentality of patriotism. The *gorotsuki* was patriotic even in his essay in blackmail. He wanted the money in order to set up in business in Manchuria, so as to promote the interests of the Empire. The pair of them got off with farcical sentences—terms of imprisonment with stay of execution of sentence—which means no punishment at all. Had such a thing happened in a country where political assassination was unknown, the judge might think it best not to minister to the vanity of a fool; but where the murder of statesmen is so common such judicial frivolity is incomprehensible. Yet this is not a unique example. When a demand sprang up for the control of patriotic ruffians, Dr. Koyama, the Minister for Justice, confessed that he found it extremely difficult to punish a man for any act which he declared to have been performed from a patriotic motive.

CHAPTER XIX

SAITO AND THE SPENDING POLICY

SAITO commanded respect, but nobody was really satisfied with his appointment. Most dissatisfied of all was the professional politician Dr. Suzuki, president of the Seiyukai, whom Saito was anxious to placate, but who refused anything short of the Premiership. He could hardly prevent other Seiyukai men from joining the Cabinet when invited; indeed, there was fierce competition between the two big parties for the loaves and fishes of office; but a day was to come when Suzuki arrogantly put loyalty to himself before public service and expelled members who consented to serve in any Cabinet not headed by himself.

It was an elderly Cabinet, the average age of the members being sixty-two, even with the almost youthful Goto's forty-nine to bring down the average. Mr. Takahashi, one of the seniors, began with a rush that looked favourable at first to the military plans. He expanded the untaxable note issue of the Bank of Japan from 250 million to 1,000 million yen, and, though he confessed that he did not like doing it, increased the import duties by one-third in order to make up for the depreciation in the yen. (Similar treatment of the yen by other countries importing Japanese goods was complained of bitterly.) An issue of Government bonds to the extent of 500 million yen helped to make things easier, but though Takahashi spoke optimistically, the Premier, in his first speech, confessed that there was no sign of prosperity and that agriculture was in great distress.

The case of the farmers assumed such prominence during the Saito régime that some account of it is necessary. Agriculture is by far the greatest industry in Japan. The tourist takes due note of the wonderful achievements of primitive implements, and of the picturesqueness of Japanese farming. Since the beginning of the century, however, there had been revolutionary changes. The fields were bearing richer crops than ever, but the farmer's difficulties increased. Some of these are characteristic of farming everywhere, notably the complaint of the tenant farmer that he cannot earn enough to pay his rent. In 1925 a law was enacted whereby a tenant farmer could borrow four thousand yen at low interest, to be repaid in the course of twenty-five years, in order that he might purchase himself a *cho* (2½ acres) of land, which the landlord was bound to sell. In the latter part of 1927, Mr. Yamamoto, Minister for Agriculture and Forestry, wanted another bill passed for giving further relief, but the Government refused to sponsor it, on the ground that the Act of 1925 was working satisfactorily; 12 million yen out of the 70 millions earmarked for the purpose had been advanced, and a thousand yeoman farmers created; but this was a phantom success, for peasant farmers owning their land were disappearing at the rate of ten thousand a year and becoming the tenants of their creditors, or, in some cases, simply deserting the land and taking a chance on what the towns were offering.

There were many factors in these troubles and the sequence of cause and effect was often difficult to trace. The standard of living on the farms had improved. In older days rice was grown largely for urban consumption, and (as Lord Redesdale tells us in his *Tales of Old Japan*) the farmer's chief complaint was always the low price of rice. Nowadays the farmer seldom eats millet, and if he more often than not mixes barley with his rice, he is all the better for it. Some townsmen, hearing that the farmer's economic position was becoming desperate, proposed that he should export rice instead of eating it, and import millet for his own use, but there was no response to this invitation to return to more spartan days.

Some capitalists who looked forward to a rice shortage through an increase in population—that deferred hope that makes the heart of the Japanese farmer sick—still harped on the possibility of rice culture in the Maritime Province of Siberia, with Korean and even Russian labour, for the supply of Japan's needs. The whole economic organisation was changing. When Dr. Suzuki was Home Minister he had put forward a plan for making 3,700 miles of motor roads, for the motor truck services were speeding up the whole of rural life; but the Finance Minister could not find the money, and the Ministry of Agriculture instead evolved a plan for the better organisation of country cart services, the expenditure on which was calculated at 650 million yen against only 200 millions in railway freights.

For many years an endeavour was made to get Japanese farmers to raise sheep, more for the sake of providing home-grown army clothing than for any economic advantage, but in 1928, in spite of a generation of propaganda, there were only 23,000 sheep in Japan, chiefly in the Hokkaido. A much brighter idea was the keeping of fowls, for which about 1929 the Department of Agriculture started an extensive propaganda, with the result that in a very few years the import of eggs was replaced by a large export. But again, the American slump of 1929 knocked the bottom out of the raw silk market, and the farmer's mainstay broke in his hands.

The profoundest changes of all were wrought by the adoption of chemical fertilisers, particularly sulphate of ammonia, of which, though patent rights had been held for many years, the large-scale manufacture did not begin till 1928. At this time it was calculated that fertiliser imports totalled 170 million yen and fertilisers made and marketed in Japan about an equal amount—a large sum for the Japanese farmers to pay for modernisation, and a constant source of complaint, as the dealers formed rings to protect themselves from competition, and so deprived the farmers of a benefit that they badly needed. The farmers became enslaved to debt, and the need of a large cash expenditure on chemical fertilisers seems to have been the chief cause. In 1930 the farmers' debts amounted to 4,000 million yen, and a year later to 5,000 millions. Industrial depression sent many city workers back to the farms, and probably their extra help contributed to the production of the greatest rice crop ever raised in Japan. Prices dropped and the Government lent a hand in exporting a large quantity at low prices. The Opposition blamed the Minseito economy; freer spending was demanded—"Food before face!" as an Opposition leader put it—though it was a glut of food that had caused the trouble.

A world slump in the price of wheat had led to restrictions of wheat-growing, and the Japanese Ministry of Agriculture began to talk of restricting the area under rice; but General Araki said he could not allow that, as military considerations had to be taken into account. It was as well, because famine conditions prevailed in part of North Japan in 1932, though crop diminution was only local and it was a money rather than a harvest failure. The social effects of agrarian indebtedness were deplorable—there was even a slump, through over-supply, in the price of virgins for the brothels—but in an age of "economic nationalism" there was consolation in the fact that the money went from one Japanese pocket to another. Only a small percentage of the five or six thousand millions of debt was advanced by the banks: the biggest creditors were landholders and money-lending farmers.

The plan for making yeoman farmers was itself blamed for some of the distress. Farmers often found it so difficult to pay off the purchase-money that they had to abandon ownership. Under stress of debt they combined and asked for a moratorium, but the Seiyukai administration (1932) proposed depreciation instead. Manufacturers for export had welcomed depreciation, and it was carelessly taken for granted that it would benefit the farmer also. A delegation of farmers was sent to the capital and interviewed the House of Representatives, to whom they explained that however much good depreciation had done the manufacturer, the agriculturist had not benefited.

In Yamanashi prefecture, it was stated, 22,000 silk reeling

girls had not been paid for months, finding it better to work for food and shelter than to get nothing. In Miyagi the electric light was abandoned; from various prefectures came reports of unpaid teachers and of local officials on reduced pay. Children were not sent to school so that the small fee, hitherto cheerfully paid by the poorest, might be saved. The army, both officers and men, was largely recruited from the rural districts, and the army pamphlets of the time took on an almost Socialistic tone, demanding relief for the farmer and a thoroughgoing social reconstruction which was, by some mysterious process, to produce money for the Manchurian campaign as well. Mr. Tokutomi proposed a cancellation of debts, but the creditors were too powerful. Mitsui's gave three million yen for relief—perhaps in the hope of moderating General Araki's denunciations.

It was a curious thing that the police precautions for preventing the disturbance of the public mind—in this case by allowing no news about the distress in the North to be published—left the Finance Minister in ignorance of the existing conditions. He was shocked when he heard of them, and became a convert to the need for relief grants, though hitherto he had recommended self-help, not realising that there was anything more serious than book debts.

Before the special session closed, Mr. Mori Heibei, in the House of Peers, demanded another special session in August to consider the plight of the farmer. It was called on August 23, 1932, and the various plans for relief were hotly debated. The Government had on hand a fund of 350 million yen for stabilising the price of rice, but it was complained that there was a prospect of a bumper crop, and if this were realised it would, in spite of the stabilisation fund, complete the ruin that the record crop of 1930 had begun. With reference to the relief which it was claimed that currency depreciation had brought, it was pointed out that it made it very hard for some big concerns which had issued dollar debentures in America; but Mr. Takahashi said that no measures could be beneficial to everybody.

He confessed that much of the relief expenditure was applied to the keeping of the banks on their feet at a time when they could not recover their advances, and this, he said, was an advantage to the debtors as well as to the banks. It was rather a favourite line of argument (among capitalists) that the capitalist was a more suitable recipient of relief than the proletarian, because his relief was widely distributed, and he repaid the loan. There were also members who waxed impatient with the concentration of pity on the farming classes, and asked what was to be done about the urban debtor.

It has always been difficult to recover debt by process of law in Japan. Determined Japanophils have found this praiseworthy and have talked of a system more humane than the harsh Roman law of contract. A considerable effort was made at this session to loosen ·still further the bonds of contract, and it was proposed that debtors might appeal to the courts to mediate—that is, to reduce their debts. Bankers were rather alarmed, and pointed out to the legislators that money owing to a bank is different from other debts. The banks could hardly be blamed even if their argument was not strictly logical. Forty-nine of them had had to close because their advances were not recoverable. The Bill for Adjusting Debts fell through because the Government refused to accept the Seiyukai amendments, but another Bill passed which involved the appointment of twenty thousand mediators. It did not have much effect.

The first relief to the depression undoubtedly came about by the increase in expenditure on munition-making in connection with the Manchurian campaign—that is to say, by the squandering of the economies of the Hamaguchi Government and a reckless plunge into debt. Secondly came the increase in exports brought about by depreciation in exchange and by improvements in manufacture. But the lag in both cases was considerable—so much so that on August 26, 1932, nearly a year after the Manchurian adventure began and over eight months after Japan had gone off gold, depression was still the leading topic of the day, and the Shakai Taishuto (or "Social Mass" party) held a meeting at the Kyocho (Capital and Labour) Hall, in Tokyo, to which they brought petitions for the relief of the unemployed bearing a hundred thousand signatures. Numbers of policemen were in the hall, and the street running thence to the Diet (then in session) was heavily guarded. Every speech was stopped by the police, and there was such indignation that the meeting became a general scrimmage several times. At length fifty of the members of the party set out with copies of the resolutions demanding relief and rehabilitation of the farmers. They had to battle their way against the police to the Diet, and when they reached the parliament building they were not admitted. The best they could do was to leave the resolutions with a sympathetic member who promised to do what he could.

Some alarm was caused by a sharp fall in the deposits in the Post Office Savings Bank. It was realised, no doubt, that this was due to widespread hardship, but the chief comment was that it put the Government into a dilemma because it lessened the amount of money available for low-interest loans, by means of which it was customary to assist various necessary enterprises that were not sufficiently remunerative for the bankers.

In these days General Araki, the Minister for War, was the national oracle. He insisted that an immediate increase in the taxes was feasible and necessary. It was certainly necessary to get money somehow, for the army's irreducible minimum demand was for an allotment of 550 million yen as its share in the next year's budget, out of a revenue of 1,342 million yen, while the navy, in addition to its current expenditure, wanted 460 millions for "replenishment"— which, however, it was willing to spread over three years. The Premier, Admiral Saito, warned the Cabinet at the beginning of December 1932 that the estimates for the following year were a thousand million yen in excess of the revenue, and he begged them to make a further cut.

It was possible to raise the money by the issue of national bonds, but this might jeopardise the yen's exchange value. Mr. Takahashi, the Finance Minister, was adamant against an increase in taxes, and advanced powerful reasons in support of his stand.

But General Araki allowed nothing so base as arithmetic to stand in the way of his expensive ideals. On one occasion he gave quite an obstetrical lecture. Japan was suffering: he admitted it: but her pangs were those of travail, and would soon be forgotten in the joys of giving birth. An ignorant doctor (presumably Takahashi) might, of course, take the labour pains for gastritis and dose the patient with unsuitable drugs. But objections to taxation could not all be dismissed as bellyache. Baron Go Seinosuke, presiding at the Japan Chamber of Commerce, said that the apparent improvement in the economic situation was due only to the munitions trade and to the relief granted to farmers. Actually the country was in danger of a currency collapse like that which overtook Germany after the war.

Baron Go was Japan's foremost man of business, but Araki was not abashed. The only danger to the country, he said, was dangerous thought. In the Cabinet councils he descended to realities, and confessed that his early promises of Manchukuo being speedily remunerative had been disappointed. This was not an expression of remorse but merely a reason why his colleagues should agree to a heavy military expenditure in the independent State for some years to come. At the same time demands were being made at Geneva for a three-quarter naval ratio, but that was only a prelude to the rejection of the ratio principle altogether.

There were all sorts of nostrums for improving the financial situation, and (England having set an example) old loans were converted into new ones at lower rates of interest. Indeed, lower rates of interest were so much preached as a requirement of the patriotic spirit that high dividends came to be regarded as a sort of moral turpitude, and directors had to find ways of disposing of profits other than wasting them on shareholders. It was even suggested that patriotism was at such a high pitch that it would be feasible to issue bonds bearing no interest at all; but Mr. Hijikata, Governor of the Bank of Japan, deprecated this, saying that the bonds would merely become a sort of currency of high denomination with no safeguard against depreciation, and that they would drag the rest of the currency down with them.

From 1932 there was a complete reversal of the Hamaguchi policy of economy. Instead of balancing income and expenditure and constantly reducing the costs of government, there began a system of budget-balancing by loans of the order of a thousand million yen a year, most of which were taken up by the banks, who, by reducing their own rates of interest on deposits, hoped to be able to carry on. The currency note issue was greatly increased, and the yen was reduced in its exchange value from approximately 50 cents (American) to 20 cents. Manufacturers were not against restabilisation, but insisted on a 20 cent maximum, which they found advantageous for export, there being no increase in wages throughout Japan. When at length the United States went off gold as well, there was some dismay lest the bottom had been knocked out of the depreciation game. But Mr. Takahashi handled the situation firmly and "managed" the currency successfully, fixing it at 1s. 2d. instead of the 2s. of the golden age. He had to be careful, however. Several European countries had aligned their currencies on that of England, but an open declaration that Japan had set her standard by that of Britain instead of being independent would have evoked indignant protests from the patriots.

When the 1933 budget was presented and new features of a size unexpected and a recurrence unanticipated had evidently become permanent, the *Asahi* was, as usual, the only big newspaper to offer any reasoned criticism. Neither the Press nor the political parties had any real policies.

The Seiyukai still had a large majority, and its president, Dr. Suzuki, wanted to be Premier, but the Government might dissolve the Diet at any moment so as to get an amenable House. The *Asahi*, remarking that the Seiyukai must soon make up its mind one way or the other, said:

If it makes up its mind to fight the Government, there is no lack of subjects on which to join issue. In the first place, there is the huge budget of 2,238,000,000 yen, which is predominantly military. Of the total the army and navy estimates amount to 820 millions, or about 40 per cent. If to this are added the interest on war bonds, pensions, and allowances for bereaved families, the percentage will rise to 50. The army and navy estimates are equivalent to 70 per cent of the ordinary State revenue of 1,288,000,000 yen. Referring to the new expenditure, it will be seen that of the total, amounting to 730,000,000 yen, 56 per cent, or 409,000,000 yen, is absorbed by the new war expenditure. Is it the correct attitude of political parties to indulge in sordid party strife, while swallowing these disproportionate figures of war expenditure? Common sense forbids one to believe in the efficiency of national defence provided in such a way. . . . National loans are mounting up at an alarming rate. They are expected to reach the ten thousand million yen mark in the fiscal year 1935-6, by which time 90 per cent of the tax revenue will have to be devoted to tax payments.

But neither party could agree upon a programme for itself, and naturally when they tried to combine against the Saito Government, agreement was no easier to reach. There was a good deal of dissension in the Cabinet not only over matters of policy but over appointments in the gift of the Government. Takahashi and Araki quarrelled openly over the question whether the army was the ruin or the salvation of the country. Goto, the Minister for Agriculture, wept when he told his subordinates how he had striven for the amelioration of the farmers and had failed.

It was felt that the "National Government" was far from satisfactory, but the chief popular complaint, because it was safest to make, was that it was suffering from senile decay. But the break-up began with one of its youngest members—the flamboyant Araki, who could not tolerate criticism. Few dared criticise him, but among the few was Baron Wakatsuki. Araki was always prating of the "crisis year" that Japan was about to face—apparently in 1936, about when the Washington treaties expired, Japan finished with the League of Nations, and so on. Baron Wakatsuki ridiculed the crisis and said that anyhow it was three years off and it was impossible to keep people in a state of excitement so long. Wakatsuki defended the London Treaty, and pointed out that if, as was often said, it was one of the causes of the May 15th murder, then the murderers had killed the wrong man. As for the militarists' attempt to destroy party government, he said, the Emperor Meiji had granted the country a democratic constitution, and this attempt to impose an imitation Fascism on Japan was a breach of the Peace Preservation Law.

Many threats of assassination and two or three actual attempts followed this plain speaking, but Wakatsuki refused to keep quiet. He asked what was wrong with the naval treaty and how it justified the monstrous replenishment programme foisted on the nation. Araki declared that Wakatsuki had taken leave of his senses. He insisted that Japan's relations with her neighbours were unsatisfactory, and demanded an international peace conference at which *Kodo* should be explained to the nations. He was always talking about *Kodo*, the Imperial Way, and was its self-appointed apostle if not its inventor. But he never explained it to his own nation. It was not a dictatorship, and it was not economic nationalism, but he found the effort to explain what it was too much for him.

He managed to get the Minister for the Navy (Osumi having returned to the post that he had resigned) to join with him in issuing a statement denouncing the endeavours being made to estrange the army from the people, especially by declaring that the "crisis" was only propaganda. One allegation that roused Araki's wrath was that in war only common soldiers and sailors were killed and not high officers. This recalled a bitter article that appeared in a

Japanese paper during the Great War, in which, after naming a number of highly placed young men in Europe who had been killed, the writer said that in the Russo-Japanese war the two sons of General Nogi were the only men of distinction killed. This was an exaggeration: besides, the European papers were already calling attention to the "over the top" technique whereby officers were economised in the slaughter. Criticism of the army and of the army estimates, said Araki, could only be inspired by the Third International.

Araki's proposed peace conference, which, he said, would put them on good terms with Russia, received no support outside the army; his plans for agrarian relief did not even gain agrarian support; and not even the army could work up any enthusiasm for his military-economic plans for Manchuria. A mild attack of pneumonia gave him time to reflect; he saw that his "song and dance" had come to an end, and he resigned. It takes more than vanity to make a successful Minister for War, and Araki had not the other necessary qualities.

The Cabinet seemed to please nobody. There were so many cases of "dangerous thought" in educational circles that Mr. Hatoyama, Minister of Education, was driven into resignation. His enemies also charged him with corruption, and a ladies' social reform society waited on Viscount Saito and asked him to see that his next Minister of Education neither ill-treated his wife nor kept a concubine. Presently there was a hue and cry after Baron Nakashima, Minister for Commerce and Industry. Many years before he had written an essay in praise of Ashikaga Takauji, a great man in his day several centuries before, but one who backed the wrong horse when there were rival claimants to the throne. The exigencies of loyalty had become so great that it was now disloyal to admire the fine qualities of this fourteenth-century dictator.

But the fatal blow at the Cabinet came from within. Mr. Kuroda, Vice-Minister of Finance, became implicated in some serious corruption, and in the midst of the uproar that followed the Cabinet resigned, on July 3, 1934. It had been a patchwork affair, and certainly no improvement on the party system; but it had had to carry on in an atmosphere darkened by murder, and with a national economy destroyed by a military conspiracy.

CHAPTER XX

TRIALS EXTRAORDINARY

EVEN in cases where the arrests are made on the spot and there are no difficulties about the evidence, it takes a long time to bring criminals to justice in Japan. In the case of political murders there are long consultations as to what attitude the court shall take, and the crimes committed in the early part of 1932 provided no more sensation for the newspapers until the latter part of 1933. The time was spent in working up the cases for the benefit of the accused. One of them, who had been taken ill, was released on parole and died. His funeral, on December 9th, was attended by every reactionary who could get there, and there were speeches on the high calling of political assassination. Two days later a Communist was buried, and of those who came to pay their last respects, the police arrested two hundred, on the ground that their presence on such an occasion placed them under suspicion.

Some months before the trials began, Mr. Koyama, Minister of Justice, reported progress. He explained the connection between the murders. Mr. Inoue and Baron Dan, he said, were murdered by members of the Ketsumeidan, or Blood Brotherhood, of whom a Buddhist priest, Inoue Nissho, was the leader. Priest Inoue's immediate followers, seeing that the enterprise was a dangerous one, shirked further action, whereupon the Aikyojuku took up the task. Concerned in the murder of the Premier were thirteen naval officers (one of them retired) and twelve military cadets (of whom one had already been expelled). Another group had raided Count Makino's house, and some more threw bombs at banks and tried to put the power houses out of action.

Priest Inoue, who instigated the simplest of his disciples

to murder, was a type perhaps peculiar to Japan. He had long been a spy, first in South Manchuria for the Army General Staff, later in Peking for General Banzai, Japanese military adviser to President Yuan Shih-kai, and in the Shantung campaign of 1914–15. Thereafter he became a Buddhist priest and built himself a Nichiren temple, where he attracted a following of young men. His instincts were bloodthirsty, and he formed his patriotic Blood Brotherhood, who mixed their blood and drank it as an accompaniment to their initiation oath. Besides the victims whose death he had compassed, Inoue had a list of twenty more eminent men whom he had decided to persuade his followers to murder.

The Aikyojuku, or Native-land-loving Society, who participated in the murder of the Premier when Inoue's men began to fight shy, attempted to make a "direct appeal to the Throne" on behalf of the murderers, but were arrested and charged with this grave offence. The news of this was not allowed to get out, but a much better example of police efficiency in the suppression of news was the silence maintained for many months over the Shimpetai, or "God's Soldiers" affair. This was a conspiracy on a much larger scale than the others, and the murders which it had arranged to commit in July 1932 would have made the earlier crimes look pale and almost bloodless. But the conspirators were apparently men of less calibre than Tachibana and Priest Inoue, and in any case they failed entirely to carry out their design.[1]

In Japanese trials everything of importance takes place at the preliminary examination, and the court proceedings are little more than a formality, though often a tedious one. The preliminary trial was not, therefore, accounted unduly long. Though the army did not claim the credit of the murders, it acted as though they had vindicated its

[1] Towards the end of 1937 most of the Shimpetai men were discharged, without sentence, but the trial of others was still dragging on in the early months of 1938.

own opinions. In April 1933 the *Asahi* said that though the army's indignation against party politicians, which culminated in the bloody deed of May 15, 1932, was moderated, the army was not yet disposed to permit the creation of a party Cabinet. This was generally accepted as a simple statement of fact, and nobody raised the question whether the army was acting within its constitutional rights. Discussions took place which would be impossible where *sub judice* trials are kept as free from prejudice as possible. Were the service men guilty of rebellion or murder? was a favourite subject of debate. The Minseito found it easy to bear the murder of a Seiyukai president with fortitude, and issued a manifesto in which they said that "the motive for their crimes was their solicitude for the welfare of the State. They cannot properly be viewed in the same light as ordinary murderers." Rumour had it, the manifesto concluded, that the accused were to be tried on a charge of murder, lest treating them as patriots might encourage future murders, "but this is surely sacrificing the dignity of the law on the altar of expediency."

The trials began at last, that of the Blood Brotherhood on June 28th, the naval court-martial on July 24th, and the military court-martial on July 25th, with the full assurance that none of the accused would suffer the extreme penalty.

Ordinarily the trials of yesteryear are very cold mutton in retrospect, but these throw such light on points of view incomprehensible to the Occidental that their salient features are worth recalling. Open discussion of *sub judice* cases generally tells against the accused; the newspapers quote the police and even judges as affirming his guilt. On this occasion it worked the other way. Cabinet Ministers extolled the murderers. When the hearing came on, Mr. Hiramatsu, for the military murderers, pointed to an enormous heap of papers piled before him, saying that they were petitions on behalf of his clients from every part of the country. An "opinion census," he said, had been taken in many places, and always showed an enormous majority praising their acts. Mr. Hiramatsu proceeded to attack the judicial authorities for their proclivity for acting upon Western theories, and demanded of the President of the Court, "which is more important, the nation or the law?" Nor did he wait for an answer, but said that, the nation being the more important, and the murderers' motives evident, they should be acquitted. He cited historical cases of amnesties being granted after rebellions as clinching his argument.

It has to be remembered that practically all Communist trials in Japan are conducted *in camera*, so that no affirmation of Communist principles made by the accused shall be heard by the public or get into print. In these cases the trials were public, and the accused were encouraged to air their views at unlimited length.

Priest Inoue made no attempt to gain any advantage by altering the charge from murder. He had, he said, a high regard for constitutional procedure, but the emergency which the country faced justified strong measures. He gave a list of those he had intended to murder, and it included (with the names of those already killed): Prince Saionji, Count Makino (Keeper of the Privy Seal), Baron Wakatsuki (President of the Minseito), Mr. Inukai (Premier), Count Ito Myoji (Privy Council), Dr. Suzuki (President of the Seiyukai), Mr. Tokonami, Mr. Inoue, Baron Shidehara, Baron Dan, Mr. Ikeda (Mitsui firm), and Mr. Kimura (Mitsubishi firm).

As the murders were professedly a preliminary to political reforms, the Court asked Inoue what was the nature of the reforms contemplated. He replied that he had no idea. It was his part to see to the killing. He left reconstruction to others. But, he said, such acts are not murder, and "But for me, there would have been no Fifteenth of May." Another of the accused, Furuichi Shoji, said that he was inspired with disgust by the prevalent individualism, and believed the State could be reformed by bloodshed.

At the naval court-martial, which was held at Yokosuka,

the naval port, Lieutenant Nakamura stated that the object of the essay in murder in which he had participated was to get a Cabinet with Baron Hiranuma and General Araki in it. He hated the Mitsui and Mitsubishi firms. Lieutenant Mikami, another murderer, declared that Count Makino and Prince Saionji had exploited for their own profit the rivalry between the two firms. Lieutenant Kuroiwa declared that he shot Mr. Inukai, the Premier, because he was boiling with indignation at the Nanking affair (over five years before). As for Baron Shidehara, witness considered him no better than a Chinaman. Clear thinking was evidently not a strong point with these patriots.

At the military court-martial Cadet Sakamoto confessed to having a more constructive mind than Priest Inoue. The object of the murders and the bomb-throwing, he said, was to have the Emperor, through Admiral Togo, proclaim martial law, and to ask Gondo Seikyo to do the work of reconstruction. This Gondo was an elderly man, whose part in the conspiracies was ambiguous, but who was supposed to be a scholar and was reputed a patriot. He was sometimes mentioned as the brains of the movement, but when he was asked his opinion as to how the agrarian crisis might be alleviated, all he could recommend for the farmers was self-help!

The only other man connected with this deplorable business who was supposed to have any brains was Dr. Okawa Shumei, President of the Jimmukai, a patriotic society. Of the quality of his mental make-up some idea may be gathered from the testimony given that he had proposed the assassination of a number of Japanese traders in Manchuria, in order to get stronger action taken. Perhaps he was encouraged to think along these lines by the excellence of the results that had followed the killing of Captain Nakamura. He offered his suggestion to Lieutenant-Commander Fujii (who was killed in the fighting at Shanghai), who passed it on to Inoue; but though the spy-priest was far from squeamish, he could not agree to this.

The prisoners showed little gratitude for the indulgence of the courts. Priest Inoue broke out into violent expostulation against the manners of Judge Sakamaki, who occupied himself with some other activity than paying perfect attention to the boastings of one of the accused who was making his harangue. The accused all refused to go on with the trial, and the judge actually visited Inoue in prison to try and placate him. The judicial authorities overruled the accuseds' objections and ordered the trial to proceed. But the prisoners had their way. They reiterated their complaints and at length the judge resigned, Judge Fujii being appointed in his place. Four months were lost over these extraordinary proceedings.

The military court-martial finished its business first. The accused were moderate in their orations, one of them having a fling at the police, who, he said, were too cowardly to arrest him when he threw a bomb into their headquarters. The procurator declared that they were prompted throughout by patriotism pure and simple, though of course their acts were of an impermissible irregularity. He asked for a uniform sentence of eight years, and the court gave them four years, saying that their faith in *Kodo* led to their improper actions—which was rather a reflection on General Araki, the exponent-in-chief of the doctrine.

The naval court-martial was more loquacious. In the course of it there was an announcement, for instance, that at the next hearing Procurator Yamamoto would discourse on the misunderstood naval treaty. On September 11th, the procurator demanded sentence, death in three cases, and terms of imprisonment down to three years in the rest. All the accused were young men between twenty-five and twenty-nine, and Lieutenant Asada, as their class-mate, made an oration in their defence. The Cabinet, he said, for lust of power and gain, deceived the nation; the Diet had become an arena for the contests of drunkards and outlaws; foreign policy was weak-kneed, following the lead of the Western Powers and calling it co-operation; hence the fiascos of Nanking and London. Morale was declining at home and contempt was increasing abroad. Scholars were full of cranky theories, and the spirit of Japan was in danger of extinction. Rightism and Leftism had run to extremes; the farmers were impoverished and unemployment was increasing. The Chief of the Naval General Staff had denounced the London naval treaty. Finally, he eulogised the purity of the patriotism of the accused.

Lieutenant Asamidzu had the last word: "They may perish, but the brilliance of their patriotism will never grow dim."

The death sentences, of course, were not imposed, but there was a sentence of fifteen years' imprisonment. Though more than a year had been spent in preparation for the trials, the staff work was execrable. The sentences were so disparate that there was a great deal of grumbling; but if this helped to break up the unity in the patriotic murder clubs, it was a fault for which there was good reason to be thankful.

The suspension of the Blood Brotherhood trial enabled the trial of the civilian murderers of May 15th to follow on the court-martial. The twenty accused, with Tachibana at their head, were arraigned on September 26th. Tachibana's opening address alone lasted many days. He gave the court a lengthy account of his life, and how he came to hold the convictions that inspired him to form the Aikyojuku. Here the judge interposed, asking him to describe the brotherhood in detail. Several times, indeed, during this and other long speeches, the judge asked for more details, as though he could never have enough. Tachibana described how, in spite of his agricultural brotherhood, the Aikyojuku, rural conditions became worse, so that he became convinced that drastic steps were necessary, and joined the Ketsumeidan—Priest Inoue's Blood Brotherhood. Day by day Tachibana informed the court of the subject that he would take up at the next hearing. On October 5th he was so overcome by his own pathos that the court

adjourned to give him time to recover. Another day he
dwelt on his fondness for Beethoven and Rodin, and said
that it needed a great purpose to induce him to desert these
joys for the company of bedbugs in prison. On October 14th,
still continuing his oration, he was asked some further questions by the judge. In reply to these, he said that had the
murder scheme miscarried, they all intended to flee to
Manchuria. (That, in fact, was where he did go. Manchuria,
for the Japanese, offers the "great open spaces where men
are men," except when they happen to be Chinese.) Asked
why the power houses were bombed, Tachibana said he
thought it would do the luxurious good to be in darkness
for a spell. They had not had a sufficiently severe lesson.
Ten years after the great earthquake Tokyo was more
luxurious than ever, but the farmers, how miserable! And
whom did he expect to succeed the murdered Inukai? He
wanted Araki!

It is possible that this remark brought Araki's career to
an end.

Tachibana's followers were allowed to harangue the court
on whatever subjects they chose, and they all denounced
the shortcomings by which the country fell short of perfect
patriotism. But they did not mention among these murder
or the military usurpation of power: rather they assumed
that these things were virtues. The trial dragged on till
February, when Tachibana received a sentence of imprisonment for life, and the rest to various terms, the sentences
being on an average much heavier than those inflicted on
the naval men, just as these were heavier than those received
by the soldiers. It rather looked as though the accused had
been punished according to their loquacity in court, but
nobody suggested that this was the case. The navy felt sore
at the army letting itself off lightly, and the civilians thought
both services were unduly favoured. Mr. Hatta, in the Diet,
declared that the military murderers had worn their uni-
forms in order to put Inukai off his guard, and he accused
the Minister for War of echoing the sentiments of a gang

of murderers who should at least have slit their bellies by way of apology for their crimes: but things like this, that needed saying so badly, hardly ever were said except under protection of parliamentary privilege.

The murder of Inukai revived interest in the murders of other premiers and admiration for the murderers. Early in 1933, while the trials were eagerly awaited, the confederate of Hamaguchi's assassin was released from prison and was interviewed by the newspapers, to whose representatives he complacently declared that he had emerged from his two years' confinement "more patriotic than ever." An eminent lawyer, Dr. Uzawa, defending Sagoya Tomeo, the first murderer, one of the dullest fools who ever pulled a trigger, found justification for doing to death one of Japan's most courageous and devoted public servants in the fact that during his premiership Japan concluded the London Naval Treaty and permitted the export of gold. Mr. Hiramatsu, defending the military murderers, said that Sagoya's foresight was proved by the murders of 1932. No doubt it was hoped that clemency for Sagoya would automatically bring clemency for the rest. The Supreme Court confirmed the death sentence on November 6, 1933, two years after the crime, and the propaganda for pardon became more insistent than ever, even the younger Hamaguchi being subject to pressure in order to make him plead for the life of his father's murderer. There is no indecent hurry about hanging a condemned murderer in Japan, and as the Crown Prince was born on December 23, 1933, there was great rejoicing because all the murderers would benefit. Thirty thousand prisoners in all did benefit by the amnesty which was proclaimed on February 11, 1934, but not, of course, those who were in prison for dangerous political opinions. Premier Hara's murderer, another excessively stupid man, who had been serving his "life sentence" since 1922, did not benefit by the amnesty, for he had already, on February 7th, been liberated and lionised. All Japan loves a murderer.

The Shimpeitai, or God's Soldiers case, has already been mentioned; while this was being investigated, yet another murder club came to light, the Kokoku Seinen Horyukai, whose programme seemed to be to murder everybody, making a start with Dr. Suzuki, president of the Seiyukai, who was to be sent to his account at a party meeting on November 14, 1934, but the plot was betrayed and thirty participants were arrested on November 13th. They were sent to prison in due course, but the case was not taken very seriously.

The Ketsumeidan or Blood Brotherhood trial, interrupted so long by the murderers' complaints of the judge's inattention, was begun again on March 27, 1934, under Judge Fujii. At the outset, Priest Inoue gave a very boastful account of himself. It was still dragging its slow length along in August, when some of the witnesses who had testified already in the May 15th case (Premier Inukai's murder) were examined, among them General Sakanishi, who described Inoue fervently as "a very great man." In November sentences of imprisonment were pronounced. The procurator in demanding sentence extolled their patriotism, but said the law must not be broken. The judge spoke kindly to the prisoners, advising them to take care of their health in prison—which was equivalent to a promise that the terms would be shortened. Petitions for clemency came in a flood, and Priest Inoue's patronising approval of Judge Fujii had much more "news value" than the Judge's opinion of the murderers.

Before the year was out three youths were arrested who said that, "greatly encouraged by the May 15th affair," they had formed a Shonen Ketsumeidan (Young People's Blood Brotherhood) for the purpose of killing all prominent men, and had made two or three attempts. Most prominent men, however, were by this time taking precautions.

Modern murderers who, like the men of May 15th, enter an undefended house to kill an old man, are naturally compared with the Forty-seven Ronin, who did this very thing in 1702, and have become Japan's favourite heroes. They are familiar to a multitude of English readers through Lord Redesdale's *Tales of Old Japan*. In the sixty-six years that have passed since Redesdale wrote, the story has become more popular than ever. The new year is ushered in with its dramatic performance at the principal theatres, and the great Japanese historian Tokutomi Soho devotes a whole volume of his tremendous work on the Tokugawa period to the Forty-seven. The literature of the heroic episode is enormous. The Forty-seven waited long and patiently in order to consummate their revenge, their object being to kill their lord's enemy. They adopted every precaution against failure, and finally broke in to an all but deserted mansion, and raged through it till they found their victim cowering in a cupboard. They cut off the dotard's head and made off, without any resistance being offered. If anybody asks what there is admirable or heroic in this, the reply is that they knew that they would all be ordered to commit *hara-kiri*, as in fact they were. The modern political assassin is more fortunate in that he lives in an age more appreciative of murder and very tender towards the murderer.

Except that the excuse of a feudal vendetta and the prospect of a painful death were lacking, there was a considerable resemblance between the two murders of helpless old men in 1702 and in 1932, and the question was argued, not for the first time, whether it was consistent to give the murderers heroic honours without exacting the lawful penalty of their deed. On this occasion the *Miyako*, a Tokyo paper, produced an ingenious argument. At the time of the Ako vendetta, it said, there was a strong feeling in favour of clemency, which would doubtless have been exercised but for the influence of Sorai Ogyu, a great scholar of the time, who insisted on the lawful punishment. Therefore the murder itself is the heroic act, not the suffering of the punishment. The doing of the aged Kotsuke-no-Suke to death was the feat to be admired; the forty-seven simultaneous belly-slashings were a matter only for tears.

At the time of the Forty-seven Ronin there were no newspapers and the discussion of public events was forbidden: hence the famous drama is put back to an earlier period in history. This was recalled by an order given out in 1932 that no theatrical or cinematographic representations of the affair of May 15th would be permitted. But the large crop of murder clubs must have made the police wish that there were no newspapers.

Some interesting details emerged about the Shimpeitai. It was financed by business men whose plans on the Stock Exchange were laid in accordance with the results to be expected of the contemplated orgy of murder. But the affair lost public interest, not so much because it dragged on too long, but because there were no murders. The Japanese are realists and like results.

CHAPTER XXI

JAPAN'S AEGIS OVER THE MAINLAND

DESPITE the League of Nations, which was unwilling to take warlike action against Japan, as provided for in Article XVI. of the Covenant, and which shrank from the untried experiment of an international boycott, Japan successfully wrested Manchuria, Jehol and part of Chahar from China, and occupied them in sufficient strength to deter China from any attempt at their recovery. Under the Tangku Truce Japan was in a semi-occupation of a large area in North China, there was a demilitarised zone in which the Japanese did as they liked, and according to the Japanese interpretation of the Tangku Truce, they could ask for the removal of any Chinese officials of whom they did not approve. It was hoped that the Central Government, after this demonstration of its weakness, would break up and that the Kuomintang would be discredited. This, however, did not happen. General Chiang Kai-shek devoted himself to the consolidation of his power wherever the Japanese did not intrude, and to the suppression of the peasant revolt—the "Communist-bandits" as they were officially called.

When the conquest of Jehol was determined upon but not yet accomplished, the Japanese newspapers, under military inspiration, were full of scorn and contempt for the "opium province," Jehol having indeed a bad name as the worst backslider among the Chinese provinces. But when the conquest was effected, the strange announcement appeared that the downtrodden Chinese farmer would now get a fair price for his poppies. The truth was that Jehol opium had competed with the opium monopoly in Dairen. For years past the opium poppy had been cultivated in Formosa, Japan, and Korea, and the distribution of its products all over the world was a scandal for which Japan offered very inadequate excuses every year at Geneva. Unquestioned dominance over Manchuria, Jehol and a large part of North China offered her a market for heroin and morphia where nobody would be able to complain, and this market she proceeded sedulously to cultivate. The Japanese Concession in Tientsin became the chief centre of manufacture of the derivative drugs, and the Japanese army was the protector of drug-shops wherever they were set up under its aegis. Often these were run by Koreans, upon whom any attaching obloquy could be placed. They assisted materially in demoralising the inhabitants and lessening any danger of revolt, and the trade brought in more money than any honest business.

But while Japan was demoralising that part of China over which she had gained control, there was disconcerting progress where it had been supposed that there was only hopeless corruption and poverty. The New Life movement, though its rules and maxims sound naïvely simple, was touching and renewing the lives of a people who had begun, at last, to be conscious of their nationality and anxious to preserve it. The League of Nations, disappointed over its failure to protect China against aggression, was continuing its other work, notably the organisation of the Committee for Technical Assistance, with Dr. Rajchman at its head, and this Committee, which neither offered gratuities nor pushed loans, but which helped with expert advice, and had no axe to grind, was also impressed with China's recovery and will for progress. This was particularly hateful to the Japanese, who could no longer co-operate with the League of Nations and regarded all its acts as hostile. Animadversions against the Committee of Technical Assistance appeared in the Press, and personal slanders against Dr. Rajchman and the Secretary, Mr. Haas. Japanese strategists regarded the progress shown as inimical to the maintenance of peace in the Far East.

Mr. Huang Fu, Chairman of the Peiping Political Council, had come to an agreement with the Nanking leaders, more favourable to Japan than they liked, yet recognised by them as the necessary price of peace; but it was expected that, with the making of a settlement, the inclination of the League to assist China would grow, with the result that Western influence would be increased, and Nanking would act more independently towards Tokyo. Early in April 1934, Mr. Amau, the head of the Foreign Office Intelligence Bureau, gave the foreign journalists, at one of the regular gatherings, an outline of the Japanese view regarding Chinese affairs; but they apparently regarded it as only one of the essays in abstract principles in which Japanese Government Departments frequently indulge. So little notice was taken of it that it was like a *ballon d'essai* that had failed to rise from the ground, so on April 17, 1934 the *Asahi* published an inspired statement emphasising Japan's attitude in a way which could not be ignored. The Amau Statement is of sufficient historical importance to require quotation:

As a result of the Nanchang Conference the hope is now entertained that the various problems in North China will be settled in the near future. At the same time, there is a body of opinion in Nanking Government circles which is hostile to the policy of Mr. Huang Fu, and which cannot be ignored. Some of these hostile elements, desirous of stronger co-operation with America and the League Powers, are contemplating schemes to invite their financial aid on the plea of economic or technical help. Regardless of the success or failure of these schemes, the Japanese Government is firmly determined to shape its course towards China in accordance with its own view of the situation. Recognising the necessity of calling the attention of China and the Powers to this attitude of the Japanese Government, the Foreign Office authorities have just given out an informal statement. This statement says that Japan's views and assertions on the Chinese problem may not be in perfect agreement with those of the Powers, but Japan is so circumstanced that she must do her utmost to fulfil her mission and responsibility in the Far East. Her withdrawal from the League of Nations was due to the conflict of views held by herself and by the League of Nations about Japan's position in the Far East. Although Japan's attitude towards China may be at variance with that of other countries in some respects, these divergences cannot be helped, as they arise from Japan's position and mission. It is hardly necessary to say that Japan is ever mindful of maintaining and promoting friendly relations with all countries, but it is only proper that for the maintenance of peace and order in the Far East she should act independently on her own responsibility. Indeed, it is Japan's mission to achieve peace, and she is determined to do so. For the fulfilment of this mission Japan must necessarily share responsibility with China for the maintenance of peace in the Far East. There is no other country with whom she can share this responsibility.

China's integrity and unity and the restoration of order in that country are what Japan most eagerly desires. Past history shows that nothing short of China's own awakening or effort can attain this. Such being the case, if China should attempt to exclude Japan or take such steps as are detrimental to the peace of the Far East by exploiting the influence of other Powers, or if she should resort to the policy of playing off one foreign country against another, Japan would be compelled to oppose such measures stoutly. On the other hand, if the Powers, in consideration of the situation developing out of the Manchurian and Shanghai affairs, should attempt to act in concert in regard to China, such action would of necessity acquire political significance, no matter whether its nominal object is to help China financially or technically. Such a situation, if fostered, would open the way for the establishment of spheres of influence in   · China, or for the international control of China, or for the partition of that country. Not only would it bring a great misfortune on China, but it would impair the integrity of the Far East, and affect Chinese interests very seriously. Japan cannot but oppose, as a matter of principle, any such development. In the individual efforts of Powers to negotiate with China on economic and trade matters, however, Japan does not see the necessity of interfering, so long as they do not hinder the work of maintaining peace in the Far East. If they should prove disturbing to the maintenance of peace in the Far East, Japan will be obliged to oppose them. For example, Japan must oppose the attempts being made of late by Powers to supply military planes to China, to aid China in the establishment of aerodromes, to supply military organs and advisers, and to give political loans to China, as it is obvious that these measures will, after all, serve to cause estrangement between China and Japan or other countries, to the detriment of the peace of the Far East. Japan's policy, set forth above, is a natural corollary of the course which she has hitherto been pursuing, but its pronouncement at the present moment may not be out of place, in view of the fact that some countries have been acting positively of late in China, on the nominal pretext of joint action and joint aid.

This amounted to a declaration of suzerainty over China. It denied China's right to any foreign relations except such as Japan approved; and its permission to foreign traders to continue such business as Japan allowed, conveyed the hint that, when it suited Japan, that privilege might be withdrawn. The manner in which the Statement was given out to the newspaper correspondents was so offhand that it did not attract their attention; but the pointed repetition gained the notice which it sought. Europe, however, was busy with its own quarrels, and though English newspapers pointed out that the Statement tore all treaties across, Sir John Simon, the Foreign Secretary, refused to comment upon it on the ground that it had not been communicated to him by or through an ambassador. For lack of adequate protest the Amau Statement superseded all rights, treaties, and understandings with China, and left China tributary to Japan—a complaining and disobedient tributary, no doubt, but unable to enlist help in resisting. Even the peaceful and unpolitical efforts of the League of Nations were paralysed. Europe's dissensions made a convenient opportunity for this challenge to the world; but the occasion for it was the prospect that, with the help of the League of Nations, China might experience an economic and political renaissance.

Though perhaps the method was novel it called for something more than indifference. The fact that those Powers most concerned made a pretence of ignoring it greatly encouraged Japan in preparing for her next step, for she rightly regarded it as indicating that no forcible action would be taken, when she herself chose to act forcibly. Meanwhile the possibility still existing of selling aeroplanes and munitions to China and China's continuance to engage foreign instructors were assumed by the silent chancelleries to justify their silence.

For the time being Japan had her hands full with the settlement of Manchukuo. Soon after the issue of new capital for the South Manchuria Railway, a Manchukuo Telegraph and Telephone Company was started, with a guaranteed dividend of six per cent. The money could have been had cheaper, but the rush of subscribers helped to popularise the Manchukuo idea and to give a solid bourgeois backing to all plans designed for the firmer establishment of Japanese control.

Money continued to be poured into Manchuria for all sorts of industries and enterprises, and it was not long before Mr. Takahashi angered the military men by uttering a warning against too large investments in the new Empire. The amount of capital, he said, was limited, and too reckless investment might bring about a crisis. The army, it is true, disapproved in theory of exploitation by large capitalists, which seemed to be inevitable with so many new concerns starting up; but it was semi-officially explained on behalf of the Manchukuo Government, that the Government gave charters only for approved projects, and subscribed half the capital itself by way of exercising proper control. How far it actually did this is doubtful. The new Government had its own problems, and its share of the capital was probably more in evidence in the books than in the bank. The Meirinkai, a comparatively respectable body of political reactionaries, supposed to be chiefly interested in ethics, did a good deal to promote Manchurian investment.

Great hopes were entertained at one time of the cultivation of cotton, for which, only a hundred years earlier, Manchuria had been famous, but cotton had been disappointing in Korea, and it was quickly decided that Manchuria was unsuitable. To those who objected to manufactures in Manchuria it was pointed out that a purely agricultural country could never be densely populated or wealthy and so would always lack the essentials of a good market. Mitsuis at this time attracted some attention by selling to the public some of their most profitable ventures, and an obliging Press represented this as indicating a change of heart—a desire to be less of an octopus in the business world. Actually it was done to raise the money for new investments, Manchuria getting its share.

Strategic railways were hurried on, especially the connection with the North Korean ports, and lines crossing North Manchuria to the Amur, but there was a railway problem of the first importance still to settle. The Chinese Eastern Railway from Manchuli to Pogranichnaya, with the southern branch from Harbin to Changchun (Hsinking), was still under Russian management. A foreign railway running through some part of the loosely knit empire of China created no very difficult problems; but it was an entirely different matter when a highly centralised and active, not to say irritable, Japanese administration took the place of the Chinese. Parties of Japanese soldiers were surveying every nook and corner of the Four North-Eastern Provinces (except where the bandits were too formidable) and there were many complaints from Russia that these parties were not content to explore Manchuria, but were constantly crossing the border and exploring Russian territory as well. An agitation was started in Japan for the taking of the railway by force. Manchukuo was to do this, or perhaps it would be better to say that the Japanese were to do it for Manchukuo, who was to accept the responsibility. The plan was not officially approved, however. To have done this as a friendly gesture, to help the new State to establish its independence more completely, would have been too raw a pretence, and might have brought on a war with Russia, who already showed a far keener interest in the safety of the border than ever she had while there was a Chinese administration on the other side.

Russia recognised that the situation could only become worse, and at the end of April 1933 offered to sell. Difficulties were increasing. Japan, Russia complained, used the line for carrying troops but did nothing for its protection and maintenance. Under the Treaty of Portsmouth, Russians and Japanese had agreed that neither side should keep more than fifteen soldiers to the kilometre for the protection of their respective portions of the line. The Japanese railway troops together with the garrison of the Leased Territory, had become the Kwantung Army, but the Russians had left the protection of the line to the Chinese troops, whom the "independence" of Manchukuo had turned into bandits. It becoming impossible to work the line properly, the Russians withdrew a considerable part of the rolling-stock into Russian territory, which was a source of bitter complaint on Japan's part, as the Russian gauge was larger than the standard gauge, and rolling-stock could not be supplied from other lines. In reply to one of Russia's complaints about the hostile actions of Manchukuo, Japan made the usual reply that she was not responsible for Manchukuo's acts and had no influence over the new State's policy. Manchukuo sent what amounted to an ultimatum demanding the return of the rolling-stock. In spite of these quarrels the discussions regarding the sales went on, and were hardly disturbed by China's protests that she had a definite share in the ownership of the railway which could not be thus ignored.

After about a month's discussion Japan decided that she would not herself buy the railway, but would advise Manchukuo to buy it. Meanwhile the unrestricted attacks by bandits evoked Russian complaints that Japan was deliberately ruining the line so as to cheapen it. Banditry grew worse, and that part of the line from Harbin to Pogranichnaya went out of action altogether. This section, which railed Manchurian produce to Vladivostok, had competed in the past with the South Manchuria Railway, but when it was out of action Japan had her share in all trans-Siberian traffic, so Russia had reason in thinking that it was not purely by chance that bandits were ten times worse here than on the western section.

Formal negotiations for the sale started between Russia and Manchukuo, the new State's spokesman being Mr. Ohashi, the energetic Japanese gentleman who served Manchukuo as Vice-Minister of Foreign Affairs. China sought representation on the conference, but in vain. The conference began in Tokyo with speeches by Count Uchida, Foreign Minister, Mr. Yurenev, Soviet Ambassador, and Mr. Ting of Manchukuo. China talked of a North China railway project to be financed by British and Belgian capital; but Japan had her own plans for North China, and was not to be deflected from her immediate purpose. The strangest part of the protracted negotiations was the manner in which, through their inspired newspapers, Russia and Japan constantly abused each other. On September 10th, an attempt having been made to resume traffic on the eastern section, bandits held up the train near Pogranichnaya and captured over a hundred passengers.

About this time Count Uchida fell out of favour. Mr. Takahashi had declared that as the present generation would get no benefit from Manchukuo, they should not be made to pay its whole cost, and Uchida had supported him in this contention. Whether from this or other cause, Uchida found it expedient on September 14, 1934, to resign, and was succeeded by Mr. Hirota Koki, who, like himself, had been Ambassador in Russia. Hirota belonged to the patriotic school of Toyama Mitsuru, but had the discretion not to imitate his master's style of speech. Almost his first public utterance, however, was to the effect that though India received orders from Westminster (the Indo-Japanese cotton conference having just begun), it was otherwise with Manchukuo, which did not receive orders from Japan. This was so palpably untrue that the *Isvestia* thought it well to indicate that though the Japanese army might have more trust in Hirota than in Uchida, Russia had not, and it warned Japan against any attempt to seize the railway. The Japanese army responded by saying that Russia's threatening attitude necessitated an increased military expenditure. Araki, the Minister for War, declared that Russia must withdraw from the Manchurian frontier, and discoursed on the superiority of arms to amiability. After so much had been said about seizing the Chinese Eastern Railway, it was not surprising when some "documents" on the subject were published in

Russia, purporting to give the project an authoritative air; but Japan declared that the documents were impudent forgeries.

The discussion on the sale had begun with the Russians demanding 250 million yen, and the Japanese (on behalf of Manchukuo) offering 50 millions. The Russians pointed out that they were asking only half the original cost; the Japanese replied that it was declining in value every day, to which the Russians retorted that that was Japan's fault, if not her deliberate contrivance. Then there were difficult questions of the rate of exchange, and of simultaneous or prior settlement of various outstanding questions. Agreement seemed so impossible that the talks were dropped in October 1933, and were not reopened till the following May.

From that time progress was slow but fairly steady. The price was all but agreed upon when the Russians asked that Japan should guarantee payment. The dignity of the sovereign State of Manchukuo was insulted! But the guarantee was given. Then came the question of how payment should be made, and the futility of "managed currencies" suddenly came into view. Would Russia take payment in kind? Yes, but in goods that she wanted, and if Japan did not make them, she would have to buy them. This nearly wrecked the contract, but there were so few things that Japan could not make, that the Russians agreed to take Japanese goods.

Even now difficulties were not entirely removed. There would have to be a Russian buying committee, who would have the right, in respect of certain goods, to see them in process of manufacture—a common enough requirement in contracts, and the simplest way of assuring quality. This caused tremendous indignation, for Japanese manufacturers are absurdly afraid of industrial espionage.

At the last moment the army almost wrecked the whole plan. They objected to supplying the Russians with cement. Cement was used for concrete fortifications, and it was almost traitorous to supply it to a potential enemy with a long coterminous frontier. That concrete was defensive rather than offensive was a mere quibble. The best defence is offence, and Japanese cement might therefore prevent Japanese self-defence.

At length, however, an agreement was initialled on March 11, 1935, the agreed price being 140 million yen, with another 30 millions as discharge allowances to the Russian employees. Mr. Ting, the Manchukuo representative, handed Mr. Yurenev, the Russian ambassador, a cheque for 23 million yen as a first instalment, whereupon the South Manchuria Railway took over charge and paid off the Russian staff. The Nanking Government sent a last protest, pointing out to Japan that she had undertaken a grave responsibility in guaranteeing payment for Manchukuo. The South Manchuria Railway had increased its payroll by 10,000 employees in the past two years, and now it had another fourteen hundred miles of line to care for. Its first task was to change the gauge from Harbin to Changchun, which improved the service greatly.

In exchange for the railway Russia took a large variety of goods, including some ships. The bargain, which it had taken so long to conclude, was carried out with unexpected smoothness and mutual satisfaction, and probably stands on record as the largest example of barter known. Early in 1938, however, Japan repudiated the obligation to pay the last instalments, owing to Russia's disapproval of her attack on China.

CHAPTER XXII

THE BOOM IN MANUFACTURE

WE are considering a period when not only in Japan, but throughout the world great problems clamour for solution. There are population problems, for instance, including that of Japan; the problem of supplying demand without economic disaster resulting; the problem of using collective force without making the individual subhuman; and the problem of successful manufacture. That Japan offers a field for study in the first three is obvious. That success in manufacture is one of the world's major problems may not be uppermost in the reader's consciousness until he considers the craze for "protection" and for "economic nationalism." This being a chronicle of events rather than a philosophic treatise, no attempt will be made to answer questions with which many great minds are wrestling, but it may be pointed out in passing that the beating of the war-drum, audacious yet easy conquests, and a patriotic call to close the ranks against a hostile world coincided with a forward stride in successful manufacture such as had been striven for in vain for a generation. But the reason for this sudden success may lie elsewhere. The great American slump of 1929 was felt all over the world. Professor Irving Fisher, the prophet of the Permanent Boom, begged his countrymen in vain to keep on; President Hoover, casting aside three centuries of Quaker economics, exhorted them to spend their way into prosperity. Echoes of such doctrines were naturally heard when the Hamaguchi policy of thrift seemed only to increase the depression in Japan. But it may be that, without those years of sound finance and intensive propaganda for the improvement of manufacture, the expansion which seemed to scare the whole world could not have taken place. Historians will dogmatise on this point according to the experiences of the next few years. We may remember here that Baron Shide-hara, the Foreign Minister in the Hamaguchi Cabinet, in an announcement of policy, said that Japan intended to deal with the population question by industrialisation, which would absorb the increase.

European experiments in post-war depreciation had all ended disastrously; but when England went off gold in August 1931, there was a rush of orders for goods which greatly impressed Japanese manufacturers. So, when Japan followed suit four months later, she brought down the rate drastically. The result, so far as the promotion of Japanese sales was concerned, fulfilled expectations. It had generally been reckoned that such benefits exhausted themselves in about six months, after which the necessity of replacements purchased with a depreciated currency brought things back to their old level, but in spite of Japan's poverty in raw materials, her food supply was abundant, and wages were kept at their previous level. It seemed, therefore, that there was a possibility of the benefits of the depreciation being permanent; for even though raw materials cost more, manufacturing costs, in terms of foreign currencies, were incredibly low. Later on it was observed that the benefit was gradually diminishing. The amount of manu-factured goods which had to be exported to pay for a stated quantity of raw material imported, increased year by year. There are probably several causes for this, but the complex phenomenon has become an "economic law."

Undoubtedly the "home goods campaign," which had been carried on with great energy and enthusiasm by Messrs. Egi and Tawara, two of Hamaguchi's Ministers, was a factor in the new success. Everywhere Japanese manufactures, comparable in quality with imported goods and now far cheaper, helped to keep the cost of living down, and to prevent the people from feeling directly the effects of the greatly increased price of foreign goods.

Japan still found it almost impossible to export up to the value of her imports, but she was conscious of a destiny as a workshop of the world, or at least of an ambition to take this place, and she regarded with much misgiving the raising of tariff walls everywhere. Even England had put an import tax on many things and was soon to adopt a general tariff. Before the Great War Japan had been an example of heavy protection and heavy taxation, but she found herself now moderately taxed and in a position with regard to tariffs that enabled her delegates at Geneva to laud her devotion to free trade. Her salesmen thrust out into new markets with praiseworthy enterprise, but so often was a new market made difficult of access by the raising of the tariff that Japan's complaints of hostility to her trade became, in view of the actual increase, suggestive of a persecution mania.

As we have seen, complaints of depression and unemployment were still loud and bitter in 1932, yet it was in that year that a turn in the tide of international trade occurred, which brought Japan's commerce with the British Empire into the limelight. The normal course of trade with India had been greatly in India's favour from the point of view which regards it as better to sell than to buy; but for some years it had excited remark that Indian cotton could be brought to Japan, manufactured, taken back, and sold in India at prices lower than those of Indian or Lancashire manufactures. Tariffs had been revised so as to favour India and Lancashire, but Japanese cheapness still triumphed. Then it happened that there was in India a poor crop at high prices and in America an abundant crop at low prices, so that Japan bought far more of the American than of the Indian cotton. At the same time, a great advance was made in the sale of cotton goods to India, with the result that in 1932 Japan sold much more to India than she bought. There had been a good deal of propaganda in India regarding the advantages of Japanese friendship, which was to lead to the emancipation of Asia, but perhaps India remembered now the warning of Mr. Gandhi, that economically Japan was a greater menace to India than Britain. There was a great uproar about the sudden reversal of the trade balance.

The dispute with India led to the adoption of the quota system on the largest scale yet seen. India denounced the commercial treaty with Japan—in which Japanese critics naturally saw the malign hand of Britain; the Japanese Government advocated export control, but the idea that hostility could be averted by not pushing the trade was a hopeless one, when Japan was definitely making a bid for supremacy in cotton. The situation was aggravated by the reckless manner in which Japanese manufacturers competed against one another. India raised the duties still higher. Japan retaliated with a boycott,—the smaller mills, who had most to lose, participating unwillingly. The Raw Cotton Traders' Association said that the boycott might be the death of them, but that they were ready to die for their country. Mr. Adachi's small but vociferous party, the Kokumin Domei, passed a resolution declaring that Britain was squeezing the three hundred million inhabitants of India in order to keep the superannuated Lancashire industry alive, and was guilty of bad faith in this endeavour. Baron Wakatsuki warned the spinners that hasty measures of retaliation might be unwise; that Britain's action was regrettable but long views must be taken.

Except for those immediately concerned, the World Economic Conference seemed a much more important matter than the regulation of Indo-Japanese trade; but the world conference was stillborn, and the chief Japanese delegate thereto, Viscount Ishii, who had been sent so often to lie abroad for the benefit of his country, found himself on tour explaining blandly why Japanese boycotts, whether of Indian cotton, Indian pig iron, or Indian rice, were essentially different from Chinese boycotts, and adroitly casting doubt on the accuracy of the translation of the fiery speeches against England being made by his countrymen.

The Great Asians (General Matsui's crowd) called on India to rise to the occasion, but the National Congress paper, the *Bombay Chronicle*, was so tactless as to ask what Japan had done for China. Before the Japanese delegation to discuss the new problem had left for India, similar troubles were springing up in the trade with the Netherlands Indies, more especially, to start with, over the "patriotic" habit of Japanese shippers reserving their cargoes for Japanese ships; but Dutch complaints were ascribed to British instigation. The immediate sequel to the boycott of Indian cotton was a large import of coarse counts of yarn from China, which imparted a little realism to the dispute. Nevertheless, the *Yomiuri* boldly opined that if Japan boycotted Indian cotton, Australian wool, Canadian wheat, and British machinery and woollens, the British Empire would find itself in a bad way. However, lectures on interdependence are lost on a world with a craze for "economic nationalism."

An English commercial expert at this time wrote to the English Press that he found no boycott in Japan, but a sort of understanding that British goods should not be bought; the smaller mill-owners were facing charges of want of patriotism because they imported Indian cotton by devious routes. The Ambassador at the Court of St. James regretted to find critical articles in the English Press, because they might impair friendship. But the forty-fifth edition of Lieut.-Commander Ishimaru Tota's *England and Japan Must Fight* had just been published, and the Japanese reports of proceedings at Simla represented the Japanese delegates as talking very severely.

The Japanese delegation was bombarded with telegrams to be firm and to uphold the boycott. Unfortunately only a year before, Japan's chief excuse for devastating Shanghai had been the Chinese boycott, but that, it was now passionately declared, was a different matter altogether. The Chinese boycott, they said, was inspired by the Government, whereas this was a purely independent movement. It was not a boycott, but an expression of indignation, and when the cause of indignation was removed, there would be no boycott—it could not be bargained over. Again, it was not a boycott, but an abstention from buying, and Mr. Sawada, of the Foreign Office, who headed the delegation, had no control over the spinners, and could not stop the boycott. Indians asked whether, if they guaranteed purchase of a quota of Japanese goods, Japan would buy a quota of Indian cotton. The reply to this was an emphatic "No."

There was a popular legend in Japan that at Versailles in 1919, Prince Saionji moved from one hotel to another, and that, when great quantities of baggage appeared in the hall, the word went round that the Japanese were going back, with the result that the Peace Conference, as if by magic, came round to the Japanese point of view. At Simla, after two months' vain discussion, it was suddenly bruited abroad that the Japanese delegates were arranging for their return home, but Simla was undisturbed. After another month the delegates did pack their boxes, but only to come down to Delhi.

The tone gradually changed: they had to answer some unpleasant questions about the yen; they agreed that they might buy a quota as well as sell one; and Mr. Sawada found that, after all, he could call off the boycott. To India's purchase of 400 million yards of piecegoods, it was agreed that Japan should respond with a purchase of $1\frac{1}{2}$ million bales of cotton. As the 1932 purchases were 640 million yards, the larger spinning interests in Japan were far from satisfied; but the boycott was called off, the Indian duty was lowered to 50 per cent., and in 1934 the natural trends of trade reasserted themselves, and Japan bought much more from India than she sold. Had India made no fuss, the recovery of trade would probably have been about the same, and much debate would have been saved; and had the Japanese not retaliated, they would not have been committed to the purchase of $1\frac{1}{2}$ million bales of raw cotton a year.

Yet another grotesque outcome of the conference remains to be recorded. At the end of November 1933, it was reported, Mr. Matsuyama, Commercial Counsellor in London, in accordance with a plan conceived by Baron Nakashima, Minister of Commerce and Industry, called a meeting of Japanese merchants in London, and it was decided that these merchants form an importing guild, to co-operate with an exporting guild in Japan, and monopolise the import of goods from Japan. They graciously added that British merchants would be admitted.[1] Of course, it did not materialise, but no sooner was the quota of Indian raw cotton fixed than it was reported that the Big Three in Osaka had monopolised it. Trade was controlled indeed.

It brings a touch of colour into the world's greyness when great disputes produce something less dreary than official reports, and as Japan's saving grace is her artistic sense, she redeemed the follies of the cotton conference by producing a drama. Mr. Muto Sanji, who had retired from the presidency of the Kanegafuchi Spinning Company, which he had raised from a half-bankrupt state to a position unique in the world's textile trade, celebrated the occasion by writing a play, which told the history of cotton in Japan, especially in its relations to India. Mr. Muto was a free-trader (almost the only one in Japan), an apostle of mass production, an admirer of English Liberalism, and a paternalist in industry. In his retirement he led a political party—the only one which had ideas and a purpose, but it had hardly any members.

The play was called *Sangyo Nihon Koshin Kyoku* ("The March of Industrial Japan"), and dealt with real characters and events, but, like Thucydides, Mr. Muto made his dramatis personæ say what they ought to have said rather than what they actually did say. We begin with a scene in a farmhouse in May 1858. There are handlooms lying idle, and the family is obviously in the depths of despair. Shimadzu, the Daimyo of Kagoshima, has started a cotton mill, and there is no longer any profit in handloom weaving. The dutiful daughters propose that their father should repair the family finances by selling them into a brothel. The father objects. A caller says that hands are wanted at the cotton

---

[1] An attempt of the sort actually was made in Java at a later date, but the Colonial Government, instead of being intimidated, as was hoped, handled the situation very firmly.

mill. The father rages against Shimadzu, and will not hear of his daughters working there. The girls run away, and we see them next in the mill, on a day when the Lord Shimadzu is showing some officers of the Shogun's new warship round. He explains how cotton spinning is in its way as patriotic a work as creating a navy, and how he has ordered a lot of machinery from Platt Brothers. Just then there is a crash, the machinery stops working, and in the midst of a confused struggle a young man is dragged in whom the girls recognise as their brother. He has put the motive power (water wheels) out of action with a boulder. Seeing his sisters, he curses them. They should die of hunger rather than work for their enemy, he says. Shimadzu calmly asks the young man what he means, and the youth thereupon tells him of the distress into which hand spinning and weaving have fallen. Shimadzu is so distressed that he has a good mind to abandon the enterprise. Even now local suplies of raw cotton are insufficient, and it will impoverish the country to buy from abroad. But stay! Why not export the surplus manufacture and enrich the country? Yes, that is the idea!

Then we have the early troubles of the industry. Would-be manufacturers have more enterprise than caution, and are taken in by foreign experts who know nothing. One proprietor in the play is on the point of bankruptcy; his wife goes mad; the latest expert, who is a ship's engineer, feels compunction, returns his pay, and swears he will work for nothing and make a job of it. He studies books, sets to work, and presently the machines are running, yarn comes forth, sorrow is turned into gladness, and the proprietor's wife recovers her sanity.

From the early 1870's we proceed at a bound to 1893. Viscount Shibusawa (Japan's patriarch of banking and industry, who died in 1930), Asabuki (Managing Director of the Kanegafuchi Mill), and Morioka (President of the Nippon Yusen Kaisha), are confronted on the stage with Messrs. Joseph, Shields, and Rickett, of the P. & O. Co., and a debate ensues. The Englishmen are rude and none too reasonable regarding the N.Y.K.'s intention to start in the cotton-carrying business. There are several references to Jamsetji Nusserwanji Tata (founder of Tata, Sons & Co.), without whose aid at the Bombay end the N.Y.K. could not have succeeded. The sextette ends with compliments and with commercial war, and the scene changes to the Kobe pier, piled up with cotton bought speculatively by the P. & O., which no Japanese spinner will buy. Messrs. Joseph and Shields confess themselves beaten, and return to their own place.

Two scenes follow in which Mr. Muto is himself the chief character—which is surely unique in dramatic literature. He appears as the exponent of high quality, and damn the customers who want rubbish and the shareholders who want dividends. In the main the two scenes were historically true. Appreciation of high quality had been won, and in spite of world depression in 1932, Kanegafuchi was paying 25 per cent, had enormous reserves, and treated its employees better than any other mill, though with extreme paternalism.

The last scene is on the pier in Calcutta, in December 1933, when the Japanese delegates to the Simla-Delhi Conference are leaving for London. Mr. Kurata, the head industrial delegate, standing half-way up the accommodation ladder, addresses a vast crowd of Indians. He thanks everyone for their courtesy, is gratified at reaching an agreement, but he regrets that there was not a single delegate who represented the true interests of the Indian masses: throughout the negotiations the true voice of the people of India was not heard. (Loud cheers from the Indians.) For the promotion of human happiness by industry, freedom of trade is necessary, but unhappily England, once the home of free trade, is now excluding Japanese cottons from the Empire. Cobden's spirit must mourn, and must look towards Japan as the only country still upholding his principles. Some think the boycott against Indian cotton will soon break down (the speaker on the steps goes on), but remember the struggle against the P. & O. Japanese industrialists are much more united than in those days. They can get cotton elsewhere, but even if Lancashire takes twice as much as at present, how can the Indian cotton-growers live? "We did not come to fight; we did not come to cause suffering to the Indian people; Japan has no desire to threaten Indian industry, or to demand special treatment for her own goods. We depart, our task unsatisfactorily ended. Behold, the sun is setting: it will rise again. Farewell, people of India. We await the time when we can join hands for the peace of the world." (Frantic cheers as the curtain falls.)

The Thucydidean method of composing speeches that were never delivered reaches a climax when it relates to the history of the month before last. The literary experiment is interesting; and it provokes thought when we find so very liberal and widely read a Japanese setting forth the idea of Asia under Japan's aegis, and so earnest a student of free trade regarding Japan as an exemplar of Cobdenism. Muto's play was to have been staged in Osaka, but, like so many of Japan's best men, he was murdered. His assassin stabbed him while he was taking a morning walk near his house at Ofuna on March 9, 1934. The murderer committed suicide, and it was believed that he bore a personal grudge, but there were plentiful speculations as to whether there was not a political society at the bottom of it.

It would be wearisome to make a complete survey of the commercial disputes and conferences which Japan had with other countries at this period. The one—or the series—with the Netherlands Indies was even more prolonged than that with India, and was carried on with wide departures from the usual international amenities. It involved freight wars, shipping boycotts, and various other drastic measures. It had been merely a *façon de parler* when General Araki, as Minister for War, declared that the three hundred millions of India were groaning under white oppression; it had a rather more sinister significance when articles appeared in the Japanese Press about the Dutch oppression in the East Indies and the burning desire of the Javanese to have

Japanese educationists and teachers, and to learn the Japanese language, as this was most suitable for people of an Oriental culture. Articles also appeared about the equally reprehensible oppression practised by the French in Indo-China and about the high mission of saving Siam from the British maw.

As for the dispute with the Netherlands Indies, there was no such argument available on the Japanese side as there had been in the discussion with India. The Dutch colonies had become very large buyers from Japan, without any reciprocity on Japan's part. Japan regretted that she could not, as requested, buy sugar, as she had her own industry to think of. On two or three occasions in the course of the disputes Japan started boycotts, cutting off supplies of goods in which Dutch liberality of trade had allowed her to secure almost a monopoly. It was a dangerous game, but it scored sometimes. As regards shipping, one of Japan's lesser shipping magnates, Mr. Ishihara, who ran a line of steamers to Java, was particularly belligerent, and insisted that the official language of the conference called to settle the disputes that had arisen, must be Japanese. Owing to the peculiar nature of the Japanese language, this would have meant that in the case of any dispute it would have been impossible to do anything but accept the Japanese interpretation, for the Dutch delegates would have signed an agreement which none of them could read. The Dutch wanted English to be the official language. Mr. Ishihara's refusal to budge from his position held up the conference for many months. The large number of Japanese traders in Java was another source of trouble, as they endeavoured to monopolise the imports and, of course, to restrict them to Japanese vessels. In Osaka the premises of a leading glass-maker were wrecked by a party of roughs under the leadership of Mr. Ishihara's manager, for failure to participate in one of the boycotts. In spite of these and other obstacles to harmony, however, quotas both of goods and shipping were settled at last.

With Canada there was a somewhat bitter dispute. The Canadian Government had been one of the first to impose excessive duties on Japanese goods, especially rayon, and it was a very arbitrary imposition of supplementary charges at the discretion, apparently, of any Customs official, which brought about a crisis in the trade. Japan's Trade Protection Law enabled her to retaliate without incurring a charge of discrimination, and peace was made. In the case of Australia there was little complaint of discrimination, but insistence that Australia buy a reasonable amount of Japanese goods. Australia fell back on an appeal to population. Australians bought vastly more per head from Japan than Japanese,ˌper head, bought from Australia. The only remedy for Japan seemed to be to get her wool elsewhere, and this, as a commercial proposition, was difficult. Many fine merino rams were imported from Australia to improve the breed of sheep in Manchuria and Mongolia; but the success of the experiment still awaits demonstration.

The military ideal was to grab as much of China as would, with Japan, make a complete economic *bloc*, and then to return to the economic isolation of a hundred years ago. The manufacturers' ideal was very different. They were themselves rather reckless in their enterprise, and, by swamping new markets and competing against each other, minimised their own profits and provoked the hostile tariffs which they so much deplored; but most of them believed that those who gave best value would win in the end and they were also very conscious that they had already reached a stage of industrial development where China could neither supply all they wanted nor buy all they had to sell. They were almost as much afraid of a foreigner catching sight of their machinery as the soldiers were of strange eyes seeing their fortifications, but on the whole had much more common sense than the soldiers.

In spite of hostile tariffs, Japan's exports continued to increase, but so did the difficulties of foreign trade. The world had changed since the Great War, and it was difficult to get new markets without taking them from somebody else. Cheapness had become an offence and abundance a bugbear, and Japan felt that her grab in Manchuria had earned her a bad name, cost her much money, and done her no good.

CHAPTER XXIII

JAPAN'S NEW EMPIRE

BEFORE the appointment of Mr. Pu Yi as Chief Executive there had been many speculations regarding the probability of the new State being a monarchy, but all mention of this was prohibited, though it was evident that the régime was only a provisional one. The delicacy of feeling regarding the discussion of the popular sentiments of a neighbouring country was amazing. First the Japanese Press was forbidden to say anything about independence movements in Manchuria; then, when it was independent, the Press was forbidden to mention monarchical aspirations. The new State was not to be called anything but its name—Manchukuo—and its ruler was not to be called by his name, but Chief Executive. Political gestation was in progress; on January 20, 1934, the police notified the newspapers that on March 1st, the second anniversary of the proclamation of the Era of Tatung, the Chief Executive would become Emperor, with the name Kang Te, which would also be the name of the new Era. The name was officially translated Tranquillity and Benevolent Virtue, and was more applicable to its bearer than to the times in which he lived. The State was given yet another name to signify its imperial character, being henceforth Manchutikuo; but this was a mouthful so lacking in euphony that it was quickly abandoned, even in official publications. The enthronement ceremony was nothing very elaborate. The Japanese newspapers gave photographs of the new throne, with the information that it had been made in Osaka.

In two years Salvador alone had recognised Manchukuo, and as Japan was flooding the little republic with cheap goods, it begged her to buy some coffee, but in vain. Announcements by the new State to foreign Governments (who took no notice of them) suggested that on recognition trade relations would be welcome. That trade does not depend on diplomatic recognition the case of Soviet Russia had shown plainly enough; but so long as there was no recognition it was so difficult to protest against the obstacles to trade which Japan put in the way of other countries, that Japan quickly realised that the refusal of recognition made monopolisation easier for her. There was, however, an eager welcome for the least sign of a disposition to depart from the Geneva resolution, and chance remarks were exaggerated beyond recognition.

At the time of the enthronement it had been announced that Manchukuo was at last clear of bandits; but almost immediately after there were several encounters in one of which twenty-four Japanese soldiers were killed. Manchurian tram-conductors showed so little sense of the privilege of being subjects of a new empire that they distributed disturbing leaflets. On March 27th, a North China Association was formed in Tokyo, with Mr. Yoshizawa Kenkichi as President. It was already clear that Japan's interests, like her soldiers, could not be prevented from spreading south of the Great Wall; but a society sufficiently respectable to have Mr. Yoshizawa at its head was not calculated to do anything very stirring, and its name was honourably absent from the record of subsequent doings in North China.

It was clear that Manchukuo had "come to stay" at least for the time being; but it was also clear that it was not going to stay at that. Both General Araki, and General Hayashi who succeeded him at the War Office, expressed anxiety lest the peaceful settlement of Manchukuo should be a prelude to the loss of martial spirit by the Japanese army. Quite frankly they expounded the doctrine of the necessity of always having a crisis on hand if the nation's spirits were not to flag. In this they were supported by Count Futara Yoshinori, in the House of Peers, who congratulated the nation on the revival of the Japanese spirit, but regretted that irresponsible talk had created an impression abroad that Japan wanted to fight. *Kodo* was an inspiration that would bring victory without fighting. Here and there was some healthy criticism. A military officer was quoted in the *Manshu Nippo* (a Japanese daily, published in Dairen) as saying that the Japanese, by their overbearing ways, made themselves so disliked in Manchuria that the Manchurians often preferred the bandits—and joined them.

A more concrete complaint was made by Okura Kimmochi in the House of Peers, who declared that the combination in one person of the duties of Ambassador, Commander-in-Chief, and Governor-General did not work well, especially in view of the fact that by the very nature of the case, it meant a neglect of the duties of Governor-General. There was certainly a sufficiency of other duties to keep the Japanese representative occupied. On the military side there was the capture, just before Kang Te's enthronement, of Mei, one of the most troublesome of the bandit chiefs, who operated on a large scale, and kept three big sailing ships in his service on the Sungari river, always ready to attack Harbin. Though the extirpation of banditry was such a long task, however, Japanese activities seemed unable to confine themselves to the bounds of the new empire. It was not merely that the Great Wall had failed once more in its long history to keep out invaders, but the Russians were constantly complaining of Japanese aeroplanes flying over Soviet territory. Sometimes the complaints were in the opposite direction. The Russians, for instance, apologised for having fired some shots at the Japanese consulate at Habarovsk.

While Japan proclaimed to the world the perfect independence of Manchukuo, she had much difficulty in concealing from herself the struggle among different Japanese authorities for power in the new empire. At a Cabinet Council on March 30, 1934, Mr. Matsui, of the Resources Bureau, explained his plan for an economic *bloc* co-ordinating the productivity and consumption of Japan and Manchuria; and Mr. Nagai, Minister of Overseas Affairs, said that he regarded the South Manchuria Railway as destined to be the chief organ of development in Manchuria. Here he was clearly seeking an alliance with the South Manchuria Railway, which the military men had plans for controlling. They also had plans for taking Manchuria out of the hands of the Overseas Ministry altogether, and these they realised by the creation of the Manchurian Affairs Bureau, which was directly under the Premier, in theory, though in practice it comes under military control.

The efforts to create a military dictatorship never relaxed, though the army was discreet enough to avoid giving them too much publicity. Military opinion was constantly quoted, however, and the military "economic experts" would have qualified as dangerous thinkers had they not been in uniform. Five months after Manchukuo became an empire, fears were expressed in the Privy Council that the army was becoming too arbitrary in the new State; but the civilian element naturally had a larger capacity for growth, and civil control was making such strides that Mr. Maeno, of the Manchukuo Department of Justice, sent to Japan in August 1934 for sixty more judges and procurators.

Similarly, when it came to exploitation, everybody was quite willing to praise the mighty works of the army in capturing Manchuria, but though some distinguished officers denounced the capitalists, investors showed no inclination to depart from the customary practices, and opposed successfully the army's desire to manage the railways. The only point on which civil and military opinion coincided was that "Manchu" opinion did not have to be consulted. In making a bid for increased authority the army had to promise economic advantages, and in setting itself up as an authority on economics it departed further and further from the Imperial Injunctions which enjoined complete dissociation of the soldier's profession from politics. Inevitably the military politicians' plans were compared with those experiments in dictatorial Socialism in Europe, which had been in large part their inspiration. A foreign student of the economics of the new State wrote, in the course of a review of the first two years of Manchukuo:

When the establishment of Manchukuo was first announced, the young officers in the Kwantung army and the Fascist politicians in Japan envisaged a State freed from the grip of the capitalists. Their expectation was that Japan would turn over the South Manchuria Railway Company and all the Japanese Government rights in the leased area to the new State; and that the new State would then be turned over to the control of the Kwantung Army. In February 1934, however, Foreign Minister Hirota made it clear that the Japanese Government had no intention of abandoning the South Manchuria Railway Company either to Manchukuo or to the Kwantung army. Nevertheless, proponents of various Fascist and Socialist plans for Manchukuo admit only temporary defeat. The Army, it is contended, has not abandoned hopes of ultimately coming into full control of the South Manchuria Railway Company, though for the present it deems it politic to avoid any outward assaults on the capitalists. The capitalists, in turn, have deemed it politic to make certain concessions to the opposition.

The weakness of military rule everywhere is that the military ruler thinks that government consists entirely in giving orders. The complaint made by Dr. Ashida in the Imperial Diet that the army monopolised Manchukuo has already been recorded; at that time it was commonly said that Mr. Komai Tokuzo, Chief Secretary of the Manchukuo Council of State, was the only Japanese with a civilian mind in high office. He, it will be remembered, was chosen to convey to the Japanese Government the new State's request for recognition. He very soon found that his position was untenable, but after he resigned he conceived a plan for serving the new State by starting a class for young men—a three years' course, with ten recruits each year, forming a small college of imperial administration. In practice the curious spectacle was presented of the civil power, under the banner of the South Manchuria Railway, struggling against the military power with the Commander-in-Chief (who was also Ambassador) at its head.

Mr. Komai's plan came to nothing, but the civilians in the

employ of the new State were stung into action by the encroachments of the military power. The most galling of these was the proposal to put the police under the control of the Commandant of Gendarmerie. Fifteen thousand Japanese officials declared that they would resign. It was pure military arrogance which had dictated the proposal, for the éxperiment in Korea had been a most unhappy one. Had Admiral Saito still been in office it might have been averted, for he had had much experience in the repair of military mistakes in Korea; but Admiral Okada had succeeded him, and held the Overseas portfolio as well as the premiership. His subordinates in the Overseas Department submitted a memorial protesting against the subordination of civilian administration to the military authorities, and warning him that the carrying out of the schemes in hand might bring about bloodshed. Many of the officials of the Department offered their resignations, though the Premier promised that there should be no change in personnel.

The army was quite ready to try conclusions, and animadverted on the civilians' lack of official discipline, so General Hayashi, the Minister for War, refused to budge from his plan, though the officials clamoured that all posts in the new Bureau for Manchurian Affairs should be filled by civilians. Admiral Okada explained that the measures to which they objected were only temporary—which was true in the sense that nothing in this world lasts for ever. He also appointed Count Kodama Minister for Overseas Affairs, and with this for a conciliatory gesture the officials had to be content. It was just enough to save their face, and they dared not carry things to a desperate conclusion. But as many of the police force in Manchuria as could get leave proceeded to Tokyo, and at the Meiji Shrine commended their case to the spirit of the great Emperor and to the Imperial Ancestors in general.

The new administration, however, had been badly shaken. It had been unfortunate that seniority and prestige caused unsuitable men to be appointed to the military ambassadorship which ruled the new Empire. The first of these, Field-marshal Baron Muto Nobuyoshi, died at his post on July 28, 1933, and was succeeded by General Hishikari Takashi, whose singular lack both of energy and ideas soon brought about a clamour for his resignation. He could not survive the crisis of the official strike, and resigned in December 1934, on the 10th of which month General Minami was installed as his successor, and General Araki left unemployed, to the relief even of some of his former admirers.

On some points of policy in the new Empire there was perfect unanimity—on that, for instance, of discouraging all enterprise except Japanese. In the autumn of 1934 a British commercial mission, with Lord Barnby at its head, toured Manchukuo under the guidance of Mr. A. H. Edwardes, formerly of the Chinese Customs, but now adviser to the Manchukuo Government, whose presence naturally made an independent survey impossible. The extreme discretion that stultified every utterance of the mission was eloquent of its conception of the value to be set upon the promises to respect foreign interests and maintain the open door.

Incidentally the open door was neatly explained away by Mr. Amau, the head of the Intelligence Department of the Foreign Office. The Barnby Mission had departed from its perfect tactfulness by making inquiries about the proposed petroleum monopoly in Manchukuo, though none of its members was directly interested in petroleum. The Governments of Great Britain, the United States, and the Netherlands had all protested against this monopoly, sending their protests to Japan, just as though she were responsible! When a group of foreign journalists followed up the Notes and the Mission with their own inquiries, Mr. Amau was distinctly nettled, and told them that they had better ask the Nanking Government about it. Recovering his courtesy, he explained the Manchukuo policy, and hazarded the opinion that people of all nationalities might subscribe to the capital of the company which would manage the business on behalf of

Manchukuo. The open door, he said, only meant that there was no discrimination among the foreign nationalities interested. So long as that condition was fulfilled, it appeared, the impossibility of doing business could not be held to indicate a closing of the door. Nevertheless, for a long time petroleum policy was not allowed to be mentioned in the Press.

Another Press embargo was that which prohibited the mention of abolition of extraterritoriality in Manchukuo. From the Japanese point of view abolition presented no terrors, for the Manchukuo police and judiciary were largely staffed by Japanese, and nothing could be done without Japanese knowledge and consent. The Japanese objection to the abolition of extraterritoriality was that it would subject them to taxation, which hitherto they had escaped. But when at length, at the beginning of 1936, the official plan was disclosed, it was found that the Japanese were so well safeguarded that it was no more than a friendly gesture towards Manchukuo. It did involve the payment of taxes, it is true, but the Japanese officials who were responsible for raising the revenue could not themselves countenance the idea of so great a number of citizens enjoying a position of unfair privilege.

Regarding the rights of other nationals, precedents were soon established for overriding them. The case of the powerful petroleum corporations has already been mentioned. The abolition of the rights of smaller men was also taken care of. In Harbin, Mr. E. Lenox Simpson, a British subject, published a newspaper and conducted a printing office and publishing agency. On the grounds that he had published something of a Communistic nature (always a safe line to take) he was turned out of his premises and railed to Dairen, his plant being confiscated. Diplomatic action was taken and the British Government demanded compensation, but when, four years after the wrong had been done, a question was asked about the case in Parliament, the only reply was that the Manchukuo Government had refused to pay and that nothing could be done. The value of British citizenship *in partibus infidelium* had reached what the stockbrokers call a "new low."

There had been a good deal of discussion as to whether it would not be right and reasonable to hand over the leased territory and the railway to Manchukuo, but Mr. Hirota gave the quietus to that idea by a pronouncement in the Diet in November 1934. Japan's rights would continue, he said. He might have added that the Railway Zone had at last become a reality, for, instead of allowing cultivation right up to the line, as before, it was set back a rifle-shot on each side so that the trains should be safe from ambuscade. Though at the same time General Hayashi defended the "armed colonies," these were dismal failures. In some of the wilder places, especially on the lower Sungari, Japan had planted out colonies of soldier-agriculturists. They were expected to till the land, to be fruitful and multiply, and to exterminate bandits in their spare time. It had been costly to give them this start, and most of them found the life intolerable. The life of the Japanese farmer is hard, and he fares but poorly for all his labour; but the armed colonists missed a thousand things that are not to be had in the wilderness; some deserted, some preyed on their Chinese neighbours (when they had any), and none relished living in a country where they were hated and might at any time be raided by bandits.

Defence was not a simple problem. Manchukuo had been represented as a country greatly desiring independence; yet, now that it was independent, Japanese life was far less safe than before, except in places where the presence and mobility of Japanese troops made it too dangerous to attack the intruders. In railway development it was far ahead of any other part of China, yet the first task before the liberators was to construct new railways so that their armies might hold the country. Simple-minded visitors who were escorted over the safer parts were told that it had always been thus— that the country consisted of nothing but bandits—whereas in reality it had been more orderly than those regions where railway development was less in evidence.

The completion of the line from Tunhua to Seishin, North Korea, and the creation of a new port, were the first tasks; then followed the link between Lafa, on the Kirin–Tunhua line, and Harbin; and in December 1934, a line from Paianchan to Taheiho was begun. Troops can now be railed straight from Dairen or Rashin to the northernmost part of the course of the Amur and to Jehol. The Russians, seeing strategic lines approach their border, and conscious of the vulnerability of the Amur Railway—their only line of communication with Vladivostok, now that the Chinese Eastern Railway had been sold, busily fortified their frontier, which they had hardly troubled to protect while the Chinese were the other side. In so doing, they played into the hands of the Japanese army. When the regular session of the Imperial Diet opened in 1935, there was an urgent demand for the reduction of the 180 million yen budgeted for Manchurian defence. The army's own reports were quoted to show that three years' unremitting man-hunt had almost exterminated the bandits, but General Hayashi refused to abate the demands by a penny. Even if the bandits were exterminated, he said, there could be no reduction, for the border was in a threatening state: and he recited a list of border incidents to prove the bad intentions of the Russians.

As it chanced, neither the bandits not the Russians were concerned with the next incidents which followed on immediately after General Hayashi's explanation. Jehol had been taken, but this only created a problem in Chahar, where fugitives from Jehol had taken refuge, and were apt at any time to make raids into Jehol. Late in January 1935, the Japanese troops came into collision with the forces of General Sung Che-yuan, Chairman of the Chahar Provincial Government, and supposed to be a friend of Japan. The Japanese, as usual, won an easy victory, dislodged the Chinese from Tatun, and drove them over the border. Their defeat was severe, and Japanese troops, as so often happened, occupied the evacuated zone as the only means of preventing anarchy there. Further north, another body of Japanese troops attacked the Mongolians at Halha Miao, north-east of Buir Nor, and drove them out. Here, it would appear, Manchurian Chinese, assured of strong backing, had harassed the Mongolians, and the affair ended in a Mongol defeat. But the further back the Mongols were pushed, the greater became the anxieties of the Japanese, who, with every advance, came nearer the area that the Russians would defend against invasion.

Japanese ideas of the strategic requirements of safety compelled them to advance continually so long as the country was weak, and these operations attracted no attention whatever in foreign countries, where people were becoming rather bored with Japanese victories in outlandish places; yet this pushing back of the Mongols was the crowning folly of the Japanese. There were Japanese who had studied the Mongols in their homes, knew that they had little love for the Chinese, and had had the prescience to engineer the Mongol petition to the League of Nations. The Mongols were very anxious to stop Chinese encroachments, and would have been good allies of the Japanese if rightly handled. But the Japanese could not leave them to manage their own affairs, which was the one thing that they insisted upon, so that, since 1935, instead of being a bulwark against Russia, they regard the Japanese as the source of all evil, and are ready to throw in their lot with the Mongols of Outer Mongolia who accept Russian direction. The Chinese and the Japanese between them can make nothing but a desert of Inner Mongolia, which responds to cultivation like the American prairie, by becoming dust under the spade of the farmer.

It was a strange way of bringing peace to Manchuria; Russia on the north and east had been converted from a neighbour into an enemy; Japan had extended her sway beyond Jehol into Chahar, which she was not eager to present to the Emperor Kang Te, but which she could use for a descent into Hopei and Shansi, if she wanted further conquests in China; but maladroit handling of the Mongols and her threat to China ensured hostility to the new Empire on the west too. Without Japanese bayonets the new Empire could not stand a day; its people were infinitely further from independence than they had been under the Chinese régime, imperial or republican; and those Japanese who gave themselves time to think were wondering what the future would be. Were they to restore Kang Te to the Dragon Throne, or divide up China into tributary States? Korea and Formosa had been difficult enough to handle. Meanwhile there was the Manchu Emperor, seated on his Osaka-made throne by grace of Japan. After his enthronement Prince Chichibu, the Emperor's brother, had paid him a state visit and congratulated him on the loyalty of the millions of Manchurians who had placed him there. The *Asahi*, to improve the occasion, said that the immediate future must be devoted to the cultivation of friendly relations, in order to show that Manchuria was not to be merely a second Korea. To those who did not know recent history this creation of an empire showed that Manchuria was completely independent. Others remembered that Japan had insisted on the King of Korea becoming Emperor as a prelude to annexation. In view of the benefits conferred on Korea by the annexation some felt that the *Asahi's* remark was a little disappointing.

The visit to Hsinking paid by the Emperor's representative had to be returned by the puppet Emperor in person—the significance of which was not lost upon a people who, though lavish in courtesies, measure them meticulously. Kang Te arrived on a Japanese warship on April 6, 1935, and sailed on the 23rd. Very elaborate preparations were made for his reception and especially for securing his safety. The streets through which he drove were lined only with school children and the members of patriotic societies, and the closed car passed quickly by. The care taken caused much embarrassment to many people. On the most capricious suspicions men would be arrested and kept in the lock-up until the new Emperor had come and gone, their friends meanwhile wondering anxiously what had become of them. Happily there were no untoward occurrences and the police were greatly relieved when the august visitor was safely back in Hsinking.

Perhaps the visit struck the popular imagination. A dethroned and fugitive Emperor of China taking refuge in a Japanese consulate was merely a romantic incident—a lesson on the impermanence of terrestrial glory; but an Emperor of China, restored to imperial state, paying homage to the Emperor of Japan as a tributary visiting his liege lord was a spectacle that the gods might well gather round to see. Even the school children and •the patriotic braves who saw the motor-car go by must have felt something of its significance.

Some matter-of-fact Japanese, however, wondered what was going to be done about the succession. The Emperor Kang Te was a young man, with a young and beautiful wife, but they had been married some years without offspring, neither had the secondary wife whom he had in earlier days been fruitful. The problem was not an urgent one, but was full of interesting speculation. More to the general taste and safer to discuss, was the story told in the Japanese Press of Yuan Chin-kai, Keeper of the Privy Seal in Manchukuo, meeting Admiral Okada, the Premier of Japan, on the occasion of the imperial visit, and challenging him to a drinking bout. Both were mighty men of valour, and could carry their liquor like gentlemen; but the Manchukuoan was the victor of the day. Perhaps the story was invented as a subtle flattery. *Toujours la politesse!*

CHAPTER XXIV

THE DETERIORATION OF THOUGHT

PATRIOTISM is supposed to be pre-eminently a Japanese quality, and love of country and native courage both exist in such measure as to justify the belief; but for the sake of creating that unity and discipline necessary to the military ideal of national strength the whole Japanese polity is founded upon fables concerning Japanese origins, belief in which on the part of intelligent men is almost as incredible as the fables themselves. Actually no educated Japanese does believe them, but all are committed to a profession of belief, and the greater the scepticism which has to be concealed, the greater is the fear that the whole national edifice will collapse if the pretence is undermined by the unbelief of those whose self-interest will not keep them silent.

Socialism as a theory seems to have been introduced into Japan in 1898, and gained a good many adherents. When it was realised that even as an academic theory it was inimical to the political structure of Japan, authority struck hard. A leader named Kotoku and twenty-three associates were prosecuted in 1911, their trial being secret. Twelve, including a woman, were executed, the other twelve sentenced to life imprisonment. Some twenty years later the last survivor was liberated, incapable of further action. To prevent any questioning of the verdict, it was given out, verbally, that there had been a plot against the Emperor, but whether this was really the case is very doubtful. Nothing was heard of militant Socialism for a long time after this; but when, in 1917, it swept away the Imperial Family of Russia and the nobility and bourgeoisie besides, fears of a doctrine so subversive became intense. The fascination of the great Russian experiment was so great that time increased these fears rather than allayed them. Count Goto, one of the first to advocate reasonable relations with Soviet Russia, scornfully asked what was the use of boasting about Japanese loyalty and at the same time living in such a state of fear of a foreign political theory; but the fact that even a few were led by reason to prefer the doctrines of Marx to the folklore of officialdom struck terror into the bureaucratic mind.

Speaking on September 1, 1929, the sixth anniversary of the great earthquake, which was celebrated with special solemnity, Mr. Hamaguchi, the Premier, deplored the "deterioration of thought" which had followed that calamity though, as large numbers were in prison on "thought" charges at the time, and 1,300 were arrested immediately afterwards, the arrest of some three thousand during the eighteen months preceding this speech indicated the persistence of a line of thought already well established rather than a novel deterioration. The deterioration was on the part of the Government rather than on that of the reformers. A few years before, it had been proclaimed that, though politics were an unsuitable subject for middle schools, thought in universities was free. Almost immediately afterwards, the weeding out of every sign of unorthodoxy in the Universities began.

By July 1928, there was hardly a liberal professor left in any high school or college in Japan; but the Department of Education called an official conference, which made various recommendations for keeping youth on the right path. This conference proposed the creation of a Social Education Bureau, with an elaborate system of espionage in order to ensure a proper foot-binding of thought. Two million yen were allotted for this purpose, and plans were made for keeping an eye on Japanese students abroad, so that they should not become a danger when they returned home. In China, at least, it became almost as dangerous for a Japanese to indulge in "thought" as at home.

The month following the Premier's earthquake-day speech (October 1929) one of the numerous mass trials of young

Communists came to an end. Counsel for the defence, pleading for clemency (for Japanese counsel hardly ever maintain the innocence or even justification of their clients), pointed out that the young men had been under a secret inquest for eighteen months, during which one had died, while two others were in hospital, and those in court were all physically and mentally exhausted, but none of that counted: their punishment still awaited them. It was typical of such trials. The Press agencies which supply photographs to the newspapers circulated some photographs of "thought" prisoners after their examination, in which, besides being unshorn and filthy, they had expressions hardly human. Yet there were judges who testified to the high mental and moral qualities of the young men brought before them for punishment on "thought" charges. So shocking were the photographs that the publication of any more was prohibited. The judicial authorities could endure such sights, but they feared that the public could not.

Japanese Cabinets have varying degrees of illiberality, but none shows any disposition towards leniency for dangerous thinkers. Some Home Ministers are worse than others, but the bureaucracy goes on, and suffers no interference with its extirpation of heresy. The converse to patriotism is thought, and in every procurator's office large enough for a subdivision of duties, there is a special "thought" section. As for the dangerous thinkers, they may roughly be divided into proletarian reformers and student reformers. It is customary to describe Korean and Formosan malcontents as Communists, though their whole mental equipment may be nothing but a dislike for the Japanese. There appears to be no connection between these rebels against alien domination and the Japanese Communists.

It was customary, after a specially large batch of suspects had been disposed of, to issue a semi-official statement about the case, but there was never any description of what the activities were for which they had got into trouble. Even South Manchuria had its Communists—a number of students

of the Port Arthur Engineering College on one occasion—
of whom it was said that they had denounced the directors
of the South Manchuria Railway!

Whatever the injustice done to the victims of patriotism,
nobody ever dared to stand up for them, and when the last
professor who could be suspected of harbouring a 'liberal
thought was dismissed from the Tokyo Imperial University,
Mr. Robert Nichols, the English poet, then holding a pro-
fessorship there, made a lonely protest. Occasionally the
voice of sanity was lifted up against the excessive fear of
Thought, as when the Dowakai, a Peers' group, complained
that the Metropolitan Police continually hunted "thought,"
to the neglect of murder, violence, and theft. And not only in
Tokyo but in other cities it was frequently all but impossible
to get the police or procurators to take up complaints against
wrongdoers, because they were too busy with "thought."
It was a happy time for the petty criminal, who dreads the
preliminaries with police and procurator far more than he
dreads the judicial punishment.

It was seldom that anything was known even of large-scale
arrests until the examination was concluded and the accused
were committed for trial, a process which sometimes took
years; and the work of the police was so efficient, that during
this time nobody even had positive knowledge of the arrests,
though the prisoners' friends and relatives knew, of course,
that they had mysteriously disappeared. Great bitterness was
added to the movement by the use of *agents provocateurs*,
against whom, when they were discovered by the Communists, fierce reprisals were carried out.

The three biggest hauls of suspected Communists were
made in March 1928, May 1929, and February 1930, on
each of which occasions about a thousand simultaneous
arrests were made. On May Day 1930 there was a pistol
fight with police at Kawasaki, near Tokyo, and on May
Day 1931 there were also some hundreds of arrests,
after which all May Day celebrations were prohibited.
Each of the three big arrests was believed to have ex-

tirpated the movement, but it invariably cropped up again.

In one of the smaller raids, Nakamoto Takako, an officer's daughter and an expectant mother, was arrested, on July 14, 1930. Her condition gained her no consideration, the police point of view being the excellent biological one that instinct would impel her to betray her confederates, so as to save the child in her womb. The method of examination is to keep it on, one questioner following another, continually bullying and threatening. They examined Takako until she aborted, but she made no admission. She was removed to hospital, where the doctors operated. She survived the operation but lost her reason, and in this condition was consigned to prison in October, where she was kept till January, undergoing further questioning. By that time the police decided that she was incapable of informative speech and therefore useless for their purposes. It was in May 1931 that they reported to this effect and disclaimed further responsibility for her.

Extraordinary punishments were sometimes meted out. One Communist who was serving a long sentence was, after eighteen months in prison, given another two years' penal servitude for writing "disrespectful" words on the wall of his cell. Another man got a long sentence for writing disrespectful words in his private diary. In another case disrespectful words were found written on the wall of a public urinal, and this was so terrible that the news was banned from the Press. Such things seem childish, but the consequences were serious.

A new idea was tried when it was suddenly anounced that Sano Gaku, one of Japan's most distinguished Communists, then serving a sentence of imprisonment, had repented. Another prominent prisoner repented almost simultaneously, and repentance became epidemic. Indeed, it was this that spoilt it, for it had been taken for granted that the sinner who repented would be released with joy; but it was impossible to believe that so many could sincerely repent at one time, and the subtle argument that the truly penitent would find a holy joy in expiation was enough at last to leave them to finish their time.

Though the fear of trade union Socialism was swept away by the flood of patriotism that the conquest of Manchuria evoked, the murders by reactionaries in 1931 rather perversely created an impression that the jacquerie was beginning. A bank hold-up by gangsters had been laid at the door of the Communists without any evidence whatever, and there was a tendency to ascribe all unpunished crimes to exponents of "thought." There were suggestions that Inukai's murderers may have been inspired by cunning Leftists. Procurator-General Hayashi, addressing a Judicial Conference a month after the death of Inukai, dwelt on the horrors of Communism. The Communists had a clean record, and the three major murders of the year awaited vengeance, so the Procurator-General, having emphasised the fact that the Communists were the worst possible variety of criminal, went on to say that even disinterested murder could not be tolerated. Extreme Rightists, he said, were in quite a different category from extreme Leftists, and the two often came into collision; but both represented a spirit of discontent and might in certain circumstances join forces. It was a subtle and ingenious speech, for it resolved the doubts that many were feeling in face of the blameless lives of the Communists compared with the outrageous crimes of the patriots. The suggestion that the Communists were really responsible enabled people to come to the customary conclusion without the labour of thought.

There were some Anti-Imperialist societies about 1932, who greatly exercised the minds of the police. They were not disloyal to the Emperor but had a prejudice against that territorial expansion often called imperialism, and were arrested in batches. A number of them who were in the Osaka Police Station lock-up asked whether they might clean out the cell, so as to be able to worship the Emperor from a distance. Their object was, of course, to get rid of some of the vermin and the foulness; but, praiseworthy as their proposal was, and though it would have been highly extolled had they been patriotic murderers, it greatly troubled the minds of the police, who thought they must have some malign intent.

The Procurator-General's lecture stirred the police to great activity. They had been embarrassed at the idea of arresting patriots, however bloodthirsty, but now their impulses were directed with increased force along the accustomed channels, and on October 10, 1932, they arrested two thousand two hundred dangerous thinkers at one haul, including a judge, whose thoughts had somehow become "reddened." Dr. Koyama, the Minister of Justice, was so shocked at the idea of a radical judge that he considered the propriety of resigning. Among those arrested was also a Professor Otsuka. His wife brought his lunch daily to the police station. On the forty-fifth day, reported one of the newspapers, the policeman at the door said, "I am very sorry." Mrs. Otsuka turned pale. It meant that her husband had made admissions under questioning that enabled the police to send him on to the procurator. She turned homewards; the lunch was no use now. One young Communist named Kobayashi Takiji, who had escaped the October round-up, was arrested early the next year, and died under examination at the Tsukiji police station the next day, a mishap over which there were some bitter recriminations. Nobody was punished: perhaps the police made an error of judgment and tried some too dangerous method of questioning, or perhaps Kobayashi was more delicate than he appeared to be. Accidents will happen.

Soon after this, four members of the Diet presented a joint interpellation in which they praised the Services, though regretting a certain lack of discipline shown in the murder of Inukai, and said that the deterioration of thought must be due to defects in the educational system. The interpellators expressed horror at a judge and a professor being included in the last big haul, and quoted "some publicists" as being of opinion that the faculties of Economics, Law and Literature in the Imperial Universities should be abolished, as they were nurseries of Bolshevism.[1] Notwithstanding the death penalty prescribed in the Peace Preservation Law, dangerous thought increased. What did the Government think was the cause?

The Government, in reply, saying nothing about the army and navy officers who indulged in patriotic murder, said that the army and navy were both doing their best to prevent dangerous thought from invading the services; that the increase in dangerous thought must be due to economic depression "and other social conditions at home and abroad"; and that Government and people must make a combined effort to apply the Peace Preservation Law more effectively.

Here, then, was the adoption not merely by the Pro-curator-General, but by the Government itself, of the dogma that all evil comes from radical thought—which meant in practice that in the case of patriotic crime, punishment must be visited on the Communists who were presumed to have inspired it rather than on the patriots who committed it. The police tried to get the path to conviction made easier by complaining that they could not hold a prisoner long enough to get a confession out of him. In practice there seemed to be no limit to the time they could get on pro-curatorial order. As we have just seen, it was not till the forty-fifth day that they sent Professor Otsuka to the pro-curator. The police asked for two months, which was the least time in which they could be reasonably sure of making a Communist confess. The procurators also asked for un-limited time, though here again the need was not apparent, as they sometimes took over three years to bring their Communists to trial. The judges, not to be behindhand, asked for the denial to Communists of the right of appeal; and Communists had already been denied the right of trial by jury—lest the jury be corrupted. The judges also wanted the scope of the Peace Preservation Law widened; but as

[1] The patriotic Baron Kikuchi Takao proposed that the universities be closed altogether.

they were ready to regard the giving of a meal to a hungry
Communist as a contribution to the Communist funds, the
necessity, again, is not clear.

There were constant complaints of torture at the police
stations, and Dr. Koyama, the Minister of Justice, at a
conference of chiefs of perfectural police held in March 1933,
warned them against the infringement of personal rights—
the polite form which is used for all kinds of physical
maltreatment. The conference decided that under the existing laws the police could not do anything against Rightists,
so it passed on to discussing means for exercising greater
severity against Leftists. A plan was drafted for enrolling
two hundred thousand "volunteer police"—apparently for
giving information about "Thought," but it was not carried
out.

Perhaps the "preaching burglar" might be regarded as
an exception to the usually clean record of the Communists.
This man committed many burglaries in 1927, taking no
care whatever not to be heard. He went masked and armed,
and would give the household a lecture on the unequal
division of property and other social injustices—dangerous
thinking of the worst kind. At the end of the year he was
caught, and was no more heard of until he was sentenced in
June 1933. The procurator demanded the death sentence,
but the court gave twenty years' imprisonment. The newspapers, recording this, said that, under examination, the
burglar's spirits flagged in the spring of 1929, and that by
the end of June in that year he was incapable of answering.
He was carried into court to be sentenced.

The question was often asked whether sound opinions and
beliefs could not be made more attractive than political
heresies, and the fact that apparently they could not greatly
intensified the animus with which the heresies were pursued.
The Home Minister regretted that despite three thousand
years of Kokutai[1], Marxism found a fertile soil in Japan,

[1] A very "round number," the mythical foundation of the Empire
being in 660 B.C.

and he advised the starting of a Propaganda Department "like Germany's." The Education Department, like the Home Department, took up the question of making ortho-doxy more attractive, and promised an improvement in the teaching of history, so that the "spirit of the foundation of the country" (again the precious "Kokutai") and the "national idea" might be inculcated. Actually this meant the substitution of fiction for history. At present the Depart-ment considered there was too much science and not enough morals in the curriculum.

Of the brutal attitude adopted towards "thinkers" one more example must suffice. Professor Kawakami Hajime, of the Kyoto Imperial University, who in England or France would pass for a very mild Liberal, wrote to his wife express-ing regret that he had followed a course which had brought trouble upon him and his family, but concluded with the confession that even seven months' suffering in prison could not obliterate the convictions and labours of thirty years. At his trial on August 1, 1933, the procurator used this letter in evidence against him, saying that as seven months' incar-ceration had done him so much good, he would recommend a sentence of seven years to give him time for further contemplation of his errors. The judge gave him five years. Nor was the family forgotten. His young daughter had gone away, changed her name, and got employment: the police ferreted her out and made her employers discharge her.

An official "Thought Committee" opined that poverty helped to produce "thought," an idea which was partly borne out by the fact that hundreds of elementary school teachers were accused of thinking, especially in the poorer provinces, where their salaries were frequently unpaid owing to the difficulties of the local administration.

The tribulations of the Communists were increased by the growing difficulty of getting counsel to defend them. A lawyer who defended thinkers was himself in danger of being suspected of " thought." It became disloyal to defend people charged with disloyalty, and the Minister of Justice added to the difficulty when he exhorted the Osaka Barristers' Association, in November 1933, to support the authority of the law, and to realise the danger of subversive thought. The two years following the 1932 murders were bad ones for everybody suspected of liberal opinions. Partly to distract attention from the patriotic anarchy with which they dare not try to cope, and partly to satisfy themselves that they were acting energetically in dangerous times, the police and judiciary pursued " thought" with an implacable and almost insane severity.

The police stretched the law considerably by holding it an offence to "sympathise" with Communists or Communism, and the Department of Justice sought sanction of the Diet for almost unlimited powers. One item in the proposed new law gave the courts power to punish those who had committed political offences beyond Japanese jurisdiction, whoever such persons might be. This was an attempt to override the consensus of opinion of the best authorities on international law, who held that this could not be done. Much more serious was the provision that, after a Communist's prison term was finished he could still be kept in preventive confinement, lest he repeat his offence. This confinement was to be in a special prison where the necessary measures were to be adopted to procure repentance and reform. No indignation was expressed at the introduction of a law so monstrous. Curiously, the reactionaries saved it from passing. They could not agree that there was any need for the Peace Preservation Law to take any action against Rightists, however flagrant their offences.

Truth, though not much of it, could still be spoken within the walls of the Diet. A Representative who declared that the growth of Communism was due to the atrocities committed by the police was compelled to withdraw his remarks, but when Mr. Matsumoto, Director of the Police Bureau in the Home Office, declared that the police tried to preserve the freedom of speech, another Representative said, without reproof, that he did not believe it. Viscount Okochi, in the

House of Peers, went further; he said there was no freedom of speech except for soldiers, who continually denounced the politicians. The Defence Ministers protested that they only wanted purity; but the Viscount retorted that even the leader of a political party dared not make a speech on disarmament for fear of offending the army.

It was the firm belief of the rulers of Japan that the Empire could only endure if every spark of intellectual honesty were relentlessly stamped out. This dread of truth is a phenomenon found all over the world, but seldom in such strength and abundance as in modern Japan.

CHAPTER XXV

THE FAR EAST AND EASTERN ASIA

A SANE man may twiddle a coat-button, but an expert alienist has sometimes detected dementia through this act. People therefore wondered how serious was the symptom when the Foreign Office in Tokyo let it be known in 1935, to all who were interested, that henceforth the name Nippon would be preferred, and that the official practice in future would be to speak of the region hitherto known as the Far East by the name Eastern Asia. It appeared at first as though the question of Nippon was merely the settlement of a fine point in philology. Though the fame of the Nippon Yusen Kaisha was worldwide, the foreigner in Japan was generally informed that Nihon was considered more elegant, and in the notification regarding the use of Nippon, it was expressly stated that in names where Nihon was sanctioned by long usage, it would remain, as in Nihonbashi. But presently Nippon began to appear on postmarks and other places where it had been customary to use "Japan." As regards Eastern Asia, there was a certain amount of reason for the change. East and west are purely relative terms, and Americans had customarily taken trips to "the Orient," since the United States is so big that "the East" and "the West" are in common speech both comprised in its own boundaries. But there was also the suggestion of a feeling of annoyance that the position of Japan on the mundane sphere should be merely relative to that of England, with her Near East, East, and Far East. This, indeed, was the reason for the change; but throughout many years of military aggression Japan got so thoroughly into the habit of "keeping the peace of the Far East,"—and proclaimed it so often as her sacred mission—that nothing was heard of Nippon keeping the peace of Eastern Asia. She was too busy absorbing it.

After Manchukuo had been settled, so far as an armed peace within and immunity from attacks from without constitute a settlement, pious hopes were expressed of an improvement in the relations between Japan and China. General Chiang Kai-shek was very willing for such improvement, but the Japanese terms made it impossible. Japan required as a preliminary the recognition of Manchukuo and an entire suppression of anti-Japonism, but she refused to make any promise to refrain from further aggression in return for the first, and she retained the right to decide in every instance what constituted anti-Japonism. An import tariff, a "home goods" campaign, a newspaper criticism— all were evidences of anti-Japonism; and as for aggression, Japan had never admitted that there was or could be any.

General Chiang had domestic troubles of the most serious kind to contend with, chief of which was the widespread peasant revolt. His task was to create a united and armed China; but the planes and munitions that he bought with money sorely needed for other purposes were for a long time used against Chinese. As the leaders of the revolt called themselves Communists, the Nanking Government happily escaped censure on the part of the Powers, to whom the only good Communist was a dead Communist. The very necessity of achieving unity made it inevitable that the war against dissentients should be implacable.

Times were changing in China, and Japan was finding intrigue more difficult. The old-fashioned Chinese General had his price, and the race was not extinct; but the growth of national feeling in China had led to the discovery even by the most venal, that there could be no more fatal course than toadying to the Japanese, and they were themselves becoming conscious of their national obligations. During her long history China was a civilisation rather than a nation. Recent critics, enamoured of nationalism, which has proved to be the curse of the world to-day, have reproached the Chinese with a lack of patriotism, but patriotism depends on the existence of enemies. Few Chinese ever heard of

Hideyoshi, who in the sixteenth century swore he would conquer the whole of China; but in the twentieth century the spirit of Hideyoshi is Japan's inspiring force, and Chinese nationalism has necessarily been built on a foundation of anti-Japonism, other countries being regarded as either impotent to help or as contributory to Japan's aggression.

Endeavours were made early in 1935 to bring about a *rapprochement*. Mr. Ariyoshi, the Japanese Ambassador, was reasonable and a man of good will, but he failed to agree with Mr. Wang Ching-wei, head of the Executive Yuan. Mr. Wang was ready to promise that there should be no more anti-Japonism, but asked Mr. Ariyoshi what guarantee he could give that there would be no further acts of aggression on Japan's part. Mr. Ariyoshi emphatically declared that Japan had never been aggressive, so it was evident that a common basis for discussion was lacking. The military view was even more hopeless. Lieut.-General Suzuki Yoshimichi, Japanese military attaché at Peiping, gave an interview to a group of journalists, just after a conversation with the Generalissimo. Chinese unity was now, he said, so unprecedentedly complete that Chiang could suppress all anti-Japonism with the greatest of ease. Such an utterance sounded impeccable in Japanese ears, but it could only be regarded by the Chinese as either a military menace or an invitation to the Chinese leader to ruin himself. Nevertheless, there was some truth in a remark by the *Asahi*, made at the same time as these pronouncements, that the economic system was so bad that Chinese merchants would welcome any conditions that gave a promise of peace. Japan, however, would not permit peace except under her own aegis.

Unofficially the Japanese Foreign Office informs its friends from other lands that it simply hates the methods of the War Office, and this may be true in so far as the Foreign Office must dislike having its business taken out of its hands from time to time by the military men; but the final effect of these protestations is that the army gets away with the plunder while the diplomats get sympathy instead of demands for withdrawal. In its relations with China this system permitted of the Foreign Office ignoring the rape of Manchuria as something that could not now be discussed, while it did its best to maintain ordinary relations with the rest of China.

The military view, however, was that the Manchurian adventure was not merely an accomplished fact, or closed chapter, but was part of a continuing process, and, surveying these events, it is necessary to take the military rather than the official point of view as to what was happening. At the beginning of 1935 Mr. Hirota, the Foreign Minister, definitely promised to make an effort for the improvement of relations with China; but what the Chinese regarded as the least that was due to their national self-respect the Japanese considered proof of their insincerity, and what the Japanese believed was the very least they could ask for seemed to the Chinese barefaced aggression. Approaches were made, however, and Mr. Wang Ching-wei welcomed them, saying that there was nothing in the differences between the two countries which sincerity could not solve.

Both in the Amau Statement and in her attitude towards the League of Nations Technical Committee Japan had shown a determination that nobody but herself should help China. The *Mainichi*, to assist in the agreement by sincerity, published an exposition of the Foreign Office policy towards China, which was to the effect that Japan would help China in the same measure as China showed sincerity towards Japan, but that China must not conclude agreements with other Powers, and that Japan would take steps to prevent her from implementing "most favoured nation" clauses in any agreements that she might make.

The prospects of friendship were ruined by General Doihara making a tour through the country, giving his orders. Trouble always followed in the path of this "Lawrence of Manchuria." General Chiang Kai-shek and Mr. Wang Ching-wei had both condemned boycotts as an instrument of policy; but Doihara declared that he could find no sincerity in China. He told the Chinese that they must abandon forthwith the All Nanking Native Goods Promotion Society; and even Mr. Ariyoshi said that the campaigns now popular in China to promote the use of home-made goods were a proof of Chinese insincerity. Considering that Japan had for some years past carried on just such a campaign with much enthusiasm and with powerful support, it will be seen that the sincerity required of China was of a very high order.

There had been some Anglo-American conversations on the feasibility of helping China, whereupon Mr. Shigemitsu (who had been injured in the Shanghai explosion and was now Vice-Minister for Foreign Affairs), announced that Japan was ready to negotiate separately with any Power to help China, but thought it best for China to achieve her aims without help, seeing that such help only exploited China's unhappy divisions. Articles, speeches and further Foreign Office pronouncements all reiterated Japan's suzerain rights over China, even while they expressly disclaimed them. Doihara brought the argument to an end by declaring that, now that he had seen China for himself, he was convinced that there was no sincerity there, but that China, having seen him, perfectly understood Japan's sincerity.

Though there were large tracts in China's vast area unsuited for dense population, Manchuria had been the only part which was really under-populated, and was the place for China's overflow. Her population problem was a more real one than Japan's, but it was decided that an unrestricted flow could not be allowed into the free State of Manchukuo. It was not that the Japanese settlements were anything but costly failures; but Japan considered it a better idea to settle the land with Koreans, who were increasing rapidly. The Koreans did not love the Japanese, but it was more to the point that they had no great affection for the Chinese, and were not likely to combine with them, but would prefer to look to the Japanese for protection. Moreover, the Koreans were cultivators of rice, and the Northern Chinese always annoyed the Japanese by refusing to grow rice. The economic problems in and arising out of Manchukuo were so many and difficult that it was apparent that the new State and the Japanese Empire did not form the self-contained economic unit that was sought, and there was already some speculation, especially on the part of the military economists, as to how much of China would have to be taken in to round off this ideal.

The attempt to draw China and Japan together in bonds of friendship was defeated before it began. American monetary policy had increased the price of silver, and there began a great efflux of specie from China. Ordinarily it might be supposed that it would be all to the good to have a metal currency increase in value, but there was a certain lag in the adjustment of the exchange, and Chinese silver was worth more in London or New York than it was in China. The Nanking Government prohibited export, but the technique of smuggling was too well understood for such a prohibition to be effectual. The means to defeat it had been learnt in Shantung in 1915. When the Japanese turned the Germans out in that year, they protected the import and sale of morphia and heroin and the export of currency (copper and bronze at that time), despite the Chinese law. Much the same process began again in 1934, in North China. Where military stores passed, drugs could always find a way in, and if the Japanese or Korean smugglers were interfered with, they appealed to the Japanese military authorities who always upheld them. The Chinese threatened to fine the ships which brought in the drugs, which caused an outcry in Japan, for it would, it was pointed out, amount to a discrimination against Japanese vessels. It was rather unfortunate that this outcry should have come just after Mr. Hirota had informed a conference of prefectural governors that China was now distinctly more friendly.

The drugs performed a triple function: they gave the people something other than anti-Japonism to think about; they were very profitable; and they supplied no negligible part of the silver specie that was smuggled out. There were other lines of smuggling also. After the Japanese took over the working of the Peking–Mukden Railway as far as Shan-haikwan, it became the custom to take large bundles of Japanese goods on the train, and hurl them out of the window just before the border was reached; athletic Koreans picked them up, and crossed the border with them on foot, seldom meeting with any opposition, as it was dangerous to interfere with Japanese subjects. When it became profitable to smuggle Chinese currency out of the country, it crossed the border in the same way but in the opposite direction. But this was rather primitive, and presently there was a regular line of motor-trucks running, flying the Japanese flag and refusing inspection on the ground that they carried military stores.

There was no ban on taking silver from Manchukuo into Korea, but the exports from Japan were more than double the imports from Manchukuo; so it was perfectly well known to the authorities that large quantities of Chinese silver specie were smuggled into Japan. There was nothing underhand about this: when carried by sea from China it could not be entered on the ship's manifest, and therefore when passed by the Customs in Japan it could not be entered as an import.

Smuggling became elevated to the level of poetic justice. The *Manchuria Daily News* (published by the South Man-churia Railway in English) informed its readers that from October 1934 to April 1935, 398,677 kilogrammes of Chinese silver were smuggled through the port of Antung alone into Manchukuo, most of the smugglers being Koreans, and at the same time the Japanese *Keijo Nippo*, published in Seoul, said that Koreans entering Manchukuo prided them-selves on the fact that they were subjects of the Japanese Empire, and were filled with the desire to avenge themselves for the persecutions and humiliations they had suffered under the régime of Chang Hsueh-liang. The same paper also stated that Koreans were being invited to Manchukuo to promote the harmony of the five races and "the realisation of Great Asia with Japan as a guiding spirit." To call a policy of *Divide et impera* harmony seems rather an abuse of language. The Special Service Bureau of the Kwantung Army announced in May 1935, that, after striving for three years to promote friendship between Japan and Manchukuo, it had decided that the best means was to erect a big Shinto shrine at Hsinking, dedicated to the Sun Goddess, ancestress of the Japanese Emperors, to the Emperor Meiji, and to the Manchu Ancestors. Needless to say, the Manchu Ancestors play a very small part in the matter: the shrine, like those in Korea, Formosa, Shanghai, and Tsingtao, was to be a proclamation to the world of the spread of the domain of the Sun Goddess.

Large-scale smuggling and the use of Koreans to do the dirtier part of the work naturally did not help towards the officially desired *rapprochement* with China. It had been observed with some misgiving that the Kwantung army was developing a will of its own, an idea that it was not entirely subordinate to the Tokyo Government, but had a heaven-sent mission in the new Empire; and similarly the North China Garrison Army was inclined to discover for itself a sacred duty of putting everything right in North China.

The Japanese army and Government having exercised their uncontrolled will in Manchuria, it was psychologically impossible for them to come to terms in North China on any other footing than that of complete Chinese subservience. On May 31, 1935, Mr. Hirota telegraphed to all Japanese diplomats abroad to dispel other countries' misgivings by explaining to them that Japan had no designs in North China beyond that of keeping the peace, and on that very day the *Asahi* published the demands made on the Nanking Government as the price of keeping the peace: (1) General Yu Hsueh-chung's Hopei Government must be dismissed and anti-Japonism extirpated in the province; (2) North China must be cleared of Blueshirts and adherents of the Kuomintang; (3) all troops under control of the Central Government at Nanking must be withdrawn from North China; (4) General Chiang Kai-shek must sign a formal pledge to promote friendship between China and Japan and to destroy anti-Japonism. That is to say, Japan claimed the right to expel from North China everybody that was suspected of not liking the Japanese.

The Nanking Government kept its temper diplomatically, but universal discretion under such provocation was hardly to be expected. A couple of Chinese editors in Tientsin who drew Japanese salaries and wrote accordingly were murdered and the Japanese indignation exhibited would have been excessive even had they been Japanese subjects. Attempts to utter soothing words sometimes caused offence. Mr. Ying Tung, an important Chinese official, returning to Shanghai after a visit to Tokyo, was interviewed by the Chinese journalists, to whom he said that he thought that the Japanese bark was often worse than the bite, and that the Japanese War Office and Foreign Office did not always see eye to eye. Thereupon General Isogai Rensuke, Military Attaché at the Japanese Embassy, sent for Mr. Ying and talked to him very severely. What he had stated was not only untrue but impossible, said the General, and he must be more careful what he said. Men like Isogai were never reproved by their superiors, and they deliberately made all improvement of relations impossible. They had other plans. General Hayashi went on tour in Manchukuo and came back with the information that the situation there required more Japanese troops. Without troops the State would not have lasted a day, but as the army of occupation had already shot down three-quarters of the 200,000 bandits, it was obvious that more were not required. It simply meant that they were required for the invasion, in due course, of North China. Of course, the Russian danger was cited, but that was well known for a bogey.

Doihara, the Lawrence of Manchuria, came back from his trip to China not only thoroughly convinced of Chinese insincerity, but with plans for a Japan-Manchukuo-North China *bloc*. This, he explained, would include the mines of Shansi and Shantung, while Japan would supply agricultural experts who would tell the Chinese farmers just what they would find it most healthy to grow. The Japanese garrison in North China had an Inquiry Corps which drafted economic plans whereby Japan, by expanding to the necessary extent, would be freed from all her difficulties.

For the present the Doihara plan was pigeonholed; the moment was not convenient, and the longer it was put off, the less resistance would be encountered, at least so far as the North was concerned, for drugs and disorder were weakening the possibility of resistance, and the civil war might take a turn against Nanking, though in some respects the Kuomintang Government was increasing in solidarity. The chief means of undermining the Central Government's authority in the North was a simple defiance of law. The earlier stages of the smuggling racket have already been described: it was to take on a much more menacing form. At Tientsin gangs of ruffians, Koreans, Chinese and Japanese, working together in a manner which indicated an authority behind them well capable of maintaining discipline, took charge of consignments of Japanese goods and carried them through the Customs, in defiance of the officials. They were protected in this by the Japanese military, who insisted that the Customs must not be armed. A levy was placed on the goods, much smaller than the Customs duty, for the benefit, as was alleged, of an autonomous council presided over by a Chinese who had been educated in Japan and had a Japanese wife.

The Japanese army supervised all this, proclaiming that any interference with Japanese shipping would be treated as piracy, and offering the excuse that the Customs were not interested in collecting duty which simply went to Nanking, but preferred to support the local administration. Foreign trade other than Japanese was, of course, almost extinguished, and on complaints being made to the Japanese Foreign Office, the reply was given that Japanese merchants too had complained, and that apparently it was the high duties that caused the smuggling. In April 1936, the loss to the regular

Customs revenue was estimated at eight million Chinese dollars, and it was calculated that the year's losses would amount to a hundred millions. This proved to be an over-estimate as the market became saturated and for a time could absorb no more goods, even smuggled ones. The Japanese Press referred to this gigantic "racket" as the "new trade," and found justification for it easily enough. It gave Japan a monopoly of the north China trade, it taught the people to look to Japanese rather than Chinese authority, and it deprived the Nanking Government of its revenue. Such a desirable combination hardly needed justification.

There was a check to the smuggling out of the Chinese silver currency which was regarded as an intolerable affront, and was the more annoying in that it was difficult to find any good reason or any effective means of opposing it. Sir Frederick Leith-Ross, Chief Economic Adviser to the British Government, paid a long visit to the Far East. Visiting Tokyo, he was received politely by the Japanese officials, but found them quite uninterested in any sort of co-operation. The Japanese Press was less polite, but contemptuously dismissed his mission as futile. It assumed that he had come out to see what he could save out of the wreck of British interests in China, and that he would be glad to secure the interests in the South and leave the North to Japan, but, it added, why should Japan consent to any arrangement since the whole of China would fall into her lap in the natural course of events?

Consultations at Nanking apparently were as fruitless, till suddenly in November 1935, Mr. H. H. Kung, the Finance Minister, announced that China, like the rest of the world, was henceforth to have a "managed currency." The Com-mandant of the North China Garrison was exceedingly angry: he said it would ruin the country and that he would not allow it in North China. He found, however, that he could not prevent it. The foreign banks, other than Japanese, surrendered their silver currency to the Government, and even the Yokohama Specie Bank followed suit when it was found that the new currency was generally accepted and was working quite well. Some bitter remarks were made on Mr. Kung's intention to align the value of the dollar on British sterling; but as the Japanese currency had taken the same standard (though informally) not much could be said. Indeed, nothing at all could be said in a little while, because the Japanese found it expedient to "manage" the Manchukuo currency. Before this reform China's currency had been very chaotic, and the ready acceptance of a standard currency seemed to augur well for the future and to be a weighty testimony to the general confidence felt in the stability of the Government. In Japan, however, every sign of China being able to recover her position was resented. The Amau Statement and the hostility shown to the League of Nations Committee, were equivalent to announcing that Japan would neither assist China nor allow others to assist her; and the animosity shown to every sign of self-help on China's part could bear no other interpretation except that Japan desired that China should be reduced to a state of such complete helplessness that she would willing assent to Japan coming in to reorganise the country.

CHAPTER XXVI

UNEASY NATIONALISM

ACCORDING to that eminent psychoanalyst Dr. Adler, the most disturbing element in our mental make-up is the fear that we may be looked down upon by our neighbours or that some inferiority actually characterises us. People react in various ways to this fear, not infrequently trying to overcome it by self-assertion. Mass-emotion is a far more difficult thing to dogmatise about, but those who have claimed to discover a national inferiority-complex in Japan could certainly make out a plausible case. It is not a subject on which one can afford to be censorious, for all drum-whacking is suspect. Sometimes there was no real feeling underlying an apparent display of self-conscious nationalism, but rather a search for something to commend an idea that it is desired to popularise. There may have been a well-reasoned argument, for instance, against the spending of so much time and money over the teaching of English in Japanese schools; the opposition was apt to express itself in terms of scorn; but it was particularly strong at a time when the youth of the country, at any rate, had a perfect craze for adopting foreign words, often strangely curtailed.

Some irritation was expressed from time to time at the fact that in all dealings with foreign countries, it was Japan which was expected to learn the foreign tongue; few troubled to learn Japanese. But at the same time there was a sort of pride in the language being so intricate as to be almost a secret code, while it was also deplored that this very difficulty entailed a much longer schooling than other nations needed. At a period when such great stratagems as the conquest of Manchuria were contemplated, fierce bureaucratic tussles also took place over the retention of the Roman character on the name-boards of railway stations, and also over the question whether the *kana* names should read to left or to right. The Roman names in some patriotic eyes were a truckling to foreigners, but for some purposes romanisation was necessary, and there are even men not lacking either in learning or patriotism who believe that Japanese, like the Turkish, will have to undergo a general romanisation. If that becomes necessary a little judicious Sinophobia will enable the change to be made. For some years a Romanisation Committee discussed the matter without coming to a conclusion; for half a century the Hepburn system (named after a learned American missionary) had been used, but in many quarters the name damned it. They must have Nipponshiki (Japanese system) instead, though it was rather confusing, and, if adopted, could only lead to more confusion, as there was a massive growth of Hepburn texts and dictionaries.

If civilisation survives the follies of twentieth-century statesmanship, it may go down to posterity as a period in which the rewriting of history was a major industry. Japan has done her part in this, not merely in suppression for the promotion of the patriotic cult: a quite commendable interest has been taken in the early days of foreign intercourse—also, of course, with a patriotic twist that has its peculiar charm. Hoshi Toru, a distinguished Japanese statesman, one of the long list who fell by the hand of an assassin, was the subject of a play which had quite a long run. The author's object was, as much as anything, to "debunk" Sir Harry Parkes, the masterful first British Minister to Japan. Hoshi, at the time of the play, was Commissioner of Customs, and Sir Harry, a strutting, ridiculous figure, is brought before him, and, for his impertinence, has his ears boxed and is driven off the stage. It was a somewhat belated "compensation," as psychologists would call it, as the tradition of Sir Harry's brusqueness still lives. The Embassy, without any member having seen the play, informed the Foreign Office what it had heard about it, and the Foreign Office, equally careful not to be positive, replied that it understood that the play was not at all like that. By that time it had had its day and ceased to be, so the intimation that it had not passed unnoticed was sufficient.

A different method was taken with the dramatisation of Townsend Harris, the first American Minister, whose sacred memory is always invoked as symbolic of the warm friendship between Japan and America. The chief figure in the play was Okichi, Harris's geisha-maidservant, whom Japanese tradition always regards as his mistress; but the play was so little concerned with sentimentalities, personal or international, that it recalled, with embellishments, that Harris had said in his haste that (in Japan) all men are liars. Both plays were essentially an assertion that neither of these first ministers was the hero in Japanese eyes that he was in the eyes of his countrymen.

The debunking of foreign notabilities is a harmless pursuit: nationalist sensitiveness of a much more disagreeable kind was often shown. For instance, when the Kellogg Pact was signed "in the names of their respective peoples," an amazing amount of ink and oratory was expended over the outrage, though the necessary adjustment, showing that so far as Japan was concerned, it was signed on behalf of the Emperor, was made with no trouble whatever. Another storm threatened over a treaty that was signed "in the year of our Lord," but the lightnings missed their mark—the expression had not been used.

At a time when the whole world (at Geneva) was arrayed against Japan, the Minister of Education, weary perhaps of hunting young Communists in the schools, but wanting to do his bit in the promotion of patriotism, declared that it was disgraceful for any Japanese child to address its parents as Papa and Mama. In November 1934, the appointment of a National Language Commission was decided upon, for the "control" of foreign words, but alas! "Papa" and "Mama" persisted. But their interdiction had served a useful purpose. Instead of merely heating hotter still the flame of patriotism, it afforded "relief" of the kind known to every good tragedian.

One of the most disagreeable features of a nationalism made morbidly sensitive is that suspicions of espionage become a perfect plague. It is not too much to say that in the eyes of the Japanese every foreigner is a suspected spy: it is not at all uncommon for the Japanese newspapers to announce that a special watch is being kept on foreigners. The Japanese have never discovered, apparently, that the most dangerous spy is always the native spy, and this, of course, applies to Japan just as much as to countries that advertise their patriotism less. The fuss that is made about photographing is incredible, and nearly always ridiculous. With the introduction of infra-red photography it became worse than ever, and it is taken for granted that every Brownie camera may be taking snapshots at a fifty mile range. The late Dr. Teusler, of the American Red Cross, spent his whole life in improving Japanese hospital practice, his culminating work being the erection in Tokyo of a splendid hospital and medical school; and his reward was, when the St. Luke's Medical Centre towered above the buildings in the neighbourhood, to be charged in the Press with using the tower, with which it was crowned, for photographing distant fortifications.

Tokyo became a favourite goal of foreign aviators, and if these happened to deviate from the prescribed route there was endless trouble. Pangbourn and Herndon, who in 1931 flew from Habarovsk to Tokyo, had much ado to convince the authorities that they had no photographs; and when, on their release, they crossed the Pacific in a single hop, the demonstration of Japan's vulnerability was worth millions to the air services. The leisurely visit of the Lindberghs the same year would have been much more useful if espionage had been its intention, but there was no hint of that for over two years, when an interview with Admiral Suetsugu appeared in a Japanese magazine, in which that distinguished officer was represented as saying that Lindbergh did some espionage among the Kurile Islands. This happened to get abroad and was naturally the subject of a protest. The matter being brought up in the Diet, Admiral Osumi, Minister for the Navy, said that Admiral Suetsugu had not written the interview and had been much surprised at its effect. Admiral Osumi thought the interviewer had gone too far.

Nine-tenths of the trouble is caused through amateur counter-espionage, exploits in which are incredibly fantastic, and the belief in which reflects seriously on the intelligence of the police and gendarmerie. For instance, the National City Bank of New York, wishful that its customers should see what a mighty city it was operating in when it opened a branch in Osaka, asked a Japanese photographer to supply photographs of the principal buildings. The photographer, scenting mischief, informed the police, and there was plenty of publicity for a month after. On some occasions hotel waiters, almost entirely ignorant of English, have been known to report to the police that guests whom they served had spoken of Japan in an improper manner. The Tourist Bureau, and even the Foreign Office, asked the police not to let their mania for detecting spies lead them into such foolish excesses, but it was no use. Mr. Amau, of the Foreign Office, whose business it was to give out information and hear inquiries, was tackled on the subject and loyally tried to belittle it, saying that the cases complained of all turned out to be laughable misunderstandings. That they were misunderstandings was true enough, but only on the part of the police, and they were never laughable, except in the memories of their more philosophic victims. On one occasion a prominent Rotarian from America took occasion at a Tokyo Rotary lunch to bare his soul on the subject of his own eleven days' detention. Often people suffered the greatest distress, discomfort and anxiety, and were given no opportunity of communicating with those who could have guaranteed their respectability.

In justification of all this, the *Mainichi* stated that in the first half of 1933, 232 military spies were operating in Japan, 152 Americans, 82 British, and 18 others. Later the information was published that in 1933, there were 2,346 offences, of which 311 were punished. Of those arrested eight were foreigners, some of whom were believed to be spies! None, apparently, was proved to be a spy; and as vastly more than eight were detained and questioned, had their films destroyed and their cameras confiscated, apparently none of this counted. Notwithstanding the 232 spies supposed to be at work, none was discovered.

CHAPTER XXVII

BIGGER AND BETTER MURDERS

So long as Prince Saionji survives to nominate new Premiers, there will be a certain amount of guessing as to his choice, which has often been unexpected; but when the Saito Ministry resigned in July 1934, the guessing was rather as to whom the army wanted than as to whom Saionji thought most suitable. The army had the substance of power, and it was mainly its civilian admirers who wanted a military Government. The army let fall hints that it would accept Baron Hiranuma, Viscount Kiyoura, Baron Dr. Ikki, or Prince Konoe, or would even tolerate another dose of Admiral Viscount Saito, so long as he did not keep the obstinate Takahashi as his Finance Minister. General Ugaki was the foremost soldier, and was credited with a desire to be Premier, though he had declared that he hoped to die at his post as Governor-General of Korea: but the army was not keen on Ugaki, for he had consented to a reduction of its numbers when he was Minister for War.

Saionji took everybody by surprise by nominating another admiral—Okada, who had been Saito's Minister for the Navy, but had resigned on reaching the age limit for active service. In a way there was as much objection to Okada as to Ugaki, for he had supported the London Naval Treaty, and had pleaded with Admiral Kato Kanji, the Naval Chief of Staff, to accept it as loyally as he had done himself. Okada formed a competent but by no means remarkable ministry. The most distinguished man in it, Mr. Tokonami, had one of the less distinguished portfolios, that of Communications; the Minister for Railways was Uchida Shinyu, famous in the war years as a *funa-narikin*—one who had grown wealthy in the shipping trade; Hirota Koki, a disciple of Toyama Mitsuru, the professional patriot, became Foreign Minister, having already had a successful diplomatic career; and instead of Takahashi as Finance Minister, Fujii, a capable man who had served under him and was determined to maintain his principles. Unhappily the task was more than he could cope with. The army increased its demands, and Fujii, refusing to propose new taxes, could not satisfy it. General Hayashi, the Minister for War, demanded Fujii's dismissal, but withdrew it when Okada put it to him that if Fujii went the whole Cabinet would resign.

But Fujii broke down in health after four months of office, and died after an illness of two months; and the aged but robust Takahashi was called upon again to take office.

The sentimentalities of Japanese philosophy were always much concerned with the impermanence of all mundane things; yet there was always a demand for a-definite national policy which should ensure the right course of action in any circumstances which might arise, and so free the country from the possibility of error. The demand was again heard, so Admiral Okada did his best to fulfil it. With himself as Chairman he made up a National Policy Council of sixteen members, all "elder statesmen" of a kind. But though there had been such a strong demand for the Council, it was rather the expression of an aspiration than a wish for a real council of fallible human beings. The Home Minister hailed it as a "brain trust," but nearly everybody else, when they read the names of its members, realised that transcending mundane impermanence was not to be expected of such a "crowd," as a leading politician dubbed it. It was very difficult to decide on the scope of the Council's duties, and it had only been in existence for a month when a Seiyukai member of the Diet demanded to know why the Council had been forbidden to discuss either diplomatic or military affairs. The Premier explained that these topics had not exactly been prohibited, but that it was clear that the Council could not infringe on the Imperial prerogative. A strong suspicion was voiced by a good many politicians that the Council's real function was to reduce the Diet to impotence: that, however, proved to be groundless, for the Council was so completely impotent itself that it could do nothing.

The experiment, however, was not without its lessons. At the time of the Manchurian campaign a request for a "firm offer" to withdraw the invading troops was evaded on the ground that such an order could be given only by the Throne. This was grimly laughed at in Europe as an Oriental subterfuge; but in this later development it was used as a means of keeping policy in the hands of the army, unhampered by laws laid down by any Council, however eminent. So the Council, after all, did confirm the impotence of the civil power, for by invoking the Imperial prerogative the army was able to exalt itself above all authority.

These military encroachments did not pass unnoticed. The newspapers criticised the Government with their usual freedom; but the *Asahi*, commenting on the closing of the Diet, said that the freedom of speech had almost disappeared, and that not only had it become very dangerous to criticise the army, but almost equally so to say or do anything that offended the Rightists. In some directions, no doubt, the *Asahi* went on, there was no curtailment of liberty. Everybody was free to denounce the Minobe theory, though, on the other hand, nobody dared defend it.

This was all expressed in such a manner that nobody could say it was ironical, but it was very courageous of the *Asahi* to say it. No topic was more to the fore in 1935 than the Minobe theory, and this has been so little understood that it must be explained here. Dr. Minobe was a learned expert in law, specialising on the Constitution. Two-thirds of the professors of law in the country had been his pupils and disciples, but of late he had give serious offence on no less than three occasions. First, on the question of the authority of the civil power, he maintained that it did not permit of any dispute. It was the civil power which imposed taxes, collected revenue, and passed the budget; and the power of the purse was, in the ultimate issue, the supreme power. His second offence was worse: the question was put to him whether the right of the Defence Ministers and the Chiefs of General Staff to have audience and advise the Throne as freely as the Premier himself did not put an undue power into the hands of the army and the navy. He replied that it did not; for the Defence Ministers and Chiefs of Staff only advised the Throne of the opinion of the army or the navy, as the case might be, while the Premier advised the Throne of the opinion of the nation. Thirdly, he gave great umbrage by saying that soldiers did not understand economics. At an earlier date the soldiers might have regarded this as a testimony to their superiority of soul; but they had committed themselves to the promise that Manchuria was going to pay well and to bring prosperity to itself and to Japan. The Kwantung Army and the North China army had their corps of economic experts, and in the latter days of Admiral Viscount Saito's Ministry a big meeting was held at the Tokyo Chamber of Commerce, attended by officials, military officers, and business men, to discuss national economics. A colonel presided, and he and other officers expounded the principles of healthy economic development, which, it appeared, was to be achieved only by the directive control of industry. The right industry must be in the right place, and unnecessary competition avoided.

The first two of these offences were far from recent, but the army waited: then help came: in a textbook on the Constitution, which had been used in colleges and universities for at least twenty-five years, somebody discovered that Minobe had described the Throne as an organ of the State. Here was blasphemy. Large-scale denunciations were organised. Toyama Mitsuru, whose ignorance was as encyclopaedic as Minobe's knowledge, was particularly loud. *Kokutai*, the imperial polity, was ineffable. Any words used to describe the Emperor were wrong. The army and all the patriotic societies demanded condign punishment. The Editor of the

Yomiuri ventured to take the Doctor's part, and was promptly the victim of a murderous attack by a patriotic ruffian. Not another soul said a word in his defence; but many suffered on his account. Every professor and teacher who had been his pupil lost his post. Dr. Minobe himself lost all honours, employment and emoluments, but though the Minister for War said that the army was demanding further punishment, no further official action was taken except the proscription of his books. Unofficially an independent patriot shot him, but fortunately made bad practice, only getting him in the leg; and as the Minister of Justice had recently talked about the necessity of dealing severely with law-breaking Rightists, a judge was found sufficiently courageous to give the ruffian a prison sentence.

Such was Japanese patriotism in its most fervent manifestation—a passion artificially fomented not out of regard for the Emperor, but for the sake of revenge on an eminent scholar who denied the validity of military pretensions.

The Okada Government was, in its nature, a continuation of the Saito Government, that is to say, a demonstration that the army would not tolerate a Government with the democratic flavour acquired from association with a political party. The army based its claims on its function of protecting the country and on its profession of a special loyalty, though within itself it was greatly rent by petty jealousies which masqueraded as patriotism. The appeal to loyalty was an effective one, but there was a very large number of citizens who abhorred military government. Attempts made to combine the two big parties against the "national" oligarchy were ineffectual. In such an administration, unchecked by democratic criticism, the characteristic features of bureaucracy, always evident in Japan, became more pronounced, and any resulting inefficiency was ascribed to a lack of the spirit of true patriotism as understood only by the army. Reaction continued to be more admired than progress, and efforts to check the rapscallions who pretended that their misdeeds were inspired by patriotism were spasmodic and half-hearted.

While it was to the army's interest to keep a united front to the rest of the world, its internal dissensions were so bitter as to rend the veil that hid them from the public. General Hayashi, though very much the militarist, and though he encouraged the contemptible military agitation against Dr. Minobe, was not in favour of the "young officer" movement. General Araki Sadao, whom Hayashi had succeeded as Minister for War, encouraged the super-patriotism of the "young officers" (many of whom were old enough to know better) and during his term of office got his friend General Mazaki Jinzaburo, another "idol of the young officers," appointed Inspector-General of Military Education. The great importance of this position in Japan is due to the fact that it sets the tone of the army and determines its attitude. To have a man like Mazaki in such a position was highly dangerous: the effects of super-patriotic and anti-democratic teaching had already been tragic enough. There was a dangerous military conspiracy in November 1934, which was nipped in the bud and hushed up, and was thereafter known only mysteriously as the "November affair." Whether Mazaki had anything to do with it is not known, but Hayashi considered it necessary to remove him from his post. It was not easy, even for the Minister for War, as the post of Inspector-General carried great prestige, but with the help of his principal lieutenant, General Nagata, Director of the Military Affairs Bureau, a loyal and moderate soldier, he put sufficient pressure on Mazaki to force his resignation, and appointed in his place another moderate, General Watanabe Jotaro.

There was a certain solemn fanatic, Colonel Aizawa, who considered that something must be done to save the army from degeneracy. Accordingly, three days after General Mazaki's resignation, he went to General Nagata and advised him to resign. For an inferior to tender advice of this sort is less surprising in Japan than it would be in Europe, though when the object of such advice is very exalted, the Far Eastern tradition would generally have the adviser commit

suicide afterwards. How General Nagata received these
overtures is not recorded; but Aizawa brooded over the
small chances of the army rising to heroic heights as long
as a man like Nagata was in a position of such influence. A
personal grievance supervened. Aizawa was ordered to
Formosa—an assignment which, while it was nominally in
the way of promotion, he probably thought was General
Nagata's way of side-tracking an inconvenient officer. Now
his mind was made up. He visited the Grand Shrine at
Ise—the spiritual centre of Shinto—bought a charm there,
which he sent to his family (he had four children), and on
August 12th he marched into General Nagata's room in
the War Office, and, before his victim had time to turn and
ask him what he wanted, stabbed him to death with a short
sword. Colonel Niimi, of the Tokyo Gendarmerie, who was
present, tried to intervene, but the murder was done so
quickly that he could not save Nagata, though he got
wounded in the arm himself.

The most extraordinary thing about the murder was that
Aizawa had brooded over its righteousness so intensely that
he could not believe that anybody would disapprove of it,
and directly it was done he went and reported for duty,
believing that he would be sent to Formosa as arranged.
General Hayashi remarked at the time that Aizawa had been
misled by pamphlets—presumably those issued in such large
numbers by the army itself; and a similar statement was
made in a report on the case issued by the War Office about
two months later.

A law had just come into force to curb pamphleteering,
which had become very vexatious to authority. The printer
(on discovery) was to be punished equally with the man who
ordered the printing, though he was to be spared if he
denounced his customer in time to prevent distribution. But
the greatest pamphleteers were the army men, who did not
seem to be under control even of the War Office, General
Hayashi, on occasion, having to draw distinctions between
what might be regarded as the opinions of the War Office

and what were just military opinions of undefined authority.
A week after the murder a hundred thousand copies of an
army pamphlet entitled "The International Situation on
the Turn—and Japan" were distributed. It had nothing to
do with the murder, but was a typical example of the
propaganda of preparedness constantly published by the
army. Any writings suggesting that Japan's own policy was
leading to war were, however, promptly suppressed.

General Hayashi resigned, according to the usual formula,
"to show his sense of responsibility" for such a breach of
discipline. Such was the state of military discipline that if
he had not taken this step, Aizawa might have found the
court-martial very sympathetic. Even as it was, there was
a strong bid for his vindication. The trial was postponed, and
meanwhile the "young officer" movement was seething and
bubbling. Takahashi at a Cabinet Council on November
27th, pointed out that he had been forced to compile a
budget in which the revenue was only half the expenditure,
that the Services were taking 60 per cent of the expenditure,
and that the national bonds had to be taken up by the banks
because they dared not put them on the market except by
very small instalments. The newspapers, he went on, were
intimidated and dared not criticise the military, nor did the
financiers, but there was general dissatisfaction with army
and navy extravagance. Japan was perfectly secure from
attack, but enormous sums were being spent on unnecessary armaments. He asked what the Defence Ministers
thought of it. These gentlemen replied that they must
have the money, so the Government departments cut
down their already curtailed allotments in order to placate
them.

It was difficult to make out that Aizawa's was a heroic
act: had he committed *hara-kiri* he would have passed for a
hero, but he wanted to be his own chief admirer. The
procurator, whose usual function was to affirm guilt and
demand punishment, did his best for the murderer in this
case, and produced in court letters of commendation written

by schoolgirls in their own blood. The Colonel, who had acquired some underclothes supposed to have belonged to General Nogi, got the Court's permission to wear them during these troubled days—a proof of his sincerity. He made a highly religious speech in his own defence, declaring that he had been ordered by God to act as he did, and describing his plan for the Showa Restoration. This was one of the catchwords of the time. The Meiji Restoration had swept away the Shogunate and started Japan on her career of conquest. From the time Meiji's grandson ascended the Throne, the era being called Showa, the ultra-militarists had talked much of modern degeneracy and of the necessity for a Showa Restoration.

Some sensation was caused when, on February 25th, the court-martial summoned General Mazaki whose removal from the military triumvirate was the immediate cause of the murder. He indignantly refused to reply to the questions of the court-martial, which thereupon adjourned to recover its equanimity and to consider what to do in the face of this unprecedented difficulty.

The next morning, February 26, 1936, whispers went round of tragic happenings, and there was tense excitement. Roads in the neighbourhood of the Palace were guarded by soldiers and forbidden to the public. There was a coming and going of military men, placing of guns, erection of barbed wire fences. Telephones worked spasmodically, telegraphs not at all. The mass of the population, of course, endeavoured to pursue their ordinary avocations. Men went to office, shops opened, housewives cooked the food, policemen arrested Communists.

What had happened gradually became known, with plenty of embellishments, but the essentials were given out to the public in military communiqués. Early on the morning of the 26th, while it was yet dark, bands of soldiers, each numbering about thirty, set out for the houses of Prince Saionji, the last of the Genro, Admiral Okada, the Premier, Mr. Takahashi, the Finance Minister, Admiral Viscount

Saito, Keeper of the Privy Seal, Count Makino, former Privy Seal, Admiral Suzuki, Grand Chamberlain, and General Watanabe, the Inspector-General of Military Education who had succeeded General Mazaki. Japanese houses seldom fasten very securely, and the intention was to murder all these elderly gentlemen in their beds. The chief slaughter took place at the Premier's official residence, which was comparatively well guarded, and five policemen lost their lives trying to resist the murderers' entry. At the other houses there was little resistance to overcome. Admiral Saito, who had laboured for seventeen years in repairing the blunders of military men, was stabbed to death, the Viscountess, who had shared many perils with her husband, being wounded in an attempt to throw herself between him and his murderers. Takahashi, whose financial services to his country were inestimable, was butchered by the soldiery whom he had tried to prevent from ruining the country. General Watanabe, who had dared to replace Mazaki, suffered a like fate. Admiral Suzuki was sorely wounded, but did not die. Prince Saionji, warned by a telephone call that he was in danger, drove from his villa at Okitsu to Shizuoka and claimed the hospitality of the Chief of Police for the night. Makino, whose life had been attempted several times, was adept at avoiding murder, and could not be found at the hot spring resort where he was supposed to be staying.

The Premier provided a touch of comedy in the midst of this horror. He was reported dead, and was laid out. His murderers mounted guard round the house, well satisfied that they were national heroes, and streams of friends came to pay their farewells. But Okada had sought concealment in the servants' quarters when he learnt that his brother-in-law, Colonel Matsuo, who bore some resemblance to him, had been murdered by mistake. Faithful servants smuggled his clothes to him, and provided him with the huge respirator worn by many Japanese when there is influenza about, a pair of tortoiseshell spectacles completing the disguise.

Mingling with the mourners and paying a tribute of respect to what was supposed to be his own body, the Premier passed out undetected among the numerous other elderly gentlemen in frock coats and top-hats. The first inkling of the truth was in the omission of the Okada family's name from the Imperial condolences.

Dreadful as these occurrences were, they exhibited a contemptible degree of incompetence on the part of the organisers of a conspiracy which lacked neither elaborateness of planning nor brutality of execution. There were some fourteen hundred men involved, and they showed a certain boldness of conception in their seizure of the War Office and the Metropolitan Police headquarters, but a conspiracy of this sort can only succeed in Japan if the conspirators surround the Throne and make themselves the channel for the issue of Imperial mandates. This was the historic method and as recently as the 1870's such a conspiracy had only been foiled by the courage and loyalty of the Palace guards. The conspirators had the game in their own hands. They had occupied some of the Government buildings in the immediate neighbourhood of the Palace, and there was nothing to prevent them from taking possession of the person of the Emperor, but the bigger men, who had incited the conspiracy, would not take the risk of appearing in it themselves before it was completely successful. The handful of junior officers, who had been ready enough for massacre, shrank from invading the sacred Palace without an older man to lead them—and so the Showa Restoration miscarried.

All senior officers professed to regard the murderers as rebels. Martial Law was proclaimed, and General Kashii, himself an ultra-patriot, was appointed Martial Law Commandant, and took charge of operations. Troops were placed in commanding positions, where they could reduce the conspirators by force, and handbills were distributed from aeroplanes and tanks, calling on them to surrender, informing them of the Emperor's disapproval of their action, and making it understood that there would be no great severity exercised if they surrendered without further resistance. The force of this argument was so irresistible that the affair ended on the evening of the 29th, without any more violence or bloodshed. The case of the fourteen hundred of the rank and file was soon disposed of. They had acted under the orders of their officers, it was announced, and as a soldier's first duty is to obey his officers, the question of guilty knowledge and of responsibility was not gone into: they were ordered back to their barracks. Of the officers, the only one with the rank of captain, a handsome young man with the aquiline glare frequently associated with a fanatical temperament, killed himself. The rest, all lieutenants, to the number of seventeen, were tried by court-martial, which, for some unexplained reason, took five months. With them were tried, also by court-martial, a hundred or so civilians, who had had nothing to do with the conspiracy, and whose names were not published, the majority of whom were sentenced to long terms of imprisonment. The seventeen, according to a statement issued by the War Office, were shot. Incidentally the exploit sealed the fate of Colonel Aizawa. He seemed on February 25th to be well on the way for special service in Manchuria; after February 26th it was impossible to give him favourable treatment, and he was shot also.

Documented history often errs in matters of fact, and the recorder of undocumented history cannot hope to be free from error. It is unlikely that the truth concerning the remarkable series of murders that took place on February 26th will ever be revealed, since all concerned are more interested in concealing than in revealing the truth. That the murders and the revolt were parts of the one conspiracy is certain. It was said that the navy felt bitter about it, seeing that the conspirators set out to kill no less than three admirals. If they wanted to murder one of their own generals that was their own affair, but why three admirals? It was not because they were members of a service which the army did not particularly like, but for other reasons. An examination of the list of victims affords some clue to the nature of the conspiracy.

The murder of the Premier was quite natural: it had become almost a tradition to murder the Premier as an indication of dissatisfaction with the government. Besides, Okada had consented to a weakening of Japan's defence forces, he showed no zeal in the matter of punishing Minobe, and, as a nominee of Saionji, was essentially unsatisfactory. Takahashi had again and again told the army that it was ruining the country and could not have all the money that it asked for. He had been warned when the Okada Cabinet was created that the army wouldn't have him at any price, but he took office as Finance Minister again when Fujii died. Prince Saionji had long been a thorn in the militarist side. He had gone on living to a preposterous age, and while he lived there was little hope of getting a Premier such as the army wanted, for the Elder Statesman had a congenital dislike for soldiers. General Watanabe had taken the place of the "strong man," General Mazaki, and as Hayashi, who had jockeyed Mazaki into resignation, had resigned himself, this probably saved him from the massacre. These reasons were quite sufficient in Japan to account for four of the projected murders, but we still have to account for the determination to kill Saito, Makino, and Suzuki. Makino was a civilian who had a long and distinguished record of public service. In late years he had been Minister of the Imperial Household, and then Keeper of the Privy Seal, and was still regarded as a close friend and adviser of the Emperor. Like Saionji, he had no taste for soldiers, and told the army men plainly on one occasion that he couldn't have them dragging their intrigues into the Palace. Admiral Saito had succeeded him as Privy Seal, and Saito, though not a statesman of genius, was imperturbably courageous without being fanatical, and would never consent to any extreme measures. Admiral Suzuki, Grand Chamberlain, was a man of similarly stable character. It was quite certain that while these three, to whom, with Prince Saionji, the Emperor would inevitably appeal for counsel, had the entry of the Palace, it would be useless to take possession of the person of the Emperor. Yuasa Kurahei, Minister of the Imperial Household, was a man of much less personal prestige and probably of smaller calibre, and perhaps would not object to shining in the glory of the Showa Restoration, so he was spared. The common reason for what seems at first to be a strangely assorted list of murders is sufficiently plain in the light of these considerations.

That the conspiracy was conceived and executed by a group of young men of whom the senior was Captain Nonaka, nobody even pretended to believe. It was said both in the Diet and in the Press that there were others behind it; but the subject was too dangerous to emphasise or to pursue.

How near success the conspiracy came was shown by the fact that some of the troops ordered to hem in the insurgents joined them instead, and that when the army gave out its bulletins it merely said that groups of officers had visited the houses of So-and-so, "who had died immediately." While the issue hung in the balance murder was too delicate a thing to mention. The police were as determined as the Vicar of Bray to be on the right side. They would not even allow to be published such details as the army released; they supplied body-guards to all sorts of important persons, and they began industriously to arrest Socialists. The army too gave out a proclamation that the populace must keep cool, and that the army would protect it from the "Reds." Neither police nor army referred to the murders with the least hint of reprobation.

When the insurgents surrendered and the crisis was averted, the army made a very extraordinary pronouncement. It regretted that the tranquillity of the capital had been disturbed even for a short time, and reminded the public at large that they shared the responsibility, and that it was for them to help in maintaining order and promoting correct ideas, and especially to see that adequate provision was made for defence. So the army remained the saviour of the

country and dangerous thought was still the only danger
that threatened.

No names were mentioned of men higher in rank than
those who openly led the revolt; but General Minami, only
lately appointed to the Manchurian dictatorship, was almost
immediately recalled, and five out of seven of the Supreme
War Council resigned. The Government, of course, resigned,
and General Hayashi was not reappointed Minister for
War in the new Government.

The appointment of this new Government was the first
business. Prince Saionji, once more compelled to leave his
peaceful villa, and to repair to the Palace, proposed Prince
Konoe, but the Prince declined on grounds of health. To
be Premier was certainly not a healthy occupation. Saionji
once more made a surprise choice by nominating Hirota.
It could hardly be supposed that he liked the school of
Toyama Mitsuru, but, after all, it was better than appointing
a soldier. Baron Hiranuma was almost the only other
civilian that the army extremists would accept, and Saionji
abhorred him. In place of the murdered Watanabe, General
Nishi had been appointed Inspector-General of Military
Education, and he consulted with Prince Kanin, the Chief
of the General Staff, regarding the appointment of Minister
for War. Their choice fell on General Count Terauchi, son
of the General Count Terauchi who had been Premier in
1916–18.

Meanwhile Hirota compiled his list of Ministers. When it
was complete, General Terauchi looked over it, and informed
him that it would not do—that the list included party men
and could only be regarded as an attempt to maintain the
system which must be reformed. He proceeded to reproach
the Premier. The army, he pointed out, had purged itself
by the resignation of some of its chief generals; the political
world must also purge itself, since, as the army had already
announced, it was also responsible for the untoward events
of February 26th. An example of the military criterion in
the choice of Cabinet Ministers was General Terauchi's

objection to Mr. Ohara, as Minister of Justice, whose continuance in office he would not allow because of his luke-
warmness in the matter of punishing Dr. Minobe.

With the exception of Takahashi, none of those marked
down for murder on February 26th was a party politician;
moreover, there was a "national" Government in power;
so the excuse that served for Inukai's murder, that it was the
natural outcome of party corruption, would not serve here.
The massacre was immensely popular in the army. Its
protagonists had to suffer, like the Forty-seven Ronin, but
that made the whole thing glorious and heroic. The army
acted as though the revolt was the work of the whole body
and had succeeded. It gave out a number of pronouncements
on subjects of the day. For instance, it set forth four principles
for the guidance of the new Cabinet:

(1) Vindication of the National Polity (*Kokutai*).
(2) Stabilisation of the livelihood of the people.
(3) Reform of Foreign Policy.
(4) Strengthening of National Defence.

The second of these looks like one of the "Three Principles"
of Dr. Sun Yat-sen, and, no doubt, was sincerely desired,
but for the time being it had to give way to the fourth. In
its new orders the army said that it could not tolerate
liberalism, that internationalism and individualism must be
banished, and nationalism and "the Japanese principle"
promoted.

The army let it be known that it concerned itself not only
with the physical part of defence: it was the final authority
on finance, economics, foreign policy, education, and constitutional government. Undue importance, it declared, was
ascribed to science in the universities. Rather than science,
moral ideas congruent with the ideals of the Foundation of
the Country and with the true mission of Imperial Japan
must be inculcated.

Other pronouncements guaranteed the sacred inalter-
ableness of the Constitution granted by the Meiji Tenno in

1889, but required the abolition (by amalgamation) of some
of the civilian Ministries and the creation of new military
Ministries of Air and Propaganda, as well as a new National
Policy Council like the General Staff but less trammelled.
Army economics included a new plan of taxation for "the
execution of the Asiatic policy."

Much that was thus flourished over the heads of the nation
was held over to a more convenient season: the army
contented itself for the time being with a censorship of the
Premier's choice of Ministers, and a louder voice in policy.
General Terauchi actually nominated the Finance Minister,
Mr. Baba, formerly Governor of the Hypothec Bank, who
announced, as soon as he was appointed, that the Takahashi
financial policy was mistaken and that something would have
to be done about taxation; whereupon there was such a sharp
drop on the Stock Exchange that he hurriedly declared he
did not mean anything like that, but that everybody should
remain calm and convinced that the Government would not
harm anybody. This seemed to cool the military ardour a little.
Perhaps some of the military men remembered that Marshal
Chang Tso-lin had once tried to check a decline in exchange
by lopping off heads of stockbrokers; and though their
economic ideas were as crude as the Marshal's, they remembered that the medicine had not been effectual.

Some better reason than the corruption of the political
parties had to be found for the murders of February
26th, and one which justified and gave continuity to what
was evidently a feature of military policy. The matter
proved comparatively simple. This time it was the "new
bureaucracy" which had offended. As mentioned elsewhere,
Japanese administration tends to be excessively bureaucratic,
and this tendency seemed to become more pronounced under
the "national" governments, though the cause of this may
have been the growing complications of ordinary life rather
than the abeyance into which the party system had fallen.
The "new bureaucracy" were said to be tyrannical and
selfish and to act as though the country belonged to them.

They were obstinate and would not listen to advice, and certain warm-blooded young men with their country's interests at heart could tolerate it no longer. In brief, the civilian had not the same sense of duty as the military man, and the reforms for which the murders of 1932 had called were still uncompleted in 1936. Most of Inukai's murderers were already at liberty in February 1936, but they did not participate in the new series of murders.

In the course of explaining the murders there was a new development. It had been announced soon after the murders that the civilians arrested were "notorious Rightists," but now it was discovered that they were "Leftists," and had been guilty of incitement to violence. In 1932, the Minister of Justice had made a similar charge regarding the patriotic murders of that year; yet nobody appeared to see any inconsistency in thus allocating the patriotism to the murderers and the guilt to the "Reds."

CHAPTER XXVIII

THE SUN GODDESS EXTENDS HER KINGDOM

IT is unfortunate that members of the military profession, instead of being exemplars of a courage that nothing can disturb, live in a state of perpetual panic. The citizens of Tokyo, on the 26th of February, as on other days, had their living to earn and went about their work as usual, in spite of the tramp of armed men, the efflorescence of barbed wire, the rumbling of tanks and gun-carriages, the thunder of the captains and the shouting. In three days the affair was at an end, but the army did not recover its nerve for months, but kept the capital under martial law. It may be that there was reason for this. When General Mazaki was manœuvred out of the Military Triumvirate, a number of senior officers were shelved with him. These the insurgents would have acclaimed as their leaders if their coup had been successful, and the more moderate party in the army were not easily reassured of their loyalty. The free pardon extended to the rank and file prevented discontent from manifesting itself in the ranks; but the heads of the army, moderates or extremists, did not breathe freely again until the young leaders of the insurgents were all shot. Only then could they pretend to themselves to show a united front.

Meanwhile they realised that the proclamation of martial law did not mean that the business of government was superseded. In accordance with custom the formation of a new Cabinet was followed by the summoning of a special session of the Diet, and there was much speculation as to how far the existence of martial law would be inimical to the privilege that the members enjoyed of speaking their mind. No newspaper dared say a word in criticism of the army, but, as everybody knew that the lieutenants under arrest were not the real conspirators, there was much suppressed

indignation at such doings, and enormous crowds attended
the funerals of Admiral Saito and Mr. Takahashi: it was
a demonstration far beyond accounting for as the curiosity
of sightseers.

When the Diet opened the Minister for War gave a
perfunctory and colourless statement regarding the murders,
hinting that the Communists were behind them, though
that was obviously untrue. Mr. Saito Takao, a Minseito
member, then rose, and spoke with great solemnity and
deliberation to a hushed house. He disclaimed any intention
to create prejudice against the army, but pointed out, in
regard to these political murders, that the young soldiers who
participated in them were disobeying an injunction of the
Meiji Tenno against officers concerning themselves with
politics, as a soldier's duties, properly fulfilled, took up his
whole time. The disastrous effects of young soldiers disobeying the Emperor were before them. He recalled that
dreadful day, the 15th of May, 1932, when the Premier was
murdered by young naval and military officers. The procurator at the subsequent trial did his duty. He demanded
the death penalty, with the consequence that his own life
was threatened: his family had to be secretly removed to a
place of safety and his house strongly guarded. And behold
the independence of the judiciary! The murderers all
received comparatively light sentences. Much heavier punishments were meted out to certain civilians who on that same
bloody day threw some bombs, which failed to explode, at
the power houses. The attitude of the Services over the 1932
murders was responsible for this greater tragedy they had
just witnessed. Twenty young officers were under arrest. Did
they receive no inspiration from any of higher rank than
themselves?—this was a very important question.

Those accustomed to parliamentary procedure in democratic countries can hardly conceive the high degree of
courage that it needed on the part of Mr. Saito to make this
speech. Though a big man with a hearty manner, General
Terauchi made a poor show of replying. He said that he

thought Mr. Saito's questions were very pertinent, and heartily agreed with him. The army's political views must be expressed only through the Minister for War. The rank and file in the recent trouble must be regarded as innocent: they had obeyed orders and a soldier's first duty was obedience.

Emboldened by Mr. Saito, a less discreet gentleman, Mr. Tsumura, in the House of Peers, had his say in the Upper House. The rank and file, he said, were fine fellows, as ready to die as the Three Human Bombs: he was sorry he could not say as much for the officers: here was one who murdered his superior, was condemned to death, and then appealed against his sentence. Was this *yamato damashii* (the spirit of Japan)?

There was a tremendous uproar. Nobody stood by Mr. Tsumura, who got so alarmed that he apologised abjectly, paid a round of visits, apologising everywhere, and finally resigned his membership of the Upper House, which alone saved him from consequences more dire. Yet it was true; the miserable Aizawa had appealed. But parliamentary privilege could not stand against martial law. Nor could any civil rights be protected. Under martial law the arrested civilians were tried by court-martial, in camera, without benefit of counsel or right of appeal, and sentenced, some to fifteen years and some to life imprisonment; and there is no reason to believe that they had had anything whatever to do with the rising. One arrested civilian, however, appears to have escaped the court-martial, and that was Mr. Kuhara Fusanosuke, a leading member of the Seiyukai, and a man of much wealth, whose arrest was kept secret for a long time. He was supposed to have financed the rising—for large-scale murders, however patriotic, cost money—but the charge fell through and, after some months, he was discharged.

Mr. Hirota's Government had by no means an easy time. It was engaged on a diplomatic offensive against China and an administrative defensive against the army. The army's idea of saving money was to abolish several Ministries; but it was also very insistent on the appointment of a "Minister without Portfolio" to be duly approved by the army, who would act as a sort of Dictator of Policy. The army in November issued 300,000 copies of a pamphlet on armaments, in which it pointed out not only how necessary armaments were for securing the country's safety, but how their manufacture brought prosperity to the whole country.

The basic position was that the army had to maintain its prestige and to find a diversion of the public mind from home discontents. This, of course, was found in China. As much as possible was made of the Russian menace, but the Soviet Government had been so persistently unaggressive that this was a very ineffective bogey. With China it was a different matter. There were so many Japanese there that it was always easy to find cause for complaint. There was, for instance, a Japanese sailor who apparently got killed in a Shanghai brothel; there was a Japanese journalist who, against the orders of his consul, plunged into the midst of a civil disturbance in Szechuan and lost his life; and there was a Japanese drug-seller in Kwangtung killed in some way. These set the whole Press howling against the hostility of all Chinese to Japan, though in Manchuria, after five years' peace and self-government, Japanese soldiers on an average of thirty a month were being killed.

Conversations were always being renewed at Nanking. and it was ominously declared that the price of Japan's friendship was the settlement on her own terms of over two hundred "outstanding issues." The Japanese demands regarding North China were extraordinary: all troops owing obedience to the Nanking Government were to be withdrawn; more Japanese military posts were to be created; the tariff was to be revised in accordance with Japan's wishes; and any official whom Japan found to be anti-Japanese was to be dismissed. Naturally General Chiang Kai-shek found it impossible to accede to such demands; and the *Miyako*, of Tokyo, without realising the admission that it was making, said that Chiang in the last extremity would fight rather than lose his influence in China. The steady increase of that influence had a peculiarly infuriating effect on Japanese critics. His success in getting on good terms with the Canton group was referred to as though it were the acme of treachery. His refusal to allow the Japanese to fight his battles for him against the Communists who had got round to the north was regarded as an outrage.

Then came that rather mysterious incident, the "capture" of Chiang Kai-shek at Sian, when the Japanese suddenly realised that, unaccommodating as he had sometimes been, he was the least hostile of the men at that moment constituting the Government of China. But there was a sense of injury and frustration when his captors apologised and ranged themselves under his banner, and the Communists affirmed that in the present circumstances the unity of China was the most important thing. For some time past there had been an increasing demand from the Japanese side that Japan should assist China in the suppression of the Communists. So long as the Communists were on the south or the west, indeed, the Nanking Government was welcome to go on wasting its resources in fighting them; but when they got round to the north, they might join hands with the Soviet Government, and Japan had all these years been saving the world from the devastating flood of Bolshevism which was conventionally supposed to be about to break over Asia. Without this bogey to invoke, there was no excuse at all for Japan to be pressing forward in North China except that she must have an "outlet."

Such was the position when the regular session of the Diet got to work at the beginning of 1937. The army had made little headway. Their own nominee to the Finance portfolio was a broken reed who was afraid to impose taxes with the necessary boldness; and as for the other reforms, nobody seemed to be willing to abolish ministries; the idea of a ministry for the direction of policy aroused no enthusiasm; the only army project which received any support was the nationalisation of electrical supplies, and the interested capitalists put every obstacle they could think of in the way of that. The two great political parties were more in agreement than they had ever been before, in the face of the common danger of even the semblance of democratic institutions being abolished. Mr. Hamada, a leading Seiyukai member, who had been President of the House, denounced in the strongest terms the condition to which the military dictatorship had reduced the legislative body. Even in the House of Representatives, he said, nobody dared utter a word of criticism of army policies.

General Terauchi, the Minister for War, proceeded to show that while his capacities as a dictator might be superb, his qualities as a statesman were negligible. Again and again he demanded a dissolution of the Diet, and at last he compelled his colleagues to seek imperial sanction for a suspension of the session. He had antagonised the whole Diet with the exception of Adachi's handful, the Kokumin Domei, who desired to shine in a blaze of patriotic splendour. Hardly was the session suspended when the Government resigned: it was simply impossible to work with such a Minister for War. Prince Saionji, of course, was called upon to recommend a new Premier to the Throne, and there seemed to be nothing for it but to have a military Premier. He nominated General Ugaki, whose eminence and services as well as his statesmanlike qualities, entitled him to precedence of all other officers. For four and a half days Ugaki endeavoured to obey the Emperor's command that he should form a Cabinet; but the army was against him. General Count Terauchi, lost to all sense of samurai dignity or soldierly decency, declared that if Ugaki wanted to see him he could call on him, for he was certainly not going to call on Ugaki. This, of course, amounted to a military revolt against the Premier, for no other general dared accept the War Ministry. The quarrel with Ugaki was that he had consented to a reduction in the army during Hamaguchi's premiership, being convinced that the country could not afford to keep up the existing numbers and mechanise as well.

So General Ugaki had to report to the Emperor that the army which pretended to be the fine flower of loyalty, had rejected the imperial nominee.

Saionji's advice was once more in request. This time he chose Hayashi. Nothing could be said against Hayashi's capacity for rising to a patriotic occasion. He had been prominent in the Manchurian coup. He was Commander-in-Chief in Korea in September 1931, and, without waiting for orders of any sort, he railed his troops across the border into Manchuria, an act which fitted in marvellously with the dispositions and actions of the Kwantung Army, and contributed much to the overnight seizure of Manchuria. It was reported on that occasion that the Japanese Foreign Office was astonished; but no astonishment was evinced by the War Office. Nevertheless, though he was so ready for energetic action abroad, he had no taste for homicidal policies at home, as he showed when he dispersed the group headed by General Mazaki. But though General Terauchi had declared that he would have the Diet dissolved as many times as was necessary, he was not prepared to reject as many military Premiers as Saionji cared to nominate. So Hayashi was allowed to form a Cabinet, though it was a matter of sufficient difficulty to make it necessary to swear in Ministers holding two and even three portfolios.

So passed the Hirota Cabinet, brought in by military insubordination and thrust out by military arrogance. It had accomplished one feat—the anti-Comintern pact with Germany, with its implication of moral support in continental activities; but by this very act it wrecked the Fisheries Treaty with Russia, which was very necessary if Japan's mission really was to "keep the peace of the Far East." Unfortunately for peace, General Count Terauchi had to be offered the post of Inspector-General of Military Education when General Sugiyama, who occupied it, was appointed to the War Ministry.

The Diet was summoned, but after a few meetings, at which it appeared nobody was willing to support the new Govern ment, it was dissolved, and a general election ordered for April 30th, 1937.

Meanwhile there was some talk of adopting a less blatant manner. Two commercial missions were arranged, one to Europe and America, and the other to China, and it was also reported that many of the previous demands on China were to be dropped. The impression was created abroad that the army had had a set-back, that civil government was to come to the fore, and that there was to be a "new deal" for China. Mr. Kawagoe, the Ambassador in China, had apparently reported, with approval rather than rancour, that China now was really united and that Chinese nationalism, so long a disappointed aspiration, had become an accomplished fact.

But it was mainly domestic troubles which diverted attention from foreign conquest. Munition-making might minimise unemployment, but it aggravated other ills, and since the beginning of the year prices had gone up with a rush, and there was a record number of industrial strikes. There was also an unprecedentedly unfavourable balance of trade. There was only one party pledged to support the Government—a new and feeble body called the Showakai—and when polling day came, the Hayashi Government found that its pledged supporters had dwindled from 24 to 18. Labour (the Shakai Taishuto, or "Social Mass") increased from 18 to 36. and the two big parties were almost even—the Minseito 179 and the Seiyukai 175. The Government found itself without a single popular measure to propose, and resigned, to be succeeded by Prince Konoe, who, because he belonged to an ancient and aristocratic but non-military family, was supposed to be modernly liberal in outlook, which got the new Cabinet a good Press at home and abroad. The new Government did not represent the Diet any more than the old one had done—perhaps less, as it was remarked that it included fewer party men. Indeed, Prince Konoe appealed to the Representatives to put the State above party, and especially not to let party disputes intrude into foreign affairs—but these were old slogans, and since the 1932 murders the activities of the parties had been confined to demanding a restoration of constitutional government, without getting it.

Dr. Baba, who had failed badly as Finance Minister, became Home Minister in the new Cabinet, and the militarists wanted him to be chairman of a Planning Committee—an attempt to realise the "Corporate State"—but this proposal was so unwelcome that Dr. Baba resigned, the "strong" Admiral Suetsugu taking his place—a nomination to which the militarists could raise no reasonable objection.

The endeavour to come to amicable terms with China was little affected—if, indeed, such an endeavour was being made, which was sometimes very difficult to believe. Some of the diplomatists may have personally desired such an agreement, but they were so subservient to the army, which was seeking excuses for an attack on China, that they persisted in putting forward conditions which the Nanking Government could not accept, especially in regard to jurisdiction in North China. So much was said later about China's insensate hostility that it is necessary to look back on the contemporary evidence which is conveniently forgotten. In June 1937 Admiral Takahashi, a Japanese War Councillor, returning from a tour of the Yangtse valley, spoke of his surprise at the great unification and constructive growth that he had witnessed. The "New Life" movement was making great headway; finance and defence showed a new strength; there was a social purification and a revival of the Confucian spirit. He laid special emphasis on the fact that he could detect no traces of anti-Japonism, though there was a growing resistance to Japan's penetration, and he said that the two things must be clearly distinguished. There was no evidence of a boycott anywhere, he concluded. At the same time as Admiral Takahashi returned, Mr. Munakata, a high official of the Bank of Japan, also came back from a Chinese tour. He declared that Japan must revise her

ideas of China. World conditions had improved, and, thanks
to her currency reform, China's economic outlook was now
much brighter. There was a spirit of hope and enthusiasm, and
the Chinese Government and public would welcome Japan's
help in economic reconstruction; Chinese business men and
bankers were in favour of economic co-operation with Japan.

Unfortunately, when concrete plans were discussed, the
Japanese wanted entire direction of every co-operative project, and could not bring themselves to negotiate with the
Chinese on equal terms. Moreover, the increasing economic
pressure in Japan made it necessary for the Japanese, in any
economic deal, to have a large profit and a quick one. Japan
had been carefully feeling the diplomatic pulse. She had
already suppressed all foreign interests in Manchukuo and
declined to pay damages for wrongs done there; early in
1937 she cancelled all the remaining "perpetual leases"
in Japan without compensation. British subjects were the
chief losers, but the British Government made no protest,
and the other Governments whose nationals were concerned
also remained silent.

In a country like China, overrun with many thousands of
Japanese, often of the "toughest" kind, there are always
incidents when they are required; but though the Japanese
Press may shout for vengeance, the military men choose their
own time and manufacture the necessary incident. Perhaps
sometimes the men on the spot rush their superiors a little,
but that may be only an illusion created by the pretence of
making a settlement. In this case the Japanese troops in the
north furnished the excuse. On July 7th, outside a town not
far from Peiping they indulged in some "night manœuvres"
of so realistic a character that a Chinese military post thought
an attack was in full career, and fired a few rifles. In the
skirmish that followed a couple of Japanese were killed and
at least ten times as many Chinese.

Had the Japanese had any wish for peace, an amicable
settlement could have been come to the next day; but
instead of that they tackled General Sung Che-yuan, who

was commander of the 29th Army and Chairman of the Hopei-Chahar Political Council. In the latter capacity he had been continually urged to declare his independence of Nanking, but this he steadfastly refused to do; now as commander of the 29th Army, he was ordered to send that force away from Peiping. After a slight show of resistance it withdrew, and on August 8th, the Japanese occupied the ancient capital. The Japanese army loudly announced its intention of effecting a local settlement, so that hostilities should not extend; but this was simply a denial of the authority of the Central Government, and an attempt to separate North China by force after other methods had failed.

Throughout the negotiations with Nanking, it had been constantly urged that in North China there must be no troops owing obedience to Nanking; this pressure only consolidated China; and the more consolidated China became under the direction of General Chiang Kai-shek, the more bitterly was the generalissimo assailed by the Japanese army and its satellites. With a speed that indicated full preparation, Japanese troops were hurried into North China, and, by way of creating terror, bombs were dropped into the thickly populated Chinese quarter of Tientsin.

Chinese troops were already on their way to the north, so it was decided to make an attack on the capital, though that was far inland. A couple of Japanese were sent to "take" the aerodrome at Hungjao, a piece of audacity which, a few years before, might have been successful. They were shot by the Chinese sentry, which was equally satisfactory, because it furnished an excuse for operations which had hitherto been entirely lacking. Such action, however, had to be taken at once or not at all, since an army cannot be dispatched with no better excuse than the shooting of a trespasser. But the Japanese navy was in a state of greater readiness than it had been in 1932. It had a special source of strength in the large fortified barracks, built in defiance of all treaty limitations, at Hongkew Park, at the north end of Shanghai. As in 1932, therefore, it launched its attack, and waited for the Japanese army to come to the rescue. This it did with the expected promptitude.

Thus far the 1931-2 programme had been followed—the attack in the north followed by a large-scale diversion at Shanghai in order to prevent an effective dispute of the hastily-snatched victory. But conditions had greatly changed: in 1932 Chiang Kai-shek was so uncertain of his own position that he could not effectively succour the valiant 19th Route Army, which had defended the marshes north and west of Shanghai so desperately. Now he had an ample supply of men who displayed the most desperate valour. Far inferior still to the Japanese in mechanisation, they set an example to which history could offer few parallels in the devotion with which they sacrificed their lives to hold up and even beat back troops with infinitely superior equipment. In 1932 there was hardly a plane to meet the Japanese bombers, but in 1937-8 the Chinese, though still far inferior, put up many a good air battle.

General Matsui, one of the leading chauvinists in the army, whom General Hayashi had tried to sidetrack, flew over to take command in the north, and later proceeded to Shanghai, which became the most important centre of the campaign. The liberal and pacific Premier, Prince Konoe, became the obedient echo of the army, and promised to "beat China to her knees." To double the taxes and raise the people to a high pitch of patriotic enthusiasm and an unquestioning belief in the righteousness of their cause, was an easy matter, all policy having been directed to this end for years past.

Before even Shanghai was taken, the Japanese bombed Nanking and Canton, besides many other places, and blockaded the whole coast to Canton—and beyond. The bombing was pure terrorism, but the Japanese, rather than confess that their frightful methods had failed to terrorise, declared that they were such bad marksmen that, aiming at arsenals, they had only hit dwelling-houses.

Perhaps nothing was more revealing of the Japanese objectives than the triumphal march through the International Settlement at Shanghai which they staged after the Chinese troops had been compelled to withdraw at the end of September. Its object was twofold—to demonstrate to the Chinese the contempt in which they held the Powers, against whose wishes they made this display, and to provoke such disturbances as would provide a plausible reason for putting the whole city under martial law.

The Chinese resistance after they had been driven out of Shanghai was much weaker, which was to be expected in view of the terrible losses suffered. The Japanese pushed on, committing much unnecessary destruction at Soochow, and captured Nanking, the Government retiring into the interior, but never losing its effective organisation. The Japanese excesses in Nanking were horrible, but calculated. Men under discipline must have a little relaxation now and then.

In the north, conquests were easier and movements much more rapid than in the Yangtse region; but though conquests seemed easy at the beginning, it was by no means easy to hold captured railways when guerrilla bands were constantly attacking, and movement slowed down. The vital lines in China are those from Peiping via Tientsin and Nanking to Shanghai, and from Peiping to Hankow. There is an important chord line from Hsuchow to Kaifeng. The recently completed line from Hankow to Canton makes it possible to travel from Canton to Paris by rail. Before Japan can claim to hold China she must have undisputed control of all these lines, and at the end of eight months' fighting on an unprecedented scale she was far from having that.

When the Chinese Government retreated from Nanking, the Japanese army announced that it would not in future deal with General Chiang Kai-shek; but this did not shake the country's loyalty to him—and that is the most surprising of all the phenomena in modern China. But though armies march and countermarch, destroy and devastate, the people must go on as best they can. Over large areas of China the spring-time sowing of 1938 must be impossible, and in the next twelve months there may be famine on a scale that even Asia has never seen before; but where communal life exists, civilised people will organise it. In her own defence Japan has set up puppet governments in Peiping and Nanking—without as yet setting bounds to their jurisdiction. The men composing these may not be utterly the creatures of Japan, and if not, they will become less and less so. It is possible that Japan's megalomania contemplates the formation of a federation of States like Manchukuo, all overrun with Japanese officials and all utterly subservient to Japan. There are demands already for Shinto shrines, such as have become the symbol of Japanese conquest in Korea, Formosa, Manchukuo, Shantung, and Shanghai. Shinto zealots have declared that the kingdom of the Sun Goddess covers the whole earth.

In Japan itself, a hard working and hard faring populace may not always find its heart uplifted by such a consummation, even if we presume that it will come about. The Chinese are by no means hopeless of being able to resist until an exasperated Japan pulls down its false gods. The country is not yet completely submissive, though it has little freedom left. The Shakai Taishuto, which scored so heavily in the elections of April 30, 1937, passed a vote of thanks to the army at its general meeting in December of the same year, and solemnly abjured class consciousness for "nation consciousness." The Diet in its 1938 session was tame and passed practically all the Bills set before it; but the army did not have its way completely either over the plans for economic mobilisation or the militarisation of all electrical supplies. A significant army order was one that, after six months of war, forbade assemblies at railway stations when the troop trains left, whereas up to that time it had been a sacred duty to see the heroes off.

For many years past the army has been building up its plans for the conquest of China. The dissensions in Europe have created the opportunity; but China, which formerly knew nothing of nationalism because· it knew of nothing except its own civilisation, has become a nation—late in the day but perhaps not too late to preserve its existence. Japan has tried to destroy the culture from which she drew her own civilisation. If China resists to the end, the universities and colleges that the invader has destroyed will rise again, but the world will regret the passing of a great civilisation that cared more for the gracious arts of life than for the tarnished glories of conquest.

NOTES

Page 13.—Mr. Eugene Chen (Chen Yu-jen) was born in Trinidad, and was master of a very forcible English style, though, on the other hand, he suffered from the lack of a sound Chinese education. He attracted a good deal of attention about 1913 as Editor of the *Peking Gazette*, and afterwards as a member of Dr. Sun Yat-sen's Government in Canton. In 1927 the Canton group formed a separate Government in Canton, having broken with the Nanking Government, and in 1931, when feeling was very tense over General Chiang Kai-shek's denunciations of Japanese doings in China, Chen, on behalf of the Canton group, visited Japan, where he stayed from July 22nd till August 14th, nominally on a sightseeing tour, but the newspaper reporters described him as denouncing Chiang Kai-shek bitterly. Their great leader, the late Dr. Sun Yat-sen, he said, had declared that China could only hope to prosper if she were on friendly terms with Japan, and Chiang was disobeying those injunctions. He afterwards had interviews with Baron Shidehara and the military leaders. So far as can be gathered, he proposed that if Japan would recognise the Cantonese Government as the Government of China, he was prepared to offer, in his capacity as Foreign Minister, advantageous terms for the settlement of the Manchurian difficulty. It was a strange reversal of the position when Dr. Sun Yat-sen's Japanese visitors assured him that his Canton Government would be recognised if he made a statement that he did not consider Manchuria and Mongolia integral parts of China. Baron Shidehara reminded Mr. Chen that it was Japan's accepted doctrine that Manchuria was an integral part of China, to which Mr. Chen readily assented, but proposed that, instead of continuing to allow Manchuria to be garrisoned with troops which were liable to come into collision with the Japanese, and which, while consuming the taxpayer's money, did not ensure entire immunity from bandit outrages, it would be better if Manchuria were entirely demilitarised, and the policing of the whole region left in the care of the Japanese, always with the proviso that China's sovereignty was unimpaired.

Apparently this proposal appealed strongly to Baron Shidehara, but he was not prepared to interfere so drastically in the affairs of China as to denounce the Nanking Government and recognise the Canton group in its place. In the troubled days that followed he said on more than one occasion that if it were possible to treat with a body like the Canton Government, or if the Canton Government could only amalgamate with that of Nanking, he thought there would be no great difficulty in arriving at a satisfactory settlement. With the military leaders Mr. Chen made no progress. They did not like the Cantonese and preferred to make their own arrangements about Manchuria. When at length an amalgamation was contrived, Mr. Eugene Chen was left out and General Chiang Kai-shek left in—but by that time the Japanese military party had had their way in Manchuria.

Page 16.—Michael Borodin arrived in Canton in October 1923 with a letter of introduction to Dr. Sun Yat-sen from Karahan, Soviet Ambassador in Peking (shot as a Trotskyist in December 1937). He was highly esteemed by Dr. Sun as an adviser on revolutionary method and on political organisation generally, and he was an inspiring force to the Chinese Communists and even to the non-Communist members of the Kuomintang. There was also in Canton a Soviet emissary, M. N. Roy, a headlong person of less reliable judgment than Borodin. On the strength of Roy's reports Stalin telegraphed on June 1, 1927, instructing Borodin to form a Communist army and adopt a more militant policy. Borodin, realising that this would mean an immediate and fatal break with the Kuomintang, was unwilling to make the contents of the telegram known, but Roy disclosed them. The majority of the Chinese Communists, who agreed with Borodin on the necessity of maintaining friendship and co-operation with the Kuomintang, drove Roy back to Russia. On July 15th, the Kuomintang adopted a resolution to expel the Communists, and Borodin thereupon resigned and returned to Russia. He received thereafter a much less conspicuous official appointment in the Caucasus. The Communist purge proved to be a very bloody affair, and plunged China into civil war for nearly ten years.

Pages 29, 67, 84.—Chientao, called Kanto by the Japanese, a hilly region across the border from North-west Korea, settled chiefly by Koreans, but definitely demarcated as Chinese territory in a treaty concluded in 1909. Its Korean population was greatly increased when Japan annexed Korea, and, when propagandists used to refer to the two million Japanese subjects in Manchuria who needed protection, seven-eighths of the number consisted of these emigrants. Naturally it was always a stronghold of bitterly hostile Koreans. The Japanese established con-

sulates there and did more policing than the Chinese. In 1920
they invaded the place without a by-your-leave in order to
"punish anti-Japanese Koreans," burnt churches and houses,
and killed many Koreans. There was some desperate work
there at the beginning of the "Manchurian affair" in 1931, of
which no account has ever appeared in print. And there were
monstrous mass trials of Kanto Communists which dragged on
in camera in Seoul for long after. Yet for the English reader
Chientao is a place for a pious pilgrimage—at least in fancy.
Stella Benson once lived there. The climate nearly killed her,
but she wrote a beautiful book about it—*Tobit Transplanted.*

Page 40.—Chang Tsung-chang was a thoroughly bad type of
warlord. He was a cruel oppressor, and his exactions drove many
of his suffering subjects to Manchuria in the years before
the "independence." The Japanese found it to their interest to
keep him in power in Shantung, and provided him with a
Japanese concubine, with the usual result. He was as pusil-
lanimous as he was gigantic, and always avoided a fight. He was
also a great boaster and declared that the Japanese had offered
to make him Emperor of Manchuria. When things were uncomfortable in China he used to pay a visit to Japan; but after the
creation of Manchukuo the Japanese seemed to have no further
use for him. Then he was reported as saying that if China had
ten years' peace he would undertake the reconquest of Manchuria. Perhaps a thought so dangerous was remembered against
him. He was assassinated at Tsinan station on September 3,
1932. Japanese reports said that the murder was committed at
the instance of the Young Marshal.

Page 96.—"The Soong Dynasty." Perhaps the phrase was
invented in Japan, where "dynasty" for anything Chinese was
almost a term of vituperation. The father and son who succes-
sively ruled in Mukden were spoken of as the "Chang Dynasty."
The "Soong family" would be a more appropriate term. The
three very talented and charming daughters of a mother as
remarkable as themselves married respectively Dr. Sun Yat-sen,
Mr. H. H. Kung, and General Chiang Kai-shek. Messrs. Kung
and Chiang, along with a son of Mrs. Soong, were the
mainstay and the brains of the Kuomintang Government. T. V.
Soong was probably the best Finance Minister China ever had,
and his three sisters had an immense influence for good in the
New China which they were building up but which Japan
determined to destroy.

Page 97.—In the endeavour to shape a policy, or at least to find moral support, Baron Wakatsuki, the Premier, in the early days of October 1931, paid a round of calls on Prince Saionji, Admiral Count Yamamoto, Count Kiyoura, and Mr. Takahashi. These were the four men living who had held the office of Premier, and Wakatsuki's consultations with them were interesting for this reason: When Prince Saionji laid down the reins of office for the last time in 1912, he received an Imperial Command to be ready to serve the Throne at all times. This was regarded as placing him among the Genro, or Elder Statesmen, whose few survivors were well stricken in years. When, four years later, Marquis Okuma received a similar command, it was suggested that the Genro as an institution was to be kept in being by the appointment of men who had been twice Premier. But Okuma had always spoken scornfully of the Elder Statesmen, and never attended their councils—if he was ever invited. Admiral Yamamoto's second brief and inglorious essay in premiership was followed by no such marked acknowledgment from the Throne. As for Count Kiyoura, though a man of great prestige and formerly President of the Privy Council, he had been Premier only once, briefly and unsuccessfully. Takahashi had been Premier once, taking the place of the murdered Hara in 1921. The idea of a Council composed of former premiers was no more talked of after Okuma refused to take his place among them, but Wakatsuki's round of visits suggests that to be Premier is recognised as giving some lifelong authority. One important duty of the Elder Statesmen was to advise the Throne on the choice of a Premier. Saionji, at the age of eighty-eight, still (1938) has this final word, but of late years there has been a confabulation between other elders—the President of the Privy Council, the Minister of the Imperial Household, the Keeper of the Privy Seal, etc. When in 1913 Prince Katsura, a very masterful soldier, became Keeper of the Privy Seal, it was regarded almost as a revival of the Shogunate, but he died very soon after; and though another soldier, Marshal Prince Yamagata (one of the Genro), was the real ruler of Japan till his death in 1922, he sought no office to reinforce his authority.

Page 105.—General Chang Ching-huei, though he seemed to be very disappointing at first, later became Premier of Manchukuo—a position in which lack of military qualities and initiative was a recommendation rather than a bar.

Pages 105 and 167.—"There is no South Manchuria Railway

'zone' in the sense that any international document has used the term to apply to an area specifically delimited by mutual agreement between China and Japan. Not only is the area of the South Manchuria Railway's lands not delimited by agreement, but it is constantly, though slowly, expanding in size, a procedure which is entirely in accord with the original 1896 railway contract, taken over by Japan, which provided that lands might be progressively added for the use of the railway. . . . Although the term 'railway zone' is used almost invariably by Japanese writers to refer to the South Manchuria Railway's lands, and very frequently by Chinese and foreign writers, it is, in fact, a misnomer. Its use creates a presumption of a well-defined area, limited to a uniform width on either side of the railway itself, a presumption which is entirely contrary to fact." (C. Walter Young, *Japanese Jurisdiction in the South Manchuria Railway Areas*, Johns Hopkins Press, p. 140.) The zone in some places included whole towns. It was the area, generally speaking, in which the Chinese found it more convenient to permit Japanese pretensions than to prevent them.

Page 116.—When Inukai was murdered by a gang comprising both military and naval officers, it is much more likely that they were signifying their objections to his advocacy of civilian Defence Ministers than their dislike of party corruption, Inukai being one of the least corrupt of men; but the plea of stamping out corruption was generally accepted as genuine. W. H. Chamberlin, in *Japan Over Asia*, suggests that the closeness of his connection with Toyama saves Mr. Hirota from being on the murder list. It did not save Inukai, but on the other hand, Inukai was not, like Hirota, a protégé of the Ronin leader. There was a good deal of prejudice in the Services against the great firms, and the "party corruption" plea was partly founded on the fact that their patronage of politics tended to increase and to be not merely partisan. A Seiyukai Government was at one time known alternatively as a Mitsui Government and a Minseito Government as a Mitsubishi Government; but the firms often found their interests identical, and both of them contributed liberally to both parties in order to get a suitable iron and steel policy adopted. Because there was some military dislike of the big firms, it was often assumed by writers on Japan that they were as much devoted to peace as the army was to war, but there is no reason to believe this, for they never made such huge profits as when Japan was "keeping the peace" by making war.

Page 118.—Notable murders in the previous reign: the most notable was that of Hara Takashi in November 1921, by a minor railway employee who sought heroism. He was liberated from prison early in Showa and was lionised by the Press. Well satisfied with his achievement, he announced his intention of becoming a Buddhist priest. Mr. Yasuda, a great banker, reputed to be Japan's richest man, was stabbed by a "ronin," who committed suicide. The murderer's funeral was attended by a great concourse—or rather two great concourses—one of political bullies and ruffians, and the other of class-conscious labour, the latter well pleased that a man who had a reputation for merciless hardness had met his end. In 1913 there was the murder of Mr. Abe, who had much to do in the direction of China policy. The murderer, to signify his opinion of the weakness of that policy, spread a map of China on the floor, sat on it, and disembowelled himself. Then there was Captain Amakasu, who, shortly after the great earthquake of 1923, murdered Osugi, Japan's leading Socialist, his wife, and adopted child. As soon as the conquest of Manchuria began he was appointed head of a special police force. In 1920 a lawyer, Yonemura, shot a Socialist dead without provocation, and was let off scot-free, as he was President of the Anti-Bolshevik Society. All these murders being quite "disinterested" (like that of Thomas à Becket in Mr. Eliot's *Murder in the Cathedral*) were greatly admired.

Page 119.—When untoward things happened to the Japanese exchange it was the regular thing to blame the foreign exchange banks or the "Shanghai brokers." At the time when Japan went off gold there was a campaign in the Press against the National City Bank of New York, which lodged a formal protest against the Japanese newspaper inventions regarding its gold manipulations.

Page 120.—In describing Baron Dan's murder as unique Mr. Inukai was not quite accurate. As mentioned in the note to page 118, Mr. Yasuda Zenjiro, a banker who had nothing to do with politics, was murdered on September 28, 1921, by a Rightist. Inukai's remark about the dangerousness of Rightists, however, derived point from an incident of the previous day which the Press was apparently too timid to report. Dr. Nitobe, one of Japan's greatest scholars, was known throughout the world as the author of *Bushido*—he was almost its inventor. A member of the Society of Friends, he spent a large part of his life as an apologist for Japan, especially for her militarists; but his religious associations prevented his propaganda from being entirely divorced from the truth, and he had lately remarked that in certain circumstances militarists could be as dangerous as radicals. For this he was dragged out of a sick-bed by a group of officers and taken to a hall filled with ex-service men, before whom he was made to apologise. He tried to qualify his apology and was forced to repeat it humbly in writing without qualification. Not long after, Nitobe fled to America, at the instance, it was said, of General Araki, the Minister for War, who told him that his work had always been to set Japan in a favourable light before the world, and that just now Japan needed this help. It did indeed. Nitobe's was a tragic tour. He had, when Congress passed the Immigration Bill excluding Japanese, declared that he would never visit America again; and now he pitifully toured the country, justifying to sceptical audiences the doings of the Japanese army. He died the following year in Canada, defending to the last what the Quaker side of his soul knew to be indefensible. Nitobe's strong line was the untruthfulness of the Chinese. Even the missionaries in China he found untruthful—so different from the missionaries in Japan. One of the latter wrote for the *Christian Century* an article so favourable to Japan's Manchurian policy that it was reprinted in the Japanese semi-official papers. He mentioned therein, by way of showing how vital Manchuria was to Japan, that Japan imported much of her rice from this region. The reverent writer did not, of course, intend to be as untruthful as a China missionary. He had heard so much of the "lifeline" that he took it for granted, not knowing that Japan imports no rice whatever from Manchuria, but exports much food thither. A month later it was stated that Japan was threatened with a bumper rice crop, and that the Government must take steps to keep up the price, so as to avert the ruin of the farmers.

Page 129.—The best account of Yoshida Shoin for English readers is "Yoshida Torajiro," in R. L. Stevenson's *Familiar Studies of Men and Books*: His name is still a very famous one in Japan.

Page 130.—Whether the Aikyojuku or its home town Mito really deserves credit for all these outrages is not a point on which the present writer insists. The police in Japan have a habit of crossing undetected crimes off the list when a later culprit is vain enough to boast of them or foolish enough to be cajoled into confessing them. A burglar or murderer will often confess to a long series of undetected crimes, and these are "taken into consideration," but not quite in the English sense.

Page 136.—As an example of how little the Japanese parliament was regarded by the Services, it is interesting to note that when Admiral Shiosawa told the *Asahi* representative that he was going to take reprisals in three or four days, the Minseito party, which had supported Baron Shidehara's peaceful policy, still had a large majority in the Lower House. The Diet was, in fact, dissolved the next day, in order that a Seiyukai majority might be elected to support a strong policy. Mr. Yoshizawa, the new Foreign Minister, had by that time already been in Tokyo for a week, his first task having been to reply to Mr. Stimson's Note from Washington, pointing out that Japan was recklessly violating the treaties. Mr. Yoshizawa argued that the treaties had assumed that China was a stable entity, and had not contemplated the internal disorders which modified the obligations that Japan had entered into. The Chinese retorted that he might just as well have pointed out that the High Contracting Parties had not contemplated the impotence of the Japanese Government when the General Staff took a hand. The murder, four months later, of the Premier, Mr. Yoshizawa's father-in-law, pointed to disorders in Japan which the signatories to the treaties had not contemplated.

Page 141.—The Japanese retreat was only a slight withdrawal, and undertaken too readily to be very costly—which, perhaps, is why it inspired the tragic farce of the "three human bombs." But it had a tragic sequel. Major Kuga, badly wounded, was deserted by his men, but when found next day by the advancing Chinese, was still alive. They took him to their lines, whence he was sent to Nanking and carefully nursed in the Chinese hospital. By March 15th he had recovered sufficiently to leave hospital, and the Chinese handed him over to the Japanese authorities. He returned immediately to Shanghai and reported for duty. The duty that he was assigned was to go to the place where the Chinese picked him up, and blow out his brains. (Later versions, to make it more romantic, say that he committed *hara-kiri*.) An orderly went with him to see that he killed himself. He was sacrificed to the tradition that Japanese officers are never taken prisoner. Suicide rather than capture has its logical reason in the tradition of the torture and enslavement of captives. The Chinese by the humane treatment of prisoners (for Major Kuga was not the only one) showed that they had reached a point of

NOTES 309

civilisation where the custom would be better honoured in the breach than in the observance. It was singular that suicide remained an obligation for the Japanese major, and suggests some reflections on comparative mental advance.

Page 142.—Most energetic protests were made to the United States Government against allowing its citizens to fly for the Chinese. The Japanese have some claim to be pioneers in bombing from the air: they used this means of breaking the spirit of the Formosan aborigines before the Great War; and they bombed Chinchow in 1931 and Hangchow as well as Shanghai in 1932. But a weapon which they were eager to use they greatly dreaded. Then and in 1937 they were very fearful of foreign airmen helping the Chinese. Japan's one contribution to the naval disarmament proposals was one for the total abolition of aircraft carriers.

Page 142.—Mr. Matsuoka Yosuke went to America at an early age and studied there. Later he was in the consular service, stationed at Shanghai. His conspicuous energy and masterfulness gained him an appointment as Vice-President of the South Manchuria Railway, and when the conference of the Institute of Pacific Relations met at Kyoto in 1929, his ability made a great impression on the foreign delegates, though even he was unable to answer to their satisfaction two insistent questions, "Who killed Chang Tso-lin?" and "What are you doing in Manchuria?" Officers and diplomats at Shanghai, their sensitiveness blunted by Far Eastern experience, found him less impressive. Later he went to Geneva on the hopeless mission of persuading the Assembly of the justice of Japan's cause. Eventually he became President of the South Manchuria Railway, when its functions and authority were enormously enlarged.

Page 143.—The anxiety of the Japanese semi-official news agency in Shanghai to see a decision reached in every offensive led to some strange reporting. It reported the "fiercest fighting yet" on February 17th; on the 21st the general attack excelled everything; on the 24th "the sternest battle since the beginning" was reported; on the 29th, "after the comparative silence of the past two weeks," there was a terrific attack on Chapei; and again on March 1st and 2nd the fighting was "fiercer than at any previous time." That there was a crescendo in the Japanese effort was true, and the necessity of reducing previous "terrific battles" to a "comparative silence" is a measure of the disappointment caused by the repeated failure to break down the Chinese resistance.

Page 148.—We have been dosed *ad nauseam* with Japanese loyalty—the most advertised of all human virtues. It appears in history to have been mainly for retainers, and was rare among feudal lords. In Japan's civil wars there was a constant changing of sides, and some families tried to be on both sides at once in order to save the estates, however the fortune of war might go: perhaps this was loyalty to the family.

Page 148.—Captain Amakasu is referred to in the Note on page 118. More about him may be read in the author's *Japan under Taisho Tenno*, pp. 300—301. When the author was editing the *Japan Chronicle*, Kobe, he was reproved by the police for recalling Amakasu's exploits in murder when recording the Captain's appointment to a special pacification force in Manchuria.

Page 149.—The reader unfamiliar with Japanese literature may not recognise the literary touch in the description of General Ma Chan-shan's military apparel. Heroic chronicles, such as the *Heike Monogatari*, habitually describe minutely the armour and accoutrements of a gentleman about to engage in battle.

Page 156.—Manchurian and other Northern Chinese troops had often been singularly disappointing to the lover of battle, for, when the stage was set for a conflict, they always seemed to walk off. But when they had a real cause to fight for, such as the Japanese provided, they often did very well; and an army would follow its general with extraordinary fidelity.

Page 161.—We have a glimpse of General Tang Yu-lin in Sven Hedin's *Jehol*. He entertained the Swedish explorer's party when they went there to get the measurements of the temple of which Mr. Victor Bendix had a replica made for the Chicago exhibition. It was true that there was a good deal of poppy-growing in the province—and this, though the Japanese raged against it, was one of their chief objectives. They organised the drug trade efficiently and used it for demoralising the whole of North China.

Page 162.—In an article "The Phantom of Mengkukuo," in *Pacific Affairs* for December 1937, Mr. Owen Lattimore describes how the Japanese, if they had really been concerned for Mongol liberty, could have helped the Mongols to achieve it, but have earned their hostility instead. The Mongols of Manchuria and Inner Mongolia have apparently come to the conclusion that if they have got to suffer liberation, it is better to suffer it at the hands of Soviet Russia rather than at those of Japan.

Page 163.—In the war on China which Japan began in July 1937 there were many complaints of violations of Chinese women such as belong to the most savage traditions of war. Comparatively few such complaints were heard in the Manchurian campaign. Indeed, there was little serious fighting. There were Japanese already in all the towns, and more flocked in as soon as the Japanese troops occupied them. The pimps and panders saw to it that plenty of women were supplied to Manchuria, and the exploit of getting women to Jehol the day after its capture had been paralleled many times in Manchuria. Major Usuda, of the Kwantung Army, was reported as remarking on the rapidity with which prosperity had followed the capture of Hailar. Speaking early in February 1933, he said that the Japanese colony in that town now numbered three hundred, including eighty prostitutes, and that it was evidently destined to become one of the foremost cities of Manchukuo. Similar statistics were published of several townships. The Bascom Johnson report to the League of Nations on the traffic in women in the Far East, which was published about this time, said that the trade in women was generally to provide for men of their own nationality in foreign parts; and these reports may be taken as endorsements of this conclusion. But the manner in which the reports appeared in the Japanese newspapers often conveyed the impression that procuring was regarded as an enterprise that was as vigorous and praiseworthy as that of "preserving the peace of the Far East." The only part of the Bascom Johnson report dealing specifically with Manchuria was that where it said that in most of the villages in Manchukuo were to be found a Russian woman or two living in a state of most shocking degradation and misery. Had something been done by the new régime to remedy this, it might, at small cost, have gained many friends. But it can hardly be made the subject of reproach that nothing was done, for Japan could not be expected to be more considerate in such a matter than the Western Powers who had been concerned in the intervention in Russia, and who, when that reactionary effort failed, left the people who had trusted in them naked to their enemies. There was no tradition in Japan that women should be protected, and nothing was done to remedy the many complaints that girls were hired to go to Manchuria to serve in department stores or hotels, and that when they arrived there they were treated "no better than geisha"—which was a delicate way of saying that their life was one of prostitution.

Page 166.—The Japanese always seems to be surprised when anything published in their own language comes to be known abroad. They are fully conscious of the difficulty of Japanese and always ready to deny that a statement has been published at all or that it has been correctly translated. Quite commonly officials assure foreigners that no translation in an English paper in Japan can be trusted, whereas the fact is, of course, that even an imperfect translation is better to be trusted than any official assurance.

Page 169.—The author was in Peking in May 1933 and witnessed this remarkable restraint of the Chinese troops in the face of grave provocation; Chinese friends who had soldiers quartered in their houses testified to their excellent behaviour. When the Japanese planes were flying overhead, there were exclamations of anger and contempt but none of fear.

Page 179.—In view of the fact that Japan's aggression on the mainland is constantly excused by her need for food for her excessive population, it is well to remember that a big rice crop is hailed as a national disaster; also that in January 1938 the Finance Minister, discussing Japan's ability to fight a long war in China, said that Japan was self-supplying in food.

Page 183.—In the Occident it might sound almost Sunday-schoolish to say that there was no danger except dangerous thought. In a country where patriotic assassination is so much esteemed it was almost an invitation to murder anybody who talked financial sense. Baron Go, however, was not to be deterred by Araki's fireworks. In January 1938, at a much more serious crisis, he again protested against the imposition of heavy taxes to pay for the crushing of China. Fortunately for Japan there is more courage in civilian ranks than in those of the army.

Page 190.—Nichiren was a heretical Buddhist priest in the thirteenth century who made himself so objectionable to the authorities that he was exiled to the remote island of Sado. The sect he founded continued to flourish, and is famous for its fanaticism and love of noise. They were Nichiren priests who started the trouble in Shanghai in 1932. They are very patriotic in these days, as the example of Inoue Nissho shows, and Nichiren was solemnly canonised in 1923 with the name of Rissho Daishi. A few years later a young professor who drew a comparison between Rissho Daishi and the late Prince Kropotkin, exiled from Tsarist Russia for his liberality of thought, got into serious trouble, though actually the comparison was unduly flattering to Nichiren.

Page 190.—Some great monarchs, notably Akbar, have tried to arrange things so that the humblest of their subjects might be at liberty to appeal to them. For the very different view taken in Japan the reader may be referred to Lord Redesdale's *Tales of Old Japan*, where it is related how, in the first half of the seventeenth century, a farmer, Sakura Sogoro, his wife, and three sons (two of them children) were crucified because Sakura had thrust into the Shogun's palanquin a petition against a rapacious landlord. The severity was dictated, of course, by tyrants' fears of assassination.

Page 191.—Early in 1923, in the case of a foreigner who was charged with a criminal offence, the *Osaka Mainichi* mobilised all the anti-foreign sentiment that it could foment, with the result that the police, the procurators, and the court were deluged with letters demanding condign punishment, and it published accounts of the progress of this inundation and speculations on its probable effects. It is impossible that the judges should be impervious to this mass suggestion. Justice was vindicated in the Court of Appeal, where the late Dr. J. E. de Becker, whose great services to Japanese law have never been adequately acknowledged, obtained special permission to cross-examine, proved that the charges were false, and secured an acquittal. Such vindications are very rare.

Page 196.—Bedbugs are rare in Japan, but the police-court cells are infamous for them—and for filth in other forms. They are the subject of bitter complaint by all who claim to have been unjustly consigned to the lock-up. Bugs are called Chinese insects by the Japanese. It is a strange coincidence that the police methods are notoriously pervaded by the old Chinese tradition and that the police cells have almost a monopoly of bugs.

Page 205.—It was the intellectual renaissance in Korea

springing out of a sudden realisation that the Christian missions were revealing a new world to their pupils that led to the conversion of suzerainty into annexation, just as it was the realization of a national unity in China that led to Japan in 1937 deciding to "beat China to her knees" as the Premier, Prince Konoe, elegantly put it. Every sign of progress in Siam is watched with a sinister solicitude. Progress in the Far East, except under Japanese direction, is regarded as inimical to Japan.

Page 218.—This cotton play of Mr. Muto's has several points of historic as well as literary interest which seemed to justify its rather lengthy appearance in this book. Shimadzu Saburo was the Daimyo whose followers, four years later than the scene in the play, murdered an Englishman, Richardson, just outside Yokohama. The attack on Richardson and his three friends (one of them a woman) was totally unprovoked Shimadzu did nothing to stop it, and refused to regard it as a matter worthy of his notice. This led to the bombardment of Kagoshima to enforce payment of compensation. The American Minister of the time, Pruyn, who depended on gossip and surmise for his information, sent a very untruthful account of the matter to Washington, which has been repeated by a hundred American writers since as history. It is agreeable to find the Daimyo who defied his own as well as the British Government and showed so little regard for humanity, figuring on the stage as so enlightened a person. It is of-interest to note that, when Mr. Muto was putting into Shimadzu's mouth the sentiments about manufacture being as patriotic as the military arts, Mr. Tsunata Yano, President of the First Mutual Life Office, Tokyo, said that the Japanese victory at Shanghai was won by superior arms, which were the product of industry. Industry, he went on, had as great a share in saving nations as soldiers had, and at the same time brought wealth instead of crushing the nation as the army did. So obvious a deduction from patent facts caused great offence, and some of the military men declared that they were going to take action. But Mr. Tsunata was apparently left unmurdered. In regard to Shimadzu's remark about the shortage of supplies of raw cotton, it is interesting to recall that in the old days Japan grew much of her cotton and imported much of her silk. The imported cotton, however, made cotton cultivation in Japan unremunerative, but the Japanese made a tremendous success of the scientific culture of silk.

Page 222.—There is a rather childish ambition to declare

Japanese a "world language" as well as a great satisfaction in feeling that it is a sort of national secret code. A good many years ago (about 1916) when a Sino-Japanese agreement was under negotiation, it was suddenly discovered that the Japanese ambassador and the Chinese Foreign Minister, who were both English scholars, were conversing in English. Orders were at once telegraphed to the Ambassador to speak Japanese and use an interpreter. Sino-Japanese agreements have recently been in Japanese, but always used to be in Chinese. Other agreements are generally in some well-known language, such as English or French. The Russo-Japanese Fisheries Treaty, for instance, was in English. In 1932 the Japanese explained (in English) that the Chinese were making war on them and that they were only defending themselves against the Chinese; in 1933 they explained that their refusal to buy Indian cotton did not come under the definition of a boycott; and in 1937 there were many exegetical exploits of the same kind. In these circumstances there are certain difficulties in the way of Japanese becoming a language for treaties except where the other party signs under duress.

Page 228.—While the Japanese are proud of their expansion overseas, they lack a sense of responsibility for these new possessions, which is natural, considering how recent is the endeavour to implant any democratic sense of responsibility for their domestic concerns. The somewhat rare questions asked in the Diet concerning Korea and Formosa were customarily answered by the Premier, but often received no answer at all. That this was not satisfactory was generally acknowledged, and in 1927 a Department of Overseas Affairs was created, but the Premier, General Baron Tanaka, took the portfolio himself. Much hostility was shown towards the new Department, emphatic declarations being made at various times that Korea, or Formosa, or South Manchuria, as the case might be, should not come under its supervision. The Governor-Generalship of Korea especially was considered so important that its incumbent ought not to be subject to a comparatively junior member of the Cabinet. The creation of the Manchurian Affairs Bureau effectively took this region out of the Department's purview. The Ambassador to Hsinking is not subject to the Foreign Office; he is a soldier, but not subject to the War Office; he rules Manchuria, the Cabinet having been abolished in 1937 and the Ministers made subordinate to him; and he is set in authority over the President of the South Manchuria Railway—a unique position for a Japanese subject.

Page 244.—Kobayashi Takiji was thirty years old at the time of his death, and was the author of some proletarian stories. One of these, *The Cannery Boat*, gives its title to a book of stories by him and other proletarian writers published in English by Messrs. Martin Lawrence, London, 1933. Professor M. Bickerton, of New Zealand, who was a teacher in Tokyo, and sympathised with the forward movements, though not himself a member of any Communist group, added as an epilogue to this collection of stories a brief account of the murder of Kobayashi by the police. His name did not appear on the book, but the police suspected him, and got him in 1934. They handled him very severely. He managed to escape from the country when awaiting trial. Neither the law nor the trade unions could give workers any protection in the more distant parts, and there were many gruesome stories of the treatment of the men on the fishing boats and floating canneries. In 1930 the *Etrop Maru* came back eighteen short—victims of inhuman cruelties according to the usual accounts, but officially dead of scurvy or beri beri. The collection of stories published under the name *The Cannery Boat* was, of course, prohibited in Japan.

Page 252.—Wang Ching-wei (also known as Wang Chao-ming) was in pre-revolution days the right-hand man of Dr. Sun Yat-sen, though of a rather too independent character to make the perfect disciple. On March 28, 1910, he attempted to blow up the Prince Regent in Peking by means of a bomb concealed under a bridge. The work of the conspirators, however, set the dogs in the neighbourhood barking, and the bomb was discovered. Wang himself was arrested some days later, and sent to prison for life. He preached revolution to his jailers to such effect that the authorities, hearing of it, put him in irons, which no prisoner could survive more than two or three years. The revolution set him free, however, and, rather spasmodically, he has taken a prominent part in Chinese affairs since. He and his colleagues did their best to come to terms with Japan. Wang protested that Japanese acts of terrorism were far worse than those of the Chinese, against which the Japanese demanded guarantees; and the Chinese went so far as to punish Chinese critics of Japan. But nothing was enough, and Wang Ching-wei resigned. This endeavour to meet Japan's wishes is in part admitted by Mr. Kodama Kenji, a former President of the Yokohama Specie Bank, who wrote the second of a series of propaganda booklets circulated in England and America in 1937–38. He says that Mr. Wang "responded to the policy of economic co-operation," but that after his resignation Chiang Kai-shek became hostile again. When Wang Ching-wei complained of Japanese terrorism, Mr. Hirota sent a very minatory note to him, declaring that China would be held responsible for every untoward event—a fair example of the manner in which friendly conversations were conducted.

Page 257.—It is a common belief that China takes little notice of what goes on in the world without; but it is significant that when the craze for proclaiming One Big Party by the colour of its shirt was at its height in Europe, China broke out into blue as the outward assertion of patriotism.

Page 265.—By way of placating the Services, Admiral Suetsugu was appointed Home Minister in Prince Konoe's Cabinet in 1937. It might be supposed that there was nothing for a spy to exercise his talents upon in the Kuriles, which are not fortified; but in July 1934 it was announced that a fishing base was being constructed on Horomushiro Island, just south of Kamchatka, at a cost of 21,000,000 yen. A perennial source of disagreement with Russia is found in the Japanese fishing rights on the Kamchatkan coasts.

Page 266.—Rotary was organised rather thoroughly in Japan, with a view to promoting "direct trade," that is, substituting Japanese for foreign middlemen. In the stress of war-patriotism it was proposed in some quarters at the beginning of 1938 to suppress Rotary Clubs as un-Japanese, and in others to utilise them for inculcating the correct point of view in foreign countries regarding Sino-Japanese hostilities.

Page 268.—Prince Saionji was born in 1850 of a *kuge* family— the ancient nobility attached to the Imperial Court and sharing its obscurity in the long periods when Japan was governed by military dictators. In 1868, the year of the Meiji Restoration, he was in command of an Imperial army, but despite the distinction of being a general at eighteen, he never acquired any taste for militarism. Soon after the Restoration he was sent as Minister to Prussia, quickly discovered that his spiritual home was in Paris, and had to be officially reminded that a national envoy was supposed to spend at least part of his time in the country to which he was accredited. He returned to Japan so much in sympathy with the principles of the leaders of the Paris Commune that he became rather a problem. The task of reasoning with him was entrusted to Marquis Okuma, perhaps because Saionji could not possibly charge Okuma with being old-fashioned. Prince Saionji never sought office, his ideal being a quiet and scholarly retirement, but he was so distinguished as always to be wanted for the service of the State. At the end of his second Premiership in 1912, an Imperial Message was so worded as to be regarded as the equivalent of his appointment to the council of Genro, or Elder Statesmen, and he was the only man whose counsel was ever sought as being on an equality with the original members, all of whom he outlived by many years. His position from February 1922, when Prince Yamagata died, was unique, no great decision being taken without consulting him. His last official position was when he went to Versailles in 1919 as Japan's chief delegate at the Peace Conference; and there were many threats that he would be assassinated on his return for his failure to get better terms for Japan.

Page 271.—It may be because the Japanese are so adept at explaining that black is white that they are liable to mistrust the efficacy of words. *Kokutai* is by no means the only important thing which is ineffable. The "Zen" philosophy, which its exponents have declared to be Japan's greatest gift to the world's culture, is in nothing more Japanese than in the insistence of its professors that words cannot explain it. Sir Charles Eliot says: "To a certain extent it has moulded the Japanese character, but it is also the expression of that character. . . . In the time of the Sung (the Sung Dynasty, A.D. 960–1280) Zen may have been the full flower and expression of Chinese culture, but in later periods it is characteristically Japanese and challenges us to define what this characteristic but elusive teaching is. When a sect boldly states that its doctrine must be felt and not read, and that every attempt to state it in speech or writing must be *ipso facto* a failure, the expositor need say no more. Yet the rash pen longs to formulate the ineffable and is apt to suggest that the mysteries which cannot be expressed in words are really non-existent and that the literary history of Zen, though copious, is not a heap of philosophic jewels buried in a little dust, but a farrago of anecdotes reporting grotesque and irrelevant sayings and still more grotesque and often brutal actions. I confess that I am not quite in sympathy with the Zen view of things, and that is why I wish to emphasise the great practical achievements of the sect and to point out that a creed which has produced such remarkable results must be based on something more than eccentricity." Chinese scholars are naturally very scornful of Japanese Zen, which for them begins in failure to understand and ends in abusing the understanding. Some of Japan's most notable assassins have professed a devotion to Zen, perhaps because it absolved them from explaining their actions.

Page 277.—Admiral Viscount Saito Makoto was born in 1858 and had a distinguished naval career, rising to Cabinet rank. He had already retired, and had every hope and expectation of a quiet evening of life when a crisis arose in Korea in 1919, where General Hasegawa, a military martinet of the most rigid type, had, as Governor-General, exasperated the Koreans beyond endurance. The feeble, unarmed rising was put down with cruel severity, and Admiral Saito was chosen as a man moderate enough to restore peace as well as order. More than one attempt was made to assassinate him, but he continued his work with imperturbable courage, the Viscountess accompanying him on all his tours. In 1927 he resigned, and was sent as Japan's chief delegate to the naval conference at Geneva. The aged and easy-going General Yamanashi succeeded him, and became involved in an orgy of corruption. In 1929 he returned to Japan to stand his trial, which, after the manner of such trials, lasted very long and came to nothing. Admiral Saito again shouldered the burden and disentangled another web of trouble. He resigned once more in 1931, and was called to be Premier after Inukai's murder in 1932. Thus for fifteen years after his retirement from the navy he laboured to remedy the blunders, defalcations, and crimes of soldiers. His reward was to be butchered by soldiers. Not a Japanese newspaper had a word of parting praise for him at his death. The police, waiting to be on the successful side, had warned them not to write any appreciations of the murdered statesmen.

Page 288.—Mr. Kuhara Fusanosuke, a business man of great ability and diversity of enterprise, came rather oddly into conflict with the British Government. As owner of a shipyard, the Nippon Kisen Kaisha, he took an order in 1917 for four ships, for which he received nearly two million yen in advance and facilities for importing steel (then almost unobtainable) from the United States. Messrs. Dodwell & Co., Ltd., were the agents through whom this was arranged. The ships were to be delivered late in 1917, but were not ready, so the time was extended. On November 11, 1918, they were still undelivered, so Dodwell's cancelled the contract and demanded the two million yen back. Kuhara refused on the ground that as no limit had been placed on the extension of time the contract was interminable. Actually the keels had never been laid. Having lost his case in every court to which he could appeal, Kuhara promised to pay by instalments on condition that no bankruptcy proceedings should be taken. In 1927, General Baron Tanaka, the Premier, with whom he was on very friendly terms, wanted to make Kuhara Foreign Minister, when a newspaper disclosed the fact that none of the instalments had been paid, and the British Ambassador put it to Baron Tanaka that it would be embarrassing to deal with a Foreign Minister who owed his Government money; so Kuhara, who had political ambitions, had to be content with the Ministry of Communications, for which the little affair was not considered a disqualification. A year or two after, he did pay, and he proved to be a useful "manager" for the Seiyukai party. At the time of this writing (1938) he was not quite out of the toils of the February 26th affair, a charge of "harbouring" having still to be investigated.

Page 295.—To the student of diplomacy the "perpetual leases" may be an example of the inadvisability of making contracts in perpetuity, since nothing mundane is everlasting; but in the case of the leases in Japan there was a natural course of extinction. They could be sold to Japanese subjects, and when they were so sold this extinguished their particular character. Fully half of them had ceased to exist. (In Osaka the last lease was sold in 1914.) After the Great War, the Allies encouraged the Japanese to confiscate the German leases, and, of course, the confiscation of the rest, when an equally safe moment arrived, was the inevitable sequel. The privilege attaching to the leases lay chiefly in a fixed ground-rent in lieu of ordinary house-taxes, and this, very high at the beginning, had become, in comparison with the municipal rates, very low. The Japanese Press was continually encouraged to enlarge on this as a grievance, though no Japanese editor ever troubled to acquaint himself with the facts. There were diplomatic conversations, but the Japanese Government would never make a "firm offer" for a cancellation. At length two birds were killed with one stone. The leases were cancelled (ordinary ownership being substituted), and the lack of diplomatic protest was an assurance that foreign rights in the Far East would not henceforth be protected by any of the Governments concerned, no matter to what extent they were violated.

INDEX

www.ingramcontent.com/pod-product-compliance
Lightning Source LLC
Chambersburg PA
CBHW020351100426
42812CB00001B/28